Building Your Own Web Conferences

Building Your Own Web Conferences

Susan B. Peck
&
Beverly Murray Scherf

O'REILLY™
Cambridge • Köln • Paris • Sebastopol • Tokyo

Building Your Own Web Conferences

by Susan B. Peck and Beverly Murray Scherf

WebBoard™ is a product of O'Reilly & Associates, Inc.

Printing History

March 1997: First Edition

Trademarks

WebBoard is a trademark of O'Reilly & Associates, Inc.
WebSite, WebSite Professional, and PolyForm are trademarks of O'Reilly & Associates, Inc.
Microsoft is a registered trademark, and Windows, Windows NT, Access, Front Page, Internet Explorer, Internet Information Server, and Power Point are trademarks of Microsoft Corporation.
America Online is a registered service mark of America Online, Inc.
Netscape Communications, Netscape, Netscape Navigator, Netscape Navigator Gold, FastTrack, JavaScript, and the Netscape logo are trademarks of Netscape Communications Corporation.
Purveyor is a trademark of Process Software Corporation.
Autodesk, the Autodesk logo, and 3D Studio are registered trademarks, and 3D Studio MAX, ktn.com and Kinetix are trademarks of Autodesk, Inc.
Children with Diabetes is a trademark of Children with Diabetes.
Data Supply Outlet, Inc is a trademark and The CityNet is a trademark of Data Supply Outlet, Inc.
All other names are registered trademarks or trademarks of their respective companies.

Suggestions and Support

Your suggestions for *Building Your Own Web Conferences* are welcomed. Please email your comments to *webboard@ora.com*. Technical support questions will not be answered from this email address.

WebBoard technical support is available on a per-incident basis or through an annual technical support contract. For per-incident technical support, please call one of the numbers listed below. To set up an annual support contract, contact O'Reilly & Associates Customer Service at (800) 998-9938. WebBoard technical support hours are Monday through Friday, 7 AM to 5 PM, Pacific Time. For WebBoard questions and answers, related software, and other product information, check out WebBoard Central: *http://webboard.ora.com/* and O'Reilly Software Online (*http://software.ora.com/*)

O'Reilly & Associates, Inc.
101 Morris Street
Sebastopol, CA 95472
Phone: (707) 829-0515
FAX: (707) 829-0104

ISBN: 1-56592-279-4

Contents

Section IV: Using WebBoard

Section V: Appendixes

Preface

Building Your Own Web Conferences signals the coming of age of web conferencing. Now anyone with a personal computer running Windows 95 or Windows NT can set up and run an interactive conferencing system on the Internet or on an intranet. Participants can be located down the hall or halfway around the globe. All they need to join the conferencing system is a web browser and something to contribute. Web conferencing revolutionizes communication—whether that communication is for project collaboration, idea exchange, or just to keep in touch.

Building Your Own Web Conferences walks you through the steps of setting up and maintaining a web conferencing system using WebBoard 2.0 from O'Reilly & Associates. A full copy of this program is included on the CD-ROM in the back of this book. A wealth of ideas, tips, examples, and thorough explanations will guide you as you use WebBoard to accomplish your communication goals.

At O'Reilly, we make our living as publishers. We are best known for publishing books and software that help people solve information problems. The *Building Your Own* series continues that tradition by combining useful, plain-English writing with quality software and online resources. With *Building Your Own Web Conferences* and WebBoard, you have a platform for solving information problems for yourself and others by providing open and full-featured communication from simple message posting to live chat and file attachments.

Building Your Own Web Conferences and WebBoard 2.0 are the result of a devoted team effort from people at O'Reilly & Associates. Gina Blaber and Lisa Henning headed the team. Chris Duke led the software development effort, with the assistance of developer Mark Bracewell. Many others at O'Reilly & Associates provided invaluable editorial, design, production, software testing, technical support, marketing, and sales support.

You can learn more about WebBoard and the WebBoard team at WebBoard Central, the web site dedicated to WebBoard (*http://webboard.ora.com*). You can learn more about O'Reilly & Associates by visiting *http://www.ora.com*. We encourage you to check out our own Web resources to get ideas for developing your own.

How to Use This Book

This book is divided into 5 sections, with a total of 12 chapters, 2 appendixes, and 4 WebBoard in Action case studies. We recommend you read the first three chapters before installing WebBoard from the accompanying CD-ROM and then use the remaining chapters as necessary to accomplish your specific web conferencing tasks.

Section 1: Getting Started

Before you can start using WebBoard, you need to install the software. You should also take a few minutes to become familiar with WebBoard, explore some ideas for using it, and complete the pre-installation requirements.

- Chapter 1, *Why Conference on the Web?*
- Chapter 2, *Before You Start*
- Chapter 3, *Installing WebBoard*

Section 2: Managing WebBoard

Managing a web conferencing system means creating conferences, managing users, assigning managers and moderators, and handling other administrative tasks.

- Chapter 4, *Managing Conferences*
- Chapter 5, *Managing Users*
- Chapter 6, *Advanced Management*

Section 3: Tailoring WebBoard

WebBoard's user interface is almost completely HTML-based. That means you can change the look and feel of what your users see when they visit your conferences. From simply changing the background color to rewriting and designing the pages, you can make WebBoard as individual (or corporate!) as you are.

- Chapter 7, *Customizing WebBoard Pages*
- Chapter 8, *WebBoard File Reference*

Section 4: Using WebBoard

Navigating around WebBoard, reading messages, posting responses, using spell-check, listing users, and searching conferences and user profiles are all tasks WebBoard users should master. WebBoard's rich feature set includes support for including HTML and images in message posts, file attachments, and real-time chat.

Note

This section is also available as a separate booklet, which you can make available to your users. For more information, contact O'Reilly & Associates customer service at 707-829-0515 or 800-998-9938, or visit WebBoard Central.

- Chapter 9, *WebBoard Basics*
- Chapter 10, *Participating in Conferences*
- Chapter 11, *What's Happening on Your WebBoard?*
- Chapter 12, *Chatting in WebBoard*

Section 5: Appendixes

The two appendixes cover the upgrading to the extended license version of WebBoard, WebBoard 2.0 XL, and troubleshooting tips.

- Appendix A, *Upgrading to WebBoard 2.0 XL*
- Appendix B, *Troubleshooting Tips*

Typographic Conventions

We use the following typographic conventions.

Italic
: is used for emphasis as well as for new terms where they are first defined, titles of publications, Uniform Resource Locators (URLs), email addresses, filenames, hostnames, and directory names.

`Letter Gothic`
: is used in examples to show the output from commands or the contents of files and for names of program variables and HTML tags in text.

`Italic Letter Gothic`
: is used to show variables within code examples.

Angle Brackets < >
: are used to surround the HTML (Hypertext Markup Language) tags used to structure HTML documents.

I

Getting Started

You are about to enter the world of web conferencing, where time and distance no longer restrain conversation. This section provides an overview of web conferencing and how WebBoard can make it work for you. Chapter 1, *Why Conference on the Web?*, suggests many ways to use WebBoard and describes several features including structured conferencing, virtual boards, message tracking, navigation, and security choices. Read Chapter 2, *Before You Start*, to prepare for a smooth installation of WebBoard 2.0. And then go on to use Chapter 3, *Installing WebBoard* as your guide to a successful installation.

1

Why Conference on the Web?

Welcome to the world of online conferencing! You may be thinking, "What's that?" Well, before we discuss this technology and what it can do for you and your organization, let's take a moment to explore its roots. Its origins probably began when our ancestors gathered around campfires to discuss important business—the best hunting spots, how to keep warm, and what to do with the kids. As time went on this activity shifted to the local water cooler, although the topics changed somewhat—doing our work, adjusting our schedules, finding good entertainment spots, and so forth. Nowadays we can gather around the Web to have our confabs. "How can we do that?" you ask.

In many ways, the online world mimics the real world. We send and receive mail electronically rather than through the postal service; we search for and find information in databases rather than at the local library; we buy and sell products and services with a few keystrokes rather than making a trip to the store. But what about conversing with groups of people? Exchanging ideas and information with colleagues, friends, acquaintances, and family members? Collaborating on projects, hobbies, or shared goals? High-level corporate international conferences? Does the online world support this type of group communication?

This book is titled *Building Your Own Web Conferences,* so the answer is obviously yes. But how? With WebBoard Version 2.0, the web conferencing software from O'Reilly & Associates, included on the CD-ROM in this book. This is a full copy of the software, not demonstration software. This book explains how to use

WebBoard to turn your PC into a conference center, replacing the campfire or the water cooler and bringing users from far and wide a little closer together.

WebBoard users can participate in a variety of conferences using their Web browsers to read and post messages and join chat sessions. They can share ideas, information, questions, and suggestions. You can also use WebBoard to disseminate information to users. WebBoard's elegant user interface, effortless navigation, organized topics, and linked menus make it a breeze to use. You and your users can also include HTML elements in messages, including links to other locations or graphic images. In short, WebBoard lets you create a place for an electronic community of users to flourish—whether that community is on the global Internet or on your intranet.

This book is dedicated to showing you how to build your own web conference system using WebBoard. This first chapter sets the stage with an overview of WebBoard and some ideas for using it. Take a few minutes to look at how you can use WebBoard to build your online community.

How Can I Use WebBoard?

WebBoard is a tool for fostering communication, globally or locally, among people with common interests whether they be job, civic, or personal. WebBoard is extremely flexible and convenient to use. Because it is browser-based, you can use it anywhere, anytime. All your users need is access to a browser.

Your WebBoard may be to promote discussion for developing a product, pursuing a goal, or simply having fun. Perhaps the most important thing to note about using WebBoard is that it is designed to bring people to your site and *keep* them there, unlike many web pages that have links sending users out to *other* sites on the Web. If your WebBoard is well designed and maintained, it can become an exciting destination for a variety of people.

Once you have WebBoard up and running, you're ready to get down to business. Just direct your co-workers, customers, club members, friends, or family to your WebBoard URL, and you're on your way to building an online conferencing center.

This section gives you some standard ideas as well as some you might not have thought of for using WebBoard. Whenever group participation and collaboration is appropriate, WebBoard offers a well-organized framework for managing the discussion and users. As you become more familiar with WebBoard and your online community, you can tailor these ideas accordingly. We also recommend you read the *WebBoard in Action* case studies that are sprinkled throughout this book to see how other companies and organizations are using WebBoard. And, you can always visit WebBoard Central (*http://webboard.ora.com*) for more ideas—and to share your own WebBoard use.

Note

You will need a JavaScript-enabled browser such as Netscape 3.0 or higher or Microsoft Internet Explorer 3.0 or higher to use many of WebBoard's features. See Chapter 2 for a more detailed discussion of WebBoard's requirements.

Management Meetings

We're all familiar with the often impossible task of coordinating our schedules for meetings to review time-critical information with our peers. Scheduling meetings with multiple participants from far-flung locations can often be as much work as the meetings themselves! However, WebBoard lets you arrange an effective alternative by providing a meeting place without regard to time or location.

For example, let's say that on a countywide basis all the office managers in the medical field routinely meet to exchange ideas and discuss solutions to the unique challenges in small practices. Because of schedule conflicts, some managers can't attend these meetings. Setting up a WebBoard conference devoted to these issues lets office managers participate in "meetings" without having to attend. Office managers can easily follow and participate in conferences in their "down" time. Not only does this save time, but it also makes this valuable information readily available to office managers who may join the group later. It also ensures that members won't miss information because of sickness, vacation, or emergencies. For more immediate needs or on a regular, predetermined basis, the managers can run a chat session with other conference members.

Information Management

We live in the Information Overload Age. Information overload can be useless or even counterproductive. Have you ever wondered how to effectively manage information to make it more useful to you and your peers? WebBoard helps you manage information so that it is readily available and logically organized.

WebBoard's conferences and structured hierarchy create an ideal medium for managed information. For example, a research facility can arrange conferences in much the same way as one would manage a filing cabinet. The information is made available both logically and chronologically. In addition, WebBoard's support for file attachments and links to other sites on the Internet lets users extend the message-posting and -reading capability of WebBoard. A research scientist may want to have peers review current findings stored in a spreadsheet file, or point users to images recorded during a recent observation. Adding information in a structured way provides even more control over information overload.

Publishing Development and Review Cycles

Employees in companies that publish magazines, newspapers, and books benefit from WebBoard's document-sharing capabilities. Writers can collaborate with fellow staff members by putting their documents online in a conference for review or submission. This process can greatly speed up the development and review cycles, because all posting and retrieving can be done from anywhere.

For example, a newspaper writer can follow up on a hot story and post the material to the newspaper's internal WebBoard. The editor can review the story and get it out in time for today's paper. Running back to the office to meet the deadline becomes unnecessary. The writer can instead follow up other stories, perhaps some that are even more noteworthy.

WebBoard also affords writers an exchange for collective feedback. Authors of magazine articles and books can set up a WebBoard conference that serves as a living history of the document, including all iterations of feedback and modifications. In fact, the authors of this book used WebBoard conferencing extensively not only for collaboration and review, but also as a repository of information from the developer, project team members, case study participants, and software beta testers.

Web Conference Hosting

WebBoard makes it easy for you to host web conference systems for others with its virtual board capability. Each virtual board is unique with its own set of conferences, messages, and users. It can also have its own look and feel. You may want to run separate virtual boards for different departments or locations in your company. If you are a web consultant or host web pages for others, you may want to run virtual boards for your business clients who want conferences to discuss their products and services, from public accountant agencies to culinary schools. Each client's virtual board can have its own pages with the client's own custom look. Each virtual board can also have its own managers and conference moderators.

The version of WebBoard that comes with this book supports two virtual boards and up to 10 conferences per board. The extended license (XL) version of WebBoard supports up to 255 virtual boards and unlimited conferences. For more information on upgrading to WebBoard XL, see Appendix A.

If you run WebBoard for others, you may also find it useful to provide them with copies of the WebBoard user's guide, *Using WebBoard 2.0*. This booklet covers the material in Section 4 of this book and provides both detailed and quick reference instructions for your WebBoard end users. *Using WebBoard 2.0* is an indispensable aid for new and experienced WebBoard users alike. For more information, visit WebBoard Central at *http://webboard.ora.com*.

Foreign Language Conferences

Whether you want to provide a discussion area for your international customers or simply a place to practice with your local French club, WebBoard makes setting up foreign language conferences easy. Nearly every element displayed by WebBoard is an HTML document or image that you can translate or replace. For example, you can change the images used for buttons on the menubar to display the same commands in German (or French or Japanese!). You can translate the HTML pages and the help files, as described in Section 3 of this book.

If your business serves a variety of international locations or you are head of the foreign language department for a school system, you may want to set up multiple virtual boards based on language. From the conference center home page, users can select the language they want and go directly to the appropriate board. Foreign language students can benefit by having native speakers from the country also participate in the conferences and chat sessions.

Customer/Technical Support

WebBoard is an ideal way to provide customer or technical support. A customer posts a message with a question about a particular subject. Other participants can answer from their own experience or customer/technical support staff can provide an official answer. You may choose to moderate some of these conferences to ensure that solutions are proper and won't lead to bigger problems. Once a solution is posted, it is available for other users to read. In fact, rather than repeating the same information over and over, support staff can point users to WebBoard for answers to questions.

In essence, a customer or tech support WebBoard becomes a FAQ (Frequently Asked Questions) and IFAQ (Infrequently Asked Questions) repository. New users and customers can browse the list of conference topics before contacting technical support directly or posting a new question. Truly unique or difficult situations posted by users can be handled directly with email or completely offline if necessary.

Using WebBoard for support requires constant attention and quick replies. If you decide to use WebBoard for customer support, consider the following suggestions:

- Create a separate virtual board for each product you support. Giving each product its own virtual board segregates product information and aids navigation. Each board is dedicated to updates, questions, and known problems and their solutions for specific products. However, you might want some links to other products' virtual boards so that customers who use more than one of your products can move easily between the boards. Setting up virtual boards is described in Chapter 6.

- Create a FAQ conference within each virtual board, with each question stored as its own topic. You probably should make this a moderated conference, so that new messages can be approved before being posted to the conference.

Project Collaboration

As businesses have become more flexible in reacting to changing marketplaces and the increasing pace of technological advancements, much has been said and written about "the virtual corporation." Virtual corporations or virtual teams rely heavily on electronic communication, such as email, file transfers, voicemail, pagers, and fax service, to share and track the issues that their projects face.

WebBoard's ability to store information by topic, combined with its fast search engine, makes it an excellent choice for offsite groups collaborating on the same project. In addition, WebBoard can keep a history of previous collaborations. This archiving use of WebBoard means that knowledge acquired by the team can be passed on to future teams working in similar areas. Unless you are working on an internal network, you probably want to make project conferences private, limited to the project team members.

The following scenario traces the use of WebBoard for just such project collaboration:

- Your organization sets up a virtual board for the product you're bringing to market, with several conferences: one for marketing information, one for technical discussion, one for production, and others as required. During the course of several months, each team uses the conferences that concern it the most, but also has access to the discussions the other groups are having about the product.
- At the end of the process, your new product goes to market and is a success. Furthermore, your team's use of WebBoard is lauded as a model for the corporation's future information management.
- Because the specific information is no longer active, but could be useful as reference material, the final step is to archive the conferences used for the project. To do so, simply move the virtual board's URL (Universal Resource Locator, or web address of a specific page) from the "Current Projects" page to the "Archived Projects" page.

Online Brainstorming

WebBoard makes it easy for team members to hold brainstorming sessions despite being separated by time and distance. The fundamental rule of brainstorming is never to discard ideas, but record them all. In the traditional brainstorming model, each idea may be the seed of the final, creative solution.

WebBoard's Chat feature provides a great vehicle for real-time brainstorming sessions. Set a time for the chat brainstorming session, and have the WebBoard system administrator record the session in a chat log. The log can then be posted in the conference for participants to review.

Similarly, you can brainstorm through WebBoard's conferences. Because WebBoard keeps conference postings until the administrator removes them or they reach the expiration date, participants in a WebBoard brainstorming session can refer to earlier comments, previous ideas, and the entire flow of the conversation throughout its lifetime.

Family Get-Togethers

Families with widely scattered members appreciate keeping up with one another electronically. Email has become a common way for families to communicate. WebBoard provides an even more interesting forum because family members can "drop in" to an active discussion whenever they have a few minutes. With one copy of WebBoard running on one family member's PC, other family members need only a web browser. Because the family member running WebBoard will need a special kind of Internet account (and possibly a second phone line), other family members may want to chip in to pay monthly operating costs—a small price to pay for staying in close touch with people we love and miss.

WebBoard enhances family get-togethers, because it's easy to use, is globally available and accessible, and saves money on telephone calls and postage. A special conference for each family member or location simplifies and personalizes communication. For example, Greg has relatives all over the world, so he set up a conference for his relatives in each locality. This way, his relatives can quickly get updates on what's happening. They can include photos in their messages as well as links to their home pages. WebBoard's easy navigation makes participating fun even for children. Best yet, the whole family can also take part in WebBoard's real-time chat sessions scheduled for regular times. A great way to strengthen family ties using technology!

Interactive Democracy

WebBoard is an excellent tool for giving a voice to the people, an essential goal in a democracy. For example, if your WebBoard is for a civic or hobby club, you might want to have an interactive campaign and election for club offices. You can set up a conference for candidates to share their views and answer your questions. You can also schedule chat sessions for virtual "Meet the Candidate" night. A link to a ballot form from a topic message can complete the voting process.

How Does WebBoard Work?

We've talked a lot about how you might use WebBoard, and you probably have some more ideas of your own. At this point, it may be good to take a few minutes and get the big picture overview of how WebBoard works and what its basic components are. Of course, the rest of this book explains them all in more detail.

WebBoard combines database technology with World Wide Web technology. Behind the scenes, WebBoard relies on a Microsoft Access database to keep track of virtual boards, conferences, messages, users, and WebBoard's configuration. Out on stage, if you will, WebBoard presents a web personality: HTML pages for logging in, reading and posting messages, searching, and learning more about conferences and users. The Chat feature and administrative wizards extend the browser through JavaScript programs that launch new windows. You do not need to have Access or JavaScript on your computer; WebBoard includes all the necessary pieces.

Sitting between the database and the browser is the WebBoard "script," a program that enables the two pieces to communicate. This program comes in one of two flavors: Win-CGI or ISAPI. The Windows CGI specification (Win-CGI) was developed by Robert Denny, the developer of O'Reilly's WebSite servers. Its purpose was to allow precisely the type of interaction between Web-based requests and Windows-based applications that results in dynamic pages, such as those produced by WebBoard. Chris Duke took his background in bulletin board systems and the Web, coupled it with Bob's Win-CGI spec and developed WebBoard 1.0 (see sidebar). As Microsoft's ISAPI (Internet Server API) became more widespread, Chris added support for an ISAPI script, or DLL (Dynamic Link Library), to perform the same function. Win-CGI and ISAPI support allows WebBoard 2.0 to run on a variety of web servers.

Which leads to the next component in WebBoard: the web server. The WebBoard Win-CGI or ISAPI script requires a web server, the software that handles requests from and responses to browsers. WebBoard 2.0 includes its own internal web server, so all the components you need are on the accompanying CD. WebBoard also works with a variety of other web servers as an add-on application. You can even use WebBoard's internal web server on one port and a different external web server on another port. These topics are described in Chapters 2 and 3.

That's the very quick tour of WebBoard's operation. As you learn more about WebBoard and understand the various pieces, you'll appreciate both the power and elegant simplicity of the WebBoard model.

WebBoard: A Developer Reminisces

Chris Duke, the developer of WebBoard, shares his thoughts on how WebBoard got to where it is today.

It's funny to think that when I started WebBoard back in February 1995 I could count the number of web-based conferencing systems on one hand. Now, in February 1997 there are over 120 different free, proprietary, and commercially available conferencing tools from which to choose. The product space for web conferencing has grown exponentially. WebBoard 1.0 kick-started this market, and version 2.0 continues to lead it with its advanced features such as live chat, frames, spell-checking, email notification, file attachments, and its own built-in web server. Its performance is unrivaled, with most requests being processed in less than one-tenth of a second, some in less than even one-hundredth of a second!

How did WebBoard get to this point?

WebBoard has its roots in the world of bulletin boards. The first bulletin board system was created in February 1978 by Ward Christensen and Randy Seuss. By 1990 approximately 30,000 boards existed in the United States alone. The reason for the massive popularity was simple—they were cheap to set up and maintain. With the cost of a phone line and an inexpensive computer, you essentially had your own modern Internet site. The original text-based bulletin board systems eventually got pushed into the world of Microsoft Windows and graphical user interfaces. The transition was tough, however, as users soon discovered that the "new era" of bulletin boards was tainted with proprietary Windows terminal software that worked only with the one particular board you called. If you called another bulletin board system that used different software, you had to load the terminal software specific to *that* system. It was like trying to log in to America Online using CompuServe software!

Such was the state of bulletin board systems in 1994: text-based bulletin board systems were a thing of the past, yet no standards existed for the protocols used by Windows bulletin board systems. Each developer had his own "best" way of handling data transmission. About this same time, however, the Web started to become popular, a phenomenon that would change bulletin board systems forever.

My own background in bulletin board/conferencing systems development to this point had been writing third-party applications for *other* bulletin board systems. I spent several years developing shareware tools to assist SysOps (bulletin board system operators), including an automatic message utility, a statistical trend graph utility, a system maintenance utility, an icon editor, and a file list generator. These tools were designed to improve other systems, to make them closer to what I wanted in a bulletin board system. By 1994, I had also become intrigued with the Web. Then I knew: the Web was the future direction of conferencing, a world where the terminal software is your everyday web browser.

(continued)

(continued from previous page)

I began testing my theory by moving the time-proven features of a traditional bulletin board system to the Web. Within a few days I had a crude (yet functional) bulletin board system for the Web. In February 1995, WebBoard was officially born and in the years since has grown into a fast, feature-rich commercial conferencing tool, exploiting the capabilities of the Web and yet staying faithful to its roots.

Today WebBoard is used by thousands around the world, ranging from hobbyists (the guys who started the bulletin board craze), to ISPs, to small and large companies, to universities and nonprofits, and even to the Pentagon. WebBoard's rapid acceptance is directly related to feedback from our customers. Your ideas and suggestions have prompted continued improvements and added features; I look forward to hearing your reactions to WebBoard 2.0 and ideas for future releases.

It has been a fun and fascinating adventure developing WebBoard. Thank you for helping to continue the age-old tradition of conferencing.

—Chris Duke, February 1997

Chris wishes to thank all who have been instrumental in the development of WebBoard 2.0, especially software group director Gina Blaber, product manager Lisa Henning, software developer Mark Bracewell, quality assurance manager Pat Dutkiewicz, technical support team members Laura Nordquist and Greg Goben, graphic designer Ted Meister, and all our tireless beta testers.

What Are Some of WebBoard's Features?

Now it's time to look at some specific WebBoard features. This overview should help flesh out your ideas and get you headed in the right direction for installing WebBoard and building your own web conferences.

Chat & Chat Spots

WebBoard Chat lets you have interactive, real-time conversations.You can use Chat for company meetings, company online interdepartment updates, family visits, student jam sessions, and more. Chat messages can be customized with a variety of text options, such as the size and color, and can include active links and images. Chat also allows "private" conversations with the Whisper mode and lets users page other WebBoard participants.

Chat Spots provide a way for businesses or organizations to advertise during chat sessions. Chat spots randomly or sequentially display HTML documents (typically images or short messages) at specified intervals. Displaying company logos is a common use of Chat Spots.

Structured Conferencing

If everyone spoke at once and about a variety of topics, it would be difficult to keep track of a conversation. To eliminate such pandemonium, WebBoard structures conversations into a hierarchy of ever increasing focus. At the top of the hierarchy is the *virtual board*, or what we often refer to simply as WebBoard, or the board. The virtual board contains conferences, topics, and messages. A virtual board can cover a broad range of subject matter or a focused area. You might want to think of a virtual board as being like a bookcase.

Conferences represent the next layer of the hierarchy. If a board is like a bookcase, a conference is like a book. Conferences generally deal with a specific subject area such as cooking or travel or the latest product. WebBoard supports four types of conferences:

Public conferences
: in which any user who can reach WebBoard can read and post messages.

Private conferences
: in which only a selected group of users can read and post messages. Private conferences are useful for collaboration on projects that should not be viewed by others on your WebBoard.

Read-only conferences
: in which anyone can read messages, but only the system administrator, manager, or moderator can post messages. Read-only conferences are useful for disseminating information such as policies or product news.

Moderated conferences
: in which anyone can read and post messages, but the moderator must approve all messages before they are available for general reading. Moderated conferences are useful for keeping a conference focused on the subject or goal of the conference.

If the virtual board is like the bookcase and conferences are like the book itself, *topics* are like the chapter titles within the book. A topic can be any posting within a conference. Messages responses to that topic are kept with the topic, creating what are called *threaded* discussions. *Messages*, then, are the content within the book's chapter. A posting can change the topic at any time, in essence starting a new chapter in the book or a new discussion thread.

Virtual Boards

As mentioned in the previous section, WebBoard lets you set up completely separate boards, called virtual boards, with only one copy of WebBoard running. Each virtual board has its own set of conferences, topics, and messages and can also have its own custom look and feel. Virtual boards let you offer conferencing to a broad spectrum of unrelated businesses, organizations, and individuals. Because WebBoard is browser-based, users can easily access virtual boards anywhere in the world at any time.

The version of WebBoard that comes with this book supports two virtual boards and up to 10 conferences per board. The extended license (XL) version of WebBoard supports up to 255 virtual boards and unlimited conferences. For more information on upgrading to WebBoard XL, see Appendix A.

Message Tracking

WebBoard includes a variety of options to quickly identify and retrieve new and unread messages, a significant feature for WebBoard users:

Welcome page
: As soon as you log in to WebBoard, the Welcome page displays how many new messages you have and lets you link directly to the New Messages list. Each entry on the list includes the conference name, subject, date, and time it was posted, and is a hyperlink to the text of the message.

New Messages and Today's Messages options
: These two options are available from the WebBoard More Options menu. These list all messages you have not yet read and only messages that are new today, respectively.

NEW icon
: The name of any conference or topic with a message you haven't read yet is marked with a NEW icon in the Conferences list.

Email Notification
: You can have WebBoard notify you once a day by email when new messages have been posted to conferences you specify. Email notification helps you keep track of activity in conferences that are of particular interest to you.

Mark All Read option
: WebBoard considers all messages as new (or unread) until you mark them as read. You can select conferences individually or as a group and have WebBoard mark messages in the conference(s) as read.

Search Messages feature
: WebBoard includes a search engine for finding specific text in message topics and/or message bodies. Full-text searches make finding specific information even faster on your WebBoard.

Easy Navigation and Viewing Options

WebBoard's redesigned user interface makes it easy for you and your users to get around and see several aspects of WebBoard at the same time. Some of WebBoard's navigation and viewing options are as follows:

Menubars
: WebBoard's menubar sits at the top of the browser window and provides quick access to most WebBoard commands and options. Chat has its own special menubars that help you quickly navigate among its options as well.

Frames
: You can choose to view WebBoard with or without frames. In frames mode, you can see the Conferences list while reading or posting messages. The well-designed user interface for frames lets you navigate easily among conferences and other WebBoard information.

Full topic view
: WebBoard's Full topic view gives you continuous, uninterrupted reading of messages within any particular topic, without having to ask to see the next message.

Conference Arrows and Links
: Conference list navigation arrows and links help you quickly browse topics in larger conferences. The arrows let you control large topic lists, and the links (Next, Bottom, Previous, Top) let you make large leaps from point to point in a long conference.

Message Creation and Posting Options

You can choose from a variety of options when creating and posting messages on WebBoard:

Spell-checking
: WebBoard can spell-check your messages for you, identifying possible misspelled words and suggesting replacements. You can also add words and variants to the WebBoard custom dictionary.

Preview
: Before posting a message, you can preview it and make additional changes.

Anonymous
: Users can post their messages anonymously.

Support for HTML
: Adding HTML elements—including hyperlinks and images—to WebBoard messages expands what conferencing can do. For example, if you use WebBoard as a forum for technical support issues or software beta test

groups, you can include pointers to updated information or to bug fixes. You can also set up a read-only conference that describes your products and includes a hyperlink to a sample download or demonstration copy. Including HTML elements, images, and even video and audio, enhances your own messages and those of your users.

Attaching Files/Document Sharing

WebBoard lets you attach files to your messages, including, text, audio, video, and multimedia files. You can use WebBoard's file attachment capability to encourage document sharing. Not all web servers support file attachments; see Chapter 2 for more information.

User Information

WebBoard lets you find out more about other WebBoard users, with various lists and searches:

Top 10 Users and Top 10 Posters

WebBoard lets you easily track the top 10 users of your WebBoard, with statistics on how often they log in and the number of messages they post. This information can be a way to identify key customers, opinion leaders, and valuable resources among your WebBoard participants. Any user of your WebBoard can see these lists by clicking More on WebBoard's menubar. The Top 10 Users are determined by the number of logins; the Top 10 Message Posters are determined by the number of messages each posts.

User Profile searches

Each WebBoard user must create a user profile. You can find out more about WebBoard users by searching the user database and reading their profiles. User profiles often include descriptive material about the user such as hobbies and interests. The user profile also includes the user's email address.

Current Users and Today's Users

WebBoard can also show you who has logged in on the current day. If you run special events, promotions, or other day-based activities, Today's Users lets you see who visited your WebBoard that day. You can also see who is currently using WebBoard with the Current Users feature. This feature is especially handy if you are looking to join or start a chat session.

Easy Administration

WebBoard is easy to administer through the WebBoard Properties (in the program group or Start menu folder) and the Administrator menu (click More on WebBoard's menubar). The WebBoard system administrator can perform a variety of tasks such as deleting inactive users, compacting the database, and setting user parameters. Because WebBoard is browser-based, you can accomplish many administrative tasks from a remote location.

WebBoard's separate menus for the system administrator, manager, and moderator allow for convenient maintenance and modifications, particularly if you are using virtual boards. WebBoard also includes several JavaScript-based wizards to make certain administrative tasks simpler. Section 2 covers these topics in detail.

Built-in Web Server

As noted earlier in this chapter, WebBoard requires a web server. You can use any external web server that supports Windows CGI 1.1 or ISAPI, or you can simply use WebBoard's built-in web server. You need nothing other than software on the CD in the back of this book to set up and run your web conferencing system successfully.

The built-in internal server requires no configuration or special maintenance. It supports all WebBoard features, including both security modes, file attachments, and JavaScript used for Chat and administration wizards (note that not all external servers support these features). WebBoard's internal web server also provides faster performance than the external servers, a key consideration if you expect heavy traffic on your WebBoard. You can even use WebBoard's built-in server in conjunction with an external web server—simply assign them to different ports (this is described in later chapters).

Choice of Security Mode

When a user visits your WebBoard, he or she must provide a user login name and password. This login name and password are of the user's own choosing. He or she can change this information at any time.

If you are using WebBoard's internal web server or one of the WebSite servers, you can choose one of two authentication modes: Basic Authentication requires users to enter their login name and password each time. Cookie Authentication lets users have WebBoard remember their password. If you are using a different external web server, WebBoard will use Cookie Authentication by default.

Customization of WebBoard Pages

You can easily change the look and feel of WebBoard's user interface and help system, because the source for these pages are HTML documents, which you can edit. For example, you may want to add your company's logo to the Welcome message. Or you may want to add foreign language conferences and need to translate the standard pages. WebBoard also has a number of special text-handling tags that let you include dynamic information about WebBoard. For example, WebBoard's Welcome message greets the user by name. WebBoard includes the name because the `<WB-NAME>` tag in the HTML file for the welcome page tells it to do so. How to tailor WebBoard's pages is the topic of Section 3.

WebBoard in Action: University of Tulsa

The University of Tulsa in Oklahoma is a private academic institution with over 4,000 students. The primary colleges and schools at the university are the College of Business Administration (CBA), College of Arts and Sciences, College of Engineering, and School of Law. Sean Alexander and his team developed a CBA web site with features that were not only unique, but also advantageous to fostering the academic environment. This site, developed by a student-led and staffed WebTeam, has been highly successful and has won several awards, including Microsoft's Customer Showcase, USA Today's Hot Site Award, and Microsoft's Innovative use of Technology in Higher Education Award and Grant.

Having served as the CBA Webmaster, Sean was recently appointed university webmaster, overseeing all web-related development and infrastructures on campus, as well as assisting the provost in developing a new campus-wide technology initiative. Sean took some time out of his increasingly busy schedule to discuss how the College of Business Admininstration has used—and plans to use—the Web, and WebBoard in particular.

The University of Tulsa College of Business Administration began using WebBoard in 1995, while Version 1.0 was still in beta testing by O'Reilly & Associates. WebBoard was presented as a supplement to the in-class learning environment. Previously the CBA, and university as a whole, used a proprietary text-only telnet application to access Usenet-style newsgroups set up for the campus. A few professors were using this system for out-of-class discussion, with little success. The system was too difficult, too cumbersome, and often did not present options in a clear format.

"Initially, faculty and students explored WebBoard's options. A few messages were posted here and there, mostly concerning how the basketball team was doing. The dean was using WebBoard to answer questions from enrolled and prospective students online, but a necessary link to the classroom environment was missing. The CBA faculty began requesting their own virtual boards and conferences to be used for classroom discussions and online study materials. They noticed that WebBoard was assisting them in both educational and administrative processes.

"Here are a few examples where professors found WebBoard to be beneficial:

- A student may be too shy to ask a question in class, or has difficulty with English (as is the case with some of our international students). WebBoard is enabling these students to ask questions in general anonymity.
- A professor is asked the same question by multiple students during office hours. By posting a message on WebBoard addressing a question or clarifying an issue that was discussed in class, the professor reaches a much larger audience.
- Students interested in taking a particular class the following semester browse messages and topics in the current semester's conference to get a general feeling for the topics discussed in class.
- Course project teams set up their own private WebBoard conferences to assist in tracking project deadlines and issues.

(continued)

(continued from previous page)

- Basic and Advanced HTML instruction, which has now been integrated into the curriculum of the college, is tested and presented by students in a fast and efficient manner.

"These examples are just a small picture of how WebBoard is being used in just one college within the university. However, the entire university plans to use WebBoard for university-wide discussions and topics as shown in the following figure:

University of Tulsa's main WebBoard

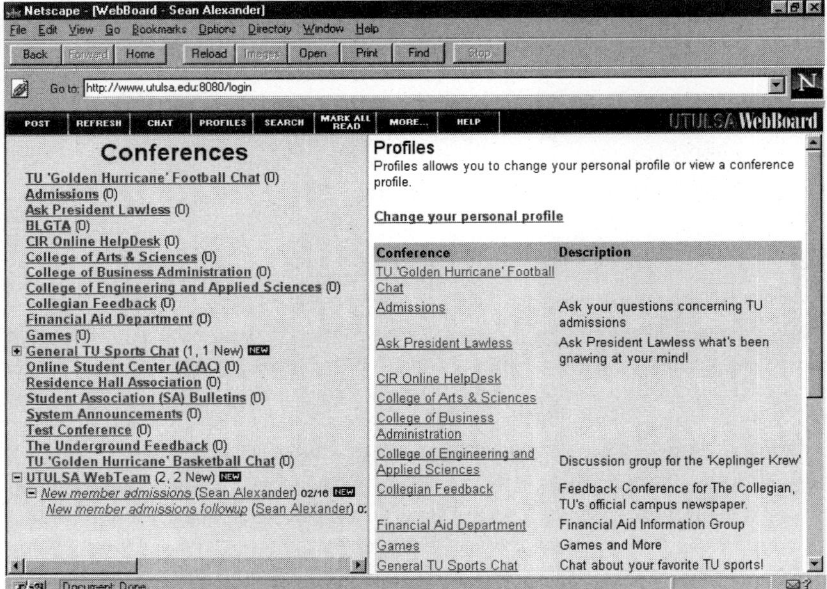

"Because of the phenomenal success of the CBA WebBoard, immediate plans have been made to roll out virtual WebBoards throughout the campus, as shown in this figure:

(continued)

(continued from previous page)

Proposed virtual board directory for the College of Business

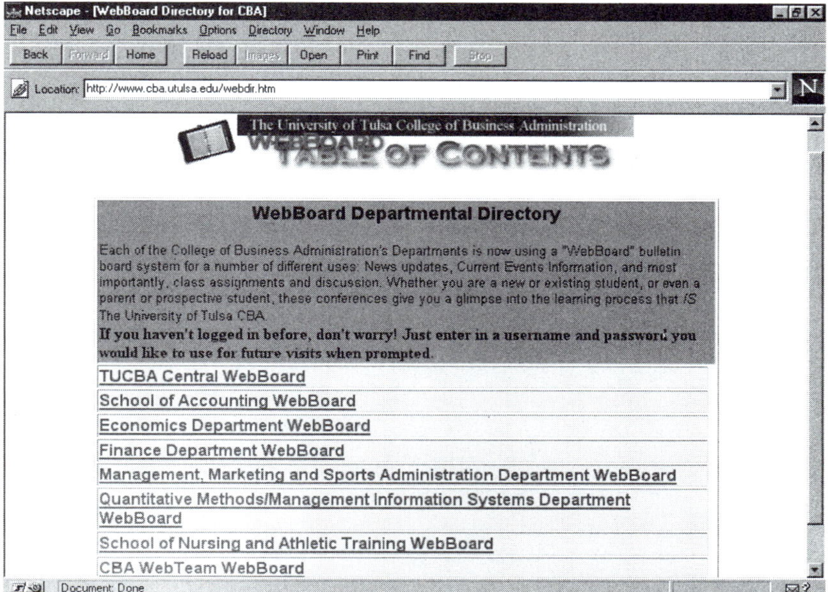

"The CBA is not the only group at the university using WebBoard. During the summer, the Russian American Oil and Gas Technology Center at the University of Tulsa (a partner with the Department of Energy) used WebBoard extensively for communication with their counterparts in the Russian Republic. WebBoard was also used to handle an online auction."

The University of Tulsa's success with the first version of WebBoard has made them enthusiastic about the new features of WebBoard 2.0. Sean further outlines the university's plans to integrate web conferencing even more fully into their online environment.

"While it is important to address how we've used WebBoard, I would also like to stress what our plans are for WebBoard 2.0. As we speak, TU is developing a university WebTeam, a "skunk works" of student developers who will be assisting in the redesign and development of a university-wide Internet and intranet presence.

"The cornerstone of this project, and the first online system, will be the University of Tulsa WebBoard Online Convocation Center (a tentative name). This WebBoard will be designed to encourage discussion at the university level between alumni, prospective employers, students, and faculty with a wide range of topic areas. Soon afterward, customized virtual WebBoards will come online for each of the colleges in the university, taking full advantage of WebBoard 2.0's new security features to distribute management of each virtual board to its particular college.

(continued)

(continued from previous page)

"WebBoard's file attachments and online chat are the most exciting new features to us. Students will upload copies of their assignments as attachments, and course materials will be distributed to students in electronic form as attachments. Once a faculty member has finished giving a class lecture, the PowerPoint presentation accompanying the lecture will be online for students to use with their notes. Office hours may be extended, where students can get together online to chat about a particular topic, or even have a guest speaker from another areas.

"We believe that the chat functions of WebBoard will be most successful with students. Having scheduled online chats or roundtables will further promote the online system in the classroom environment by familiarizing students with the WebBoard system in a fun and informative format."

You can visit the University of Tulsa at http://www.utulsa.edu.

2

Before You Start

Before You Start chapters are easy to skip. It's tempting to jump right to installing the software. However, we politely request (and strongly suggest!) that you *read this chapter before installing WebBoard.*

This chapter covers the basic information you need to successfully install and run WebBoard. Being familiar with this information up front will keep you from having to stop during the installation process to hunt for required items. Also, you'll know if your equipment and software are sufficient for using WebBoard. In essence, it's like baking a cake or changing your car's oil: Having all the tools and materials in place before you begin makes your endeavor efficient and successful.

If the idea of having your own web conferencing system is intriguing but you aren't sure you are prepared for it, this chapter will answer your questions and concerns. You'll learn about WebBoard's internal web server (as well as what other servers WebBoard works with) and what connection to the Internet is required. You'll also learn about browsers and operating system requirements, as well as what you need to know for using WebBoard's email capabilities and authentication modes.

This chapter also answers questions about running WebBoard as a desktop application or as a service, which allows WebBoard to continue running even when you aren't logged in to your computer. You can run WebBoard as a service under either Windows NT or Windows 95. Additional resources are listed if you want more detailed information about any of the topics covered.

Hardware Requirements

WebBoard requires no fancy or expensive hardware. In fact, WebBoard will install and run on almost any off-the-shelf PC. The specific hardware requirements are as follows:

- VGA video display adapter (SVGA recommended)
- CD-ROM drive
- 5 MB of free disk space for the program (more needed for your conference and user database)
- 24 MB RAM (32 MB recommended)
- Network card or modem (14.4 K bps minimum modem, 28.8 K bps recommended)

If you expect high-volume traffic or plan to run several virtual boards, your system should have the recommended values.

Operating System Requirements

WebBoard runs under two operating systems: Windows 95 or Windows NT 3.51 (or higher) Workstation or Server. Please note the following as you select your operating system for WebBoard:

- If you choose to run WebBoard under Windows NT 3.51, you must have at least Service Pack 3 installed. However, we recommend you install Service Pack 5, which fixes several NT bugs and performance issues. You can obtain service packs from the Microsoft web site (*http://www.microsoft.com*).
- If you plan to run WebBoard under Windows NT4.0 Workstation, note the license agreement that limits the number of simultaneous incoming TCP/IP connections allowed.

Connectivity Requirements

WebBoard has one simple connectivity requirement: your system must have a TCP/IP stack installed and running. TCP/IP is the suite of networking protocols that the World Wide Web—in fact, the whole Internet—requires. TCP/IP stands for Transmission Control Protocol/Internet Protocol. You don't need to understand all the nuances of TCP/IP, but to use WebBoard you need to have it running successfully on your computer. TCP/IP capability is built into both Windows NT and Windows 95 and you need no additional software.

If you are on a networked system or have an existing Internet connection, you probably don't need to worry about your TCP/IP setup. Check with your network administrator or Internet Service Provider (ISP) to make sure you have the items required by WebBoard, such as the system's Fully Qualified Domain Name and your SMTP mail server's name (both discussed later in this chapter).

If you don't have TCP/IP running, you must set it up before installing WebBoard. You can do so through the Network option on the Control Panel. For more information on installing and configuring TCP/IP on your computer, see the Windows operating system documentation.

The rest of this section discusses some pertinent TCP/IP topics.

Fully Qualified Domain Name & IP Address

One important piece of information required for WebBoard is your computer's, or web server's, Fully Qualified Domain Name, or FQDN, often referred to simply as the domain name. The FQDN is a unique name that identifies your computer on the Internet (or an intranet). For example, *webboard.ora.com*, *www.ncsa.uiuc.edu*, and *www.census.gov* are domain names used to identify computers connected to the Internet. You'll notice that these names have multiple pieces separated by periods (or dots, as they are generally called). The first piece in these domain names is the hostname; the rest is the name of the domain in which the host exists. Users will typically reach your WebBoard by using your computer's FQDN.

Usually, a Fully Qualified Domain Name is assigned to a specific IP address, which is required for setting up TCP/IP. An IP (Internet Protocol) address is a set of four numbers, one to three digits each, separated by periods (or dots), for example, 204.148.40.6. Although you do not need the IP address when installing WebBoard, an IP address must be in your computer's TCP/IP stack. The Domain Name System (DNS) keeps track of your IP address and FQDN and allows browsers to use either one when reaching a specific site.

Either your Internet Service Provider or network administrator can provide you with the FQDN and IP address for your WebBoard computer, or with more information for procuring a static IP address and domain name.

TCP/IP Connection to an Internal Network

Running WebBoard on an intranet to provide an internal conferencing system (such as for a department or departments of a company) requires that the network be running TCP/IP. Also, the computer on which you install WebBoard must have a properly configured connection to that network. If your computer is on a network, get the IP address and Fully Qualified Domain Name for it from your network administrator.

TCP/IP Connection to the Internet

If you want your WebBoard to be reachable by other computers on the Internet, you need an Internet connection that puts your computer "on the Internet." There are three primary ways a computer can be connected to the Internet, as shown in Figure 2-1.

Figure 2-1 Connecting to the Internet

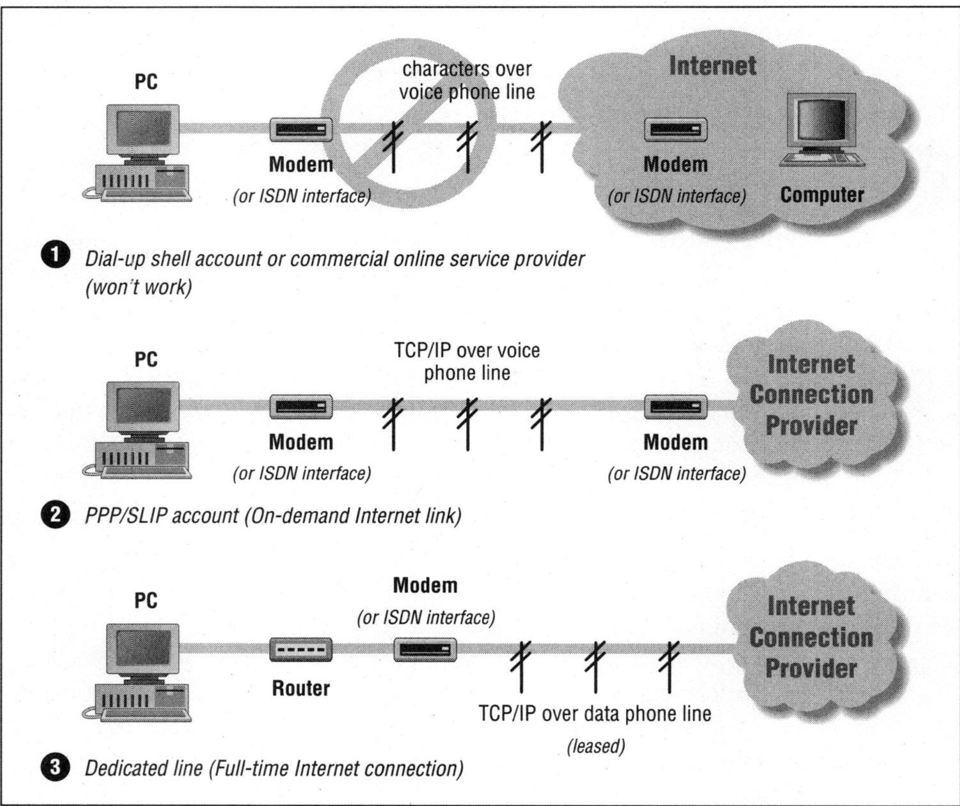

Dial-up shell account

Although inexpensive and readily available, a dial-up shell account will not work for WebBoard because it does not support the TCP/IP protocol suite.

Note

Commercial online service providers such as Prodigy, CompuServe, and America Online currently offer some type of Internet access; however, these services will not give you the kind of connection necessary to run WebBoard.

PPP or SLIP account

Also dial-up accounts, PPP (Point-to-Point Protocol) or SLIP (Serial Line Internet Protocol) accounts *can* work for WebBoard because they support TCP/IP. PPP and SLIP accounts require a high-speed modem (9600 bits per second minimum; 14.4 K or 28.8 K bps are better) to connect your computer to an Internet Service Provider. Once the connection is established, your computer is actually part of the Internet. If both types of accounts are available, we recommend a PPP account.

Many ISPs offer a PPP connection that does not give you a Fully Qualified Domain Name nor a static IP address. Rather, they assign dynamic IP addresses each time you connect to the Internet via their routers; thus each time you probably have a different IP address and no domain name. A dynamic IP address will *not* work for WebBoard. You must have an account that provides a static IP address and a Fully Qualified Domain Name. Be sure to get the details from your ISP, because this type of service usually costs more to set up and maintain. You will also need to register your domain name with the InterNIC, the organization that manages the domain name database. Your ISP can also assist you with registering your domain name.

If you choose to use a PPP or SLIP connection, you must also configure the software needed to dial the Internet Service Provider and establish the proper connection. The Remote Access Service (RAS) under Windows NT 3.51 or Dial-Up Networking under Windows 95 and NT 4.0 can handle these tasks. See the Windows documentation for more information.

Dedicated Line

The most expensive and difficult to set up, a dedicated line (such as a T1 line) gives you a full-time, high-speed connection to the Internet. If you expect a lot of traffic on your WebBoard server or you plan to offer WebBoard hosting services for your clients, you should consider a dedicated line, which requires an additional piece of hardware, a *router*, to handle Internet traffic. Your Internet Service Provider and the local phone company can help you set up a dedicated line.

If you already have full-time access to the Internet from your computer, you probably have a dedicated line. Check with your network administrator to make sure your computer is configured correctly and that you have the correct IP address and Fully Qualified Domain Name.

Note

ISDN (Integrated Services Digital Network) is a specialized type of phone line that can be used for both voice and data (at the same time). If ISDN is available from the local phone company, an ISDN line can work for either an on-demand (PPP/SLIP) or full-time (dedicated line) network and achieve speeds as great as some leased-line connections. ISDN connections require a special piece of hardware similar to a modem.

Web Server Requirements

WebBoard is an application for providing conferencing over the Web and, as such, requires a web server. WebBoard comes with its own internal web server, which means you don't need to have an additional piece of software to install and manage. However, if you are already running a web server or plan to put one in place, WebBoard will probably work just fine as an add-on application. WebBoard works with any web server that is compliant with either the Windows Common Gateway Interface (Win-CGI) specification, Version 1.1, or the Internet Server Application Programming Interface (ISAPI). The following sections provide a bit more detail about these server options.

Note

Earlier versions of WebBoard (pre-Version 1.0c) required that the web server be compliant with the Win-CGI 1.2 specification. This change in WebBoard 2.0 greatly increases the number of servers on which WebBoard can run.

WebBoard's Internal Server

A new feature with WebBoard 2.0, the internal web server provides all the functionality necessary for WebBoard to operate properly. The web server handles requests to WebBoard and returns responses to the user's browser. There are several advantages to using WebBoard's internal server:

- No additional software to install, configure, or manage
- Full support for all WebBoard features, including file attachment (some other web servers do not support file attachments)
- Enhanced performance from a tightly integrated, efficient package
- No chance of error in mapping WebBoard's executable and document space—all mapping is performed automatically during installation.
- WebBoard's address (URL) does not need to include the WebBoard path; rather, the URL is the same as the computer's domain name. For example, with the internal server running, WebBoard is reached with the URL *http://*

your.server.name/, where *your.server.name* is the FQDN of your computer. Using an external server, you must include the WebBoard path information: *http://your.server.name/webboard/$webb.exe* or *http://your.server.name/webboard/webboard.dll*.

- WebBoard's internal web server works independently of any other web server you may have installed. Note, however, that one of the servers must be assigned to a different port. We recommend you assign WebBoard's internal server to a port other than 80 (the default for web servers), such as port 8080. This change is easy to make and is described in Chapter 3.

If you choose to use WebBoard's internal server, you will be asked during installation to provide the network port number, the Fully Qualified Domain Name for the server, and an email address for the server administrator.

We highly recommend you use WebBoard's built-in internal web server. Note that this web server does not support any other web-serving activities, such as serving other documents or images; it is dedicated to WebBoard alone.

External Servers

WebBoard also runs on any Windows CGI or ISAPI-compliant web server. Among the servers that meet these requirements are

- WebSite and WebSite Professional from O'Reilly & Associates
- Internet Information Server (IIS), Peer Web Server, and Personal Web Server from Microsoft
- FastTrack from Netscape Communications
- Purveyor WebServer from Process Software

Despite the fact that WebBoard runs on all the servers listed, not all of them support WebBoard's full feature set. For example, only the WebSite servers (and WebBoard's internal web server) support WebBoard's file attachment capability. The other servers do not support HTTP file uploading, which is the method used by WebBoard. HTTP file uploading relies on the protocol of the Web—HTTP, or Hypertext Transfer Protocol—rather than on the older FTP, or File Transfer Protocol, for uploading file attachments to WebBoard. If you choose a server that does not support HTTP file uploading, you may want to disable file attachments for your WebBoard (see Chapter 4).

During installation WebBoard attempts to set up the proper mapping of the server's Windows CGI or ISAPI scripts directory to the WebBoard script directory. This mapping is essential for WebBoard to function properly and display the correct HTML pages and images. If you are using one of the WebSite servers, WebBoard automatically configures the mapping. For the other servers, you must supply the Win-CGI or ISAPI scripts directory during installation. If you are unsure of this directory's location, refer to your web server's documentation. Of course, to avoid all these configuration and feature issues, we recommend you use WebBoard's internal web server.

Note

If you plan to run WebBoard on a Netscape FastTrack web server, make sure the server has a Windows CGI directory set up before you install WebBoard. By default, FastTrack does not create this directory; rather, most FastTrack CGI scripts are placed in the *cgi-bin* directory. The *cgi-bin* directory *will not work* for WebBoard. You must create a Windows CGI directory with the proper mapping. We recommend you name the directory *cgi-win*. See your FastTrack documentation for instructions.

Browser Requirements

Taking full advantage of WebBoard's features, from its frames-based display to its JavaScript Chat, requires a browser that can support this advanced feature set. The following browsers support WebBoard's features, except as noted:

Netscape Navigator 3.0 and higher
: fully supports all WebBoard's features and is our recommended browser

Microsoft Internet Explorer 3.0 and higher
: supports all WebBoard's features except file attachments. We have also discovered some idiosyncrasies in various versions of the Internet Explorer browser, which are noted as appropriate in this book.

America Online browser 3.0 and higher
: supports all WebBoard's features except file attachments and JavaScript (the application used for WebBoard's Chat feature and administrative wizards).

Note

Browsers continue to evolve and improve. What may not have worked while we were writing this book may very well work shortly after it is published. We encourage you to test new browsers as they become available and note what problems your users encounter when using browsers other than those listed here. We are interested in hearing your feedback on browsers. Please visit WebBoard Central (*http://webboard.ora.com*) and let us know about your experiences.

Other Setup Requirements

During installation, you will be asked for some additional information, depending on which web server you chose and whether this is a new installation or an upgrade installation. This section discusses those additional requirements.

Email Settings

WebBoard automatically sends out a welcome message to new users of your WebBoard. The message contains the user's login name and password, as well as information about your WebBoard (you can edit this email file, which is called *welcome.txt*, as described in Chapter 8). WebBoard also sends email notices to alert users that new messages have been posted in conferences they have selected for email notification.

To send these email messages, WebBoard requires the following information:

Mail server name

This must be an SMTP (Simple Mail Transfer Protocol) mail server, for which you need to know the domain name or IP address. SMTP is the Internet standard for sending email messages. Typically you have access to an SMTP server through your ISP or your local network. If you are unsure of the SMTP mail server's name or IP address, please ask your ISP or network administrator.

Sender's email address

This address is used on all WebBoard email as the return address. This address is usually for the WebBoard system administrator; however, you may choose to use any email account name or create a new account for sending email messages, such as *OurWebBoard@my.server.name*.

Email account for sending wmail

All WebBoard email notifications (not welcome messages) are sent to users as blind carbon copies. That is, the users' names are listed on the Bcc line of the email so that other users do not know who else is receiving the message notifying them of new messages in a specific conference. To send email to Bcc recipients, WebBoard's mail program requires an email account for the To field of the message. Typically this account will be the WebBoard system administrator's account, but can be any account you choose. Note that any bounced emails are returned to this account.

Authentication Mode: Basic or Cookie?

If you choose to use WebBoard's internal web server or one of the WebSite servers, you have a choice of authentication mode:

Basic Authentication

This mode requires that the user enter his or her login name and password each time he or she visits WebBoard. In addition, the WebBoard system administrator must set up Basic Authentication to admit guest users (this procedure is described in Chapter 3). The benefit of Basic Authentication is that no information must be downloaded to the user's computer, as Cookie Authentication requires.

Cookie Authentication

A cookie is a small piece of information that is downloaded to the user's computer through the browser. This bit of information is retained for later use. In WebBoard, cookies are used to speed the login process: a user can request that WebBoard remember his or her password between sessions. Note that if the user's browser has cookie notification turned on, several warning messages will appear during the login process. The benefit of using Cookie Authentication is that it is faster and simpler; this is the default setting.

If you choose to use one of the other servers, only Cookie Authentication is available.

Note

If you select one authentication mode and then wish to change to the other, WebBoard's user database is not affected. Your users supply the same login name and password for either mode.

WebBoard System Administrator

The WebBoard system administrator oversees all WebBoard functions, data, and users. The system administrator performs administrative tasks such as compacting the database and resetting database counters. He or she can also create virtual boards as well as manage conferences and users. The system administrator has privileges that give him or her complete control over WebBoard's activities.

If you are upgrading from a previous version of WebBoard, the system administrator will be the same as before and you will not be asked for this information during installation. If you are performing a new installation, WebBoard requires the following information:

Login name

The system administrator will use this name to log in to WebBoard. You may want to make this name generic, such as *SysAdmin*. If a virtual board is set up to use login rather than real names, this name will appear in the system administrator's profile and all message postings.

Password

The system administrator will use this password to log in to WebBoard. *Do not lose this password!* You will not be able to recover from a lost system administrator's password.

First name

The system administrator's real first name. You may want to use your real name or a generic term. If a virtual board is set up to use real names, this name will appear in the system administrator's profile and all message postings.

Last name

The system administrator's real last name. You may want to use your real name or a generic term. If a virtual board is set up to use real names, this name will appear in the system administrator's profile and all message postings.

Email address

The system administrator's email address, used in *mailto* URLs constructed by WebBoard. You may want to use your real email address or a generic WebBoard address, such as *WebBoardAdmin@my.server.name*.

Service or Application?

If you choose to use WebBoard's internal web server or one of the WebSite servers, WebBoard can be run as a system service or as a desktop application, under either Windows NT or Windows 95. If you run WebBoard as an add-on to one of the other servers, it will run only as a service, since these servers run only as services; you will not be given this choice of run mode during installation.

There is no difference in performance or operation of WebBoard as a service or application. You can change WebBoard's mode at any time through the WebBoard Properties. The advantage of running WebBoard as a service is that it runs when no one is logged onto the computer (a security feature), and it can restart automatically without someone having to log in and launch it (such as after a power failure). If WebBoard runs as an application, its icon appears on the desktop (Windows NT 3.51) or in the status area of the taskbar (Windows 95 and NT 4.0). If WebBoard runs as a service, the icon is hidden and does not appear on the screen.

To run as a service under Windows NT, WebBoard must have administrator privileges, meaning that when you install WebBoard you must do so from an administrator-level account. Also, if you run WebBoard as an add-on to WebSite or WebSite Professional, both the web server and WebBoard must be running in the same mode—either both as desktop applications or both as system services.

With WebBoard as a desktop application, you can start it manually or have it start automatically whenever you log in (by placing it in your startup group). Although WebBoard will not stay running when you log out, you can leave it running and simply lock your screen to prevent unauthorized use. The advantages of running WebBoard as an application are that it is easier to stop and start, and the icon is readily visible, so you know at a glance that it is running. Note, too, that WebBoard's icon is animated, displaying the number of current connections or other status in the icon's caption.

Unless you are familiar with Windows NT services and the identity issues involved, we recommend you start by using WebBoard as a desktop application.

You will find it easier to set up initially and can switch it to a service later. If you are already using several other services on your computer and are familiar with how they work, you may prefer to run WebBoard as a service from the beginning.

To Learn More

If you'd like more information about these topics or about other Web and Internet topics in general, we suggest reading the online help and documentation for your operating system. We also recommend the following books published by O'Reilly & Associates, available for online ordering at *http://www.ora.com*:

- *The Whole Internet for Windows 95*, by Ed Krol and Paula Ferguson
- *Managing Internet Information Services*, by Cricket Liu, Jerry Peek, Russ Jones, Bryan Buus, and Adrian Nye
- *Getting Connected: The Internet at 56K and Up*, by Kevin Dowd
- *Networking Personal Computers with TCP/IP*, by Craig Hunt
- *DNS and BIND*, 2nd edition by Paul Albitz and Cricket Liu
- *HTML: The Definitive Guide*, by Chuck Musciano and Bill Kennedy
- *Designing for the Web: Getting Started in a New Medium*, by Jennifer Niederst and Edie Freedman
- *Inside the Windows Registry*, by Ron Petrusha
- *Win95 and WinNT Annoyances*, by David A. Karp (Spring 1997 estimated release)

Also, check out the books listed at the back of this book and other resources at O'Reilly Software Online (*http://software.ora.com/*).

3

Installing WebBoard

Before you can install WebBoard, you'll need to collect some information about your hardware, software, connectivity, and other options, as described in Chapter 2. With that information and with a properly configured system and Internet connection (either dialup or through a network), installing WebBoard is a simple job handled by the setup program.

WebBoard installation takes only a few minutes. After installation, you must test WebBoard and, if you chose not to use WebBoard's internal server, verify that mappings for the external web server are correct. Completing these tasks is important to ensure that WebBoard is installed correctly and operating properly.

During installation, WebBoard uses the information you provide, as well as information from your Windows 95 or Windows NT system Registry and configuration files, to set the basic parameters for the program. Much of this general information is recorded in the General page of WebBoard Properties. We'll look at this information and show you how to make changes to it.

We'll also show you how to set up Basic Authentication and how to change WebBoard's run mode from desktop application to system service (or vice versa). The option to run WebBoard as an application or a service is available only if you use the WebBoard internal web server or one of the WebSite servers. The other external web servers run only as services and require that WebBoard also run as a service—one more reason you should choose to use WebBoard's internal web server.

This chapter begins with a quick start summary, followed by detailed installation instructions for both a new installation of WebBoard 2.0 and an upgrade from WebBoard 1.0. Next, it walks through the tests and the general information included in WebBoard Properties. Finally, it tells you how to set up Basic Authentication, how to run WebBoard as a service, and where to find help.

Quick Start Summary

To install and test WebBoard, you must complete the following steps. These steps are listed briefly here, and explained fully in the next sections.

1. Review the WebBoard installation requirements (see Chapter 2). You may need to ask your network administrator or Internet Service Provider (ISP) for some information.
2. If you are upgrading from a previous version of WebBoard, make backup copies of your WebBoard directory (and all subdirectories) and the DUKE Registry key, located under HKEY_LOCAL_MACHINE\SOFTWARE\ in the Windows Registry.
3. If you are running other Windows applications—including WebBoard and/or your web server—close them before starting installation.
4. Start the WebBoard Setup program on the CD-ROM by double-clicking *Setup.exe* in the Windows Explorer or File Manager.
5. Choose the installation directory for the WebBoard software.
6. Choose the web server. Depending on your choice, you may need to provide additional information.
7. Enter the email settings information.
8. Choose the location for making backup copies of existing files.
9. For WebBoard and WebSite servers only, select the authentication mode.
10. Enter the WebBoard system administrator's information.
11. Enroll your copy of WebBoard at WebBoard Central (*http://webboard.ora.com*).
12. Test WebBoard's operation.
13. Verify the web server mappings.
14. Review the General page of WebBoard Properties.

Installing the WebBoard Software

WebBoard comes on the CD-ROM inserted in the back of this book. The software includes the WebBoard Server, with built-in web server, and the WebBoard Properties software. These components are installed by the WebBoard Setup program.

Note

You must have installed TCP/IP as a network protocol in order for WebBoard to operate, even if you don't plan to allow Internet access. For more information on installing TCP/IP in Windows NT or Windows 95, see your Windows documentation.

Performing a New Installation

The following procedures will install the WebBoard software. Read each installation screen for instructions and information. Some of the steps listed are specific to a Windows NT or to a Windows 95 installation.

Note

If you have a previous version of WebBoard, you have the option to upgrade to Version 2.0 or to install WebBoard 2.0 as a completely separate application. If you upgrade, all your previous conferences, messages, and users will be converted to the new 2.0 format. If you do not upgrade, you will not be able to use your old database with the new program. Unless you have a compelling reason not to upgrade, we encourage you to do so. However, if you decide to install a fresh copy of WebBoard 2.0 and not upgrade, follow the steps in this section.

To install WebBoard for the first time, complete the following steps. Remember to click Next to move to the next screen.

1. Start your computer and log on to Windows NT or Windows 95. If you are installing WebBoard under Windows NT, you must be the Administrator or have administrator privileges.

2. To avoid conflicts, close all Windows applications. If your web server is running and you plan to use that server with WebBoard, shut it down as well.

3. Insert the CD-ROM into your CD-ROM drive.

4. If you are using Windows 95 or Windows NT 4.0, display the CD-ROM in the Windows Explorer and double-click on *Setup* (or *Setup.exe)*. If you are using Windows NT 3.51, display the CD-ROM in the File Manager and double-click on *Setup.exe*. Under Windows 95 or NT 4.0, you can also use Add/Remove Programs from the Control Panel.

5. The WebBoard Setup program displays the welcome screen. Click Next to begin installation.

6. Choose the installation directory for the WebBoard software. The default location is *C:\WebBoard*, but you can install the software in another directory. Click Next to accept the default, or click Browse to choose another directory and click Next to continue.

7. Choose the web server you wish to use for WebBoard (see Figure 3-1.). If you do not have a web server, choose WebBoard's internal web server. You may also use the internal web server even if you have another web server on your computer. We recommend you use WebBoard's internal server for increased performance and ease of use.

Figure 3-1 WebBoard Web Server Selection

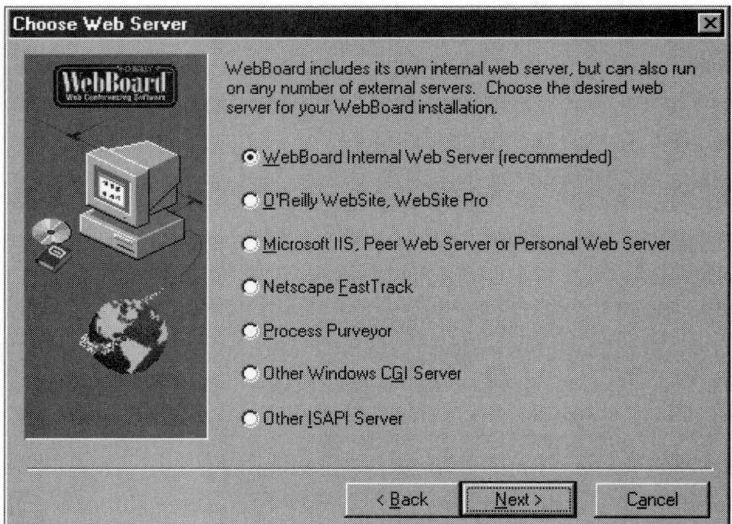

Note

If you selected any web server other than WebBoard's internal server or one of the O'Reilly WebSite servers, a warning screen appears telling you that file attachments to WebBoard postings are not supported by that server. You may select a server that does support file attachments by clicking Back to redisplay the web server selection list.

8. Depending on what server you selected in Step 7, go to the step listed here:
   - WebBoard Internal Web Server, *go to Step 9*
   - O'Reilly WebSite or WebSite Professional, *go to Step 12*
   - Microsoft IIS, Peer Web Server, or Personal Server, *go to Step 13*
   - Netscape FastTrack, *go to Step 10*
   - Process Purveyor, *go to Step 11*

- Other Windows CGI server, *go to Step 10*
- Other ISAPI server, *go to Step 11*

9. Enter the following settings for WebBoard's internal web server (see Figure 3-2):

Figure 3-2 WebBoard Internal Web Server Settings

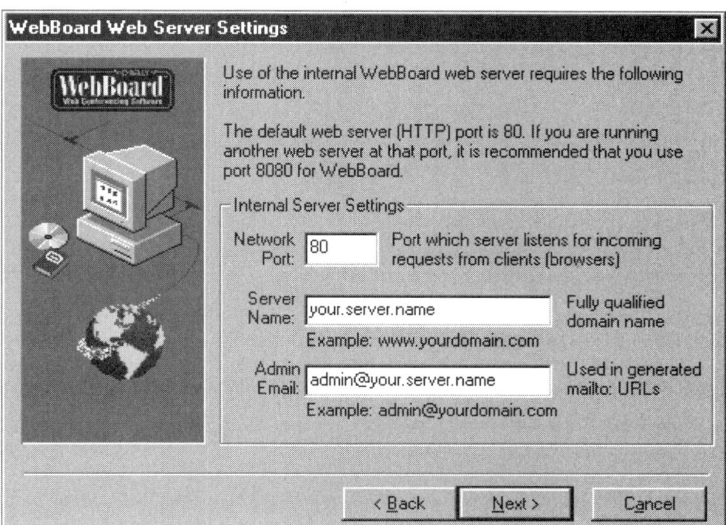

Network Port

By default, the port on which web servers listen for incoming requests is 80. If you are running another web server, it is probably using that port and you will need to assign a different port number to WebBoard's server. Typically, port 8080 is the second port used for web servers. Note that if you use a port other than 80, you must include the port number in the WebBoard URL, for example, *http://your.server.name:8080*.

Server Name

The Fully Qualified Domain Name (FQDN) by which your WebBoard will be identified on the Internet (or intranet). WebBoard tries to guess this name based on the configuration of your system.

Administrator's Email Address

The email address for the web server's administrator. It will be used in mailto URLs generated by the server (such as on error messages). You may want to use your own address or a generic one, such as *admin@your.server.name*.

10. For Netscape FastTrack and other Win-CGI servers, you must locate the directory used by the server for Windows CGI programs. This directory is often

called *cgi-win*. See your web server's documentation for more information on setting up and/or identifying the Windows CGI directory.

Note

FastTrack does not have a Windows CGI directory as part of its normal setup. You must specifically create this directory and configure all appropriate mappings. You *cannot* use FastTrack's *cgi-bin* directory for WebBoard.

---

11. For Process Purveyor and other ISAPI servers, you must locate the directory used by the server for ISAPI scripts. This directory is normally called *SCRIPTS*. See your web server's documentation for more information on setting up and/or identifying the scripts directory.
12. For both the WebBoard internal server and the WebSite servers, select how you want WebBoard to run from among these three options:
    - *Application (manual start)*. Installs WebBoard as an application that you must start each time you log in to Windows.
    - *Application (automatic start at login)*. Installs the WebBoard server as an application in the Startup Group, causing it to start automatically when you log in to Windows.
    - *Service (system start)*. Installs the WebBoard server as a service. The WebBoard icon does not appear on the Desktop.

Note

If you are installing WebBoard as an add-on application to WebSite or WebSite Professional, both WebBoard and the web server must be running either as desktop applications or as system services. You cannot mix the run modes.

---

13. Enter the email settings that WebBoard uses to send welcome and notification messages (see Figure 3-3):

Mail server
: The hostname or address of your SMTP (Simple Mail Transfer Protocol) mail server.

From address
: The email address that appears in the return address or the From field on emails sent to WebBoard users.

Via account
: The email account (address) used to send WebBoard email. This name appears in the To field, and all recipients (WebBoard users) are listed in the blind carbon copy (Bcc) field.

Figure 3-3 WebBoard Email Settings

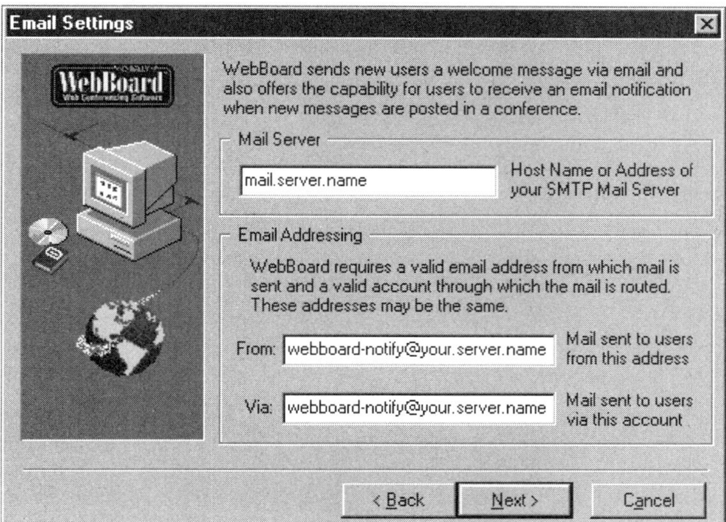

14. Setup next asks if you want backup copies made of all files replaced during installation. We recommend you answer yes, in case you need to recover the original files at any point. All actions taken by WebBoard's Setup program are recorded in the WebBoard installation log.

15. If you answered yes in Step 14, you must select the location for the backed-up files.

16. For either the WebBoard internal server or one of the WebSite servers, choose the authentication mode by which users log in to WebBoard:

    – Basic Authentication requires a login name and password each time.

    – Cookie Authentication lets users have their passwords remembered between sessions.

17. Enter the WebBoard system administrator account information (see Figure 3-4):

    Login name
    The name by which the system administrator logs in to WebBoard.

    Password
    The password by which the system administrator logs in to WebBoard. Note that when you enter the password on this screen, it is shown as plain text. When you log in to WebBoard, the password is hidden. *To maintain the security and integrity of your WebBoard, you should carefully protect the system administrator's login name and password.*

Figure 3-4 WebBoard System Administrator Account

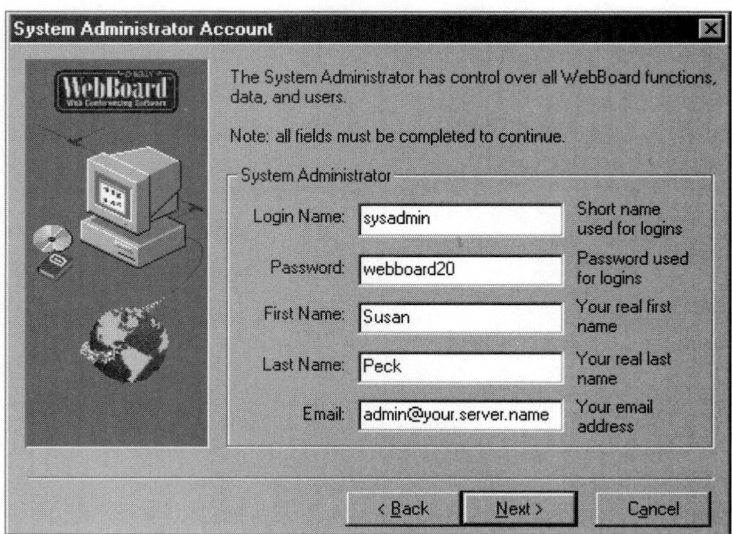

First name

The real first name of the system administrator; this name is shown in the user profile for the system administrator and is used in searches.

Last name

The real last name of the system administrator; this name is shown in the user profile for the system administrator and is used in searches.

Email Address

The email address for the system administrator. You may want to make this your real account or a generic system administration account. The system administrator's email address is used on a variety of WebBoard pages and error messages.

After you click Next, WebBoard Setup displays the system administrator login name and password you entered. Make sure you write them down. If you forget the password or login name, you will not be able to log in to WebBoard!

18. Setup installs the software on your PC. The program displays progress indicators and tells you which files are being installed. Setup also adds information to your Windows Registry and builds the program group or Start menu folder.

19. Setup then displays the WebBoard Release Notes for you to read. Click Next to continue.

20. When setup is complete, choose one of three options for continuing, as described on the final screen displayed to you:

- *Start WebBoard now.* This option is available only if you installed WebBoard under Windows 95 or as a desktop application under NT. When you click Finish, WebBoard starts.
- *Start WebBoard as an NT service.* This option is available if setup was successful and you installed WebBoard as a service. After you click Finish, you must start WebBoard from Services in the NT Control Panel or restart your computer.
- *Restart your computer.* This option appears only if Setup encountered files that were in use. To update those files, click Finish and restart your computer. If WebBoard is running as a service, it will start automatically. If WebBoard is running as a desktop application, it will start either when you log in or when you manually start it.

21. Before you begin testing WebBoard, please take a few moments to enroll your copy of the software. Enrolling WebBoard makes you eligible for product announcements, special offers, and discounts on product upgrades. You can enroll online at WebBoard Central (*http://webboard.ora.com*).

You're now ready to begin testing the installation as described later in this chapter.

Upgrading from a Previous Version of WebBoard

If you are upgrading from a previous version of WebBoard, you need to perform the following actions *before* beginning the upgrade:

- Back up the Registry keys HKEY_LOCAL_MACHINE\SOFTWARE\DUKE. To export or save this key and its subtrees, use the Registry editor (*regedt32.exe* or *regedit.exe*) supplied with Windows NT or Windows 95. These programs are usually installed in your *\Windows* directory. Save the keys under a new name.
- Back up your entire WebBoard installation, including all subdirectories (*Confs, HTML, System*, and so on). If something goes wrong with the update installation, you'll be glad you did this!

After you've completed the actions in the preceding list, perform these steps:

1. Start your computer and log on to Windows NT or Windows 95. If you are installing WebBoard under Windows NT, you must be the Administrator or have administrator privileges.
2. To avoid conflicts, close all Windows applications. If your web server is running and you plan to use that server with WebBoard, shut it down as well.
3. Insert the CD-ROM into your CD-ROM drive.

4. If you are using Windows 95 or Windows NT 4.0, display the CD-ROM in the Windows Explorer and double-click on *Setup* (or *Setup.exe*). If you are using Windows NT 3.51, display the CD-ROM in the File Manager and double-click on *Setup.exe*. Under Windows 95 or NT 4.0, you can also use Add/Remove Programs from the Control Panel.
5. The WebBoard Setup program displays the welcome screen. Click Next to begin installation.
6. The Setup program displays the Upgrade Previous Installation dialog box (Figure 3-5), which gives you two choices:

Figure 3-5 Upgrade Previous Installation?

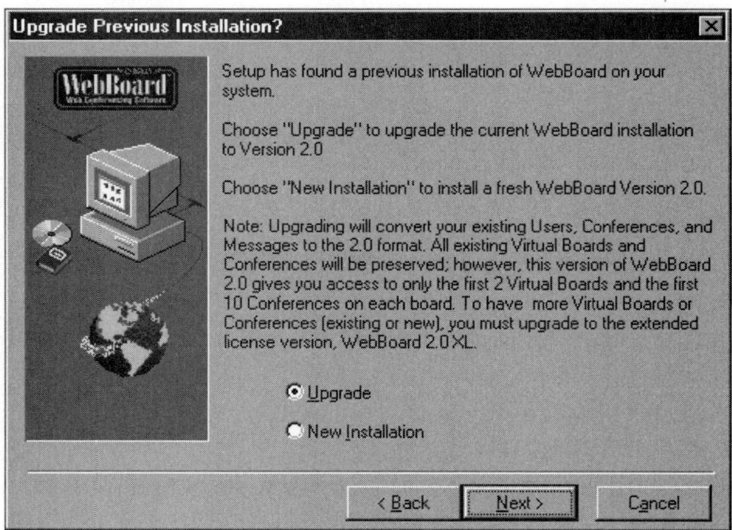

– Upgrade to 2.0. If you choose to upgrade from your previous version of WebBoard, the database of conferences, messages, and users will be converted to the new WebBoard 2.0 format. Note that if you have more than two virtual boards or more than 10 conferences per board, only the first two boards and first 10 conferences will be available after the upgrade. The other boards and conferences are also converted and ready to use, but require the extended license (XL) version of WebBoard 2.0. For more information on upgrading to WebBoard 2.0 XL, see Appendix A.

  If you choose this option, continue with Step 6.

– Perform a new installation. If you choose to install WebBoard 2.0 as a new application, none of your existing conferences, messages, or users will be converted to the new format and *cannot* be used with WebBoard 2.0. This option lets you see WebBoard 2.0 and explore its new features before deciding whether or not to upgrade. You may later upgrade by uninstalling WebBoard 2.0 completely (including the O'Reilly\WebBoard Registry key) and reinstalling it as an upgrade.

If you choose this option, complete the steps for Performing a New Installation, earlier in this chapter. *Make sure you install WebBoard 2.0 into a directory different from the WebBoard 1.0 directory; otherwise, your previous installation will be overwritten.*

7. Confirm the location of your WebBoard *Confs* directory, so your existing conferences can be upgraded. Click Next to accept the displayed location, or click Browse to choose another directory and click Next to continue.
8. Confirm the location of your WebBoard *System* directory, so your existing database can be upgraded. Click Next to accept the displayed location, or click Browse to choose another directory and click Next to continue.
9. Choose the installation directory for the WebBoard software. This should be the same directory as your current WebBoard installation. Click Next to accept the displayed location, or click Browse to choose another directory and click Next to continue.
10. Choose the web server you wish to use for WebBoard (see Figure 3-6.). If you do not have a web server, choose WebBoard's internal web server. You may also use the internal web server even if you have another web server on your computer. We recommend you use WebBoard's internal server for increased performance and ease of use.

Figure 3-6 WebBoard Web Server Selection

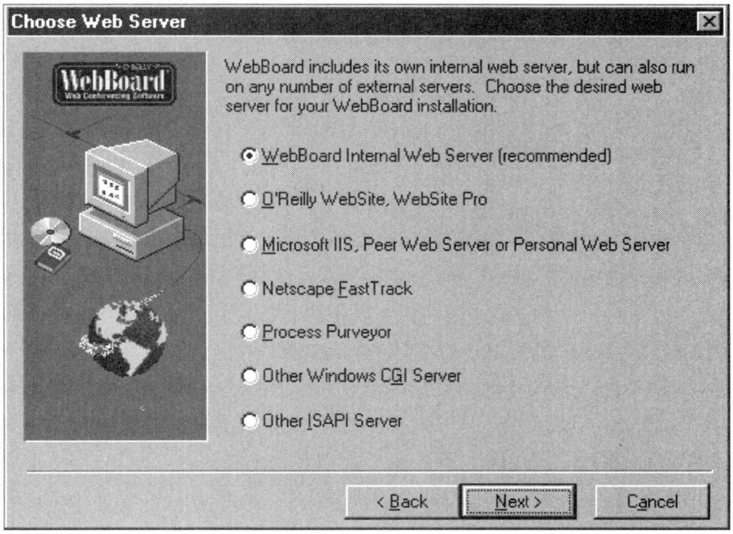

Note

If you selected any web server other than WebBoard's internal server or one of the O'Reilly WebSite servers, a warning screen appears telling you that file attachments to WebBoard postings are not supported by that server. You may select a server that does support file attachments by clicking Back to redisplay the web server selection list.

11. Depending on what server you selected in Step 10, go to the step listed here:
    - WebBoard Internal Web Server, *go to Step 12*
    - O'Reilly WebSite or WebSite Professional, *go to Step 15*
    - Microsoft IIS, Peer Web Server, or Personal Server, *go to Step 16*
    - Netscape FastTrack, *go to Step 13*
    - Process Purveyor, *go to Step 14*
    - Other Windows CGI server, *go to Step 13*
    - Other ISAPI server, *go to Step 14*
12. Enter the following settings for WebBoard's internal web server (see Figure 3-7):

Figure 3-7 WebBoard Internal Web Server Settings

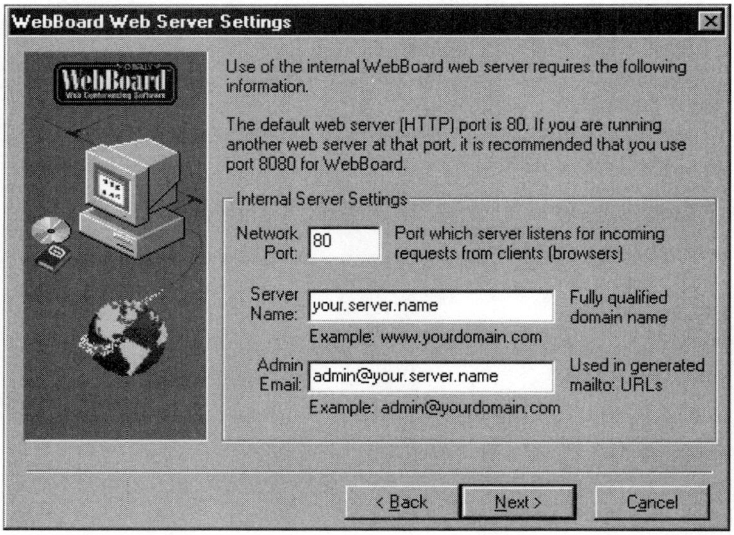

Network port

By default, the port on which web servers listen for incoming requests is 80. If you are running another web server, it is probably using that port and you will need to assign a different port number to WebBoard's server. Typically, port 8080 is the second port used for web servers. Note that if you use a port other than 80, you must include the port number in the WebBoard URL, for example, *http://your.server.name:8080.*

Server name

The Fully Qualified Domain Name (FQDN) by which your WebBoard will be identified on the Internet (or intranet). WebBoard tries to guess this name based on the configuration of your system.

Administrator's email address

The email address for the web server's administrator. It will be used in *mailto* URLs generated by the server (such as on error messages). You may want to use your own address or a generic one, such as *admin@your.server.name.*

13. For Netscape FastTrack and other Win-CGI servers, you must locate the directory used by the server for Windows CGI programs. This directory is often called *cgi-win.* See your web server's documentation for more information on setting up and/or identifying the Windows CGI directory.

Note

FastTrack does not have a Windows CGI directory as part of its normal setup. You must specifically create this directory and configure all appropriate mappings. You *cannot* use FastTrack's *cgi-bin* directory for WebBoard.

---

14. For Process Software Purveyor WebServer and other ISAPI servers, you must locate the directory used by the server for ISAPI scripts. This directory is normally called *SCRIPTS.* See your web server's documentation for more information on setting up and/or identifying the scripts directory.

15. For both the WebBoard internal server and the WebSite servers, select how you want WebBoard to run from among these three options:

    – *Application (manual start).* Installs WebBoard as an application that you must start each time you log in to Windows.

    – *Application (automatic start at login).* Installs the WebBoard server as an application in the Startup Group, causing it to start automatically when you log in to Windows.

    – *Service (system start).* Installs the WebBoard server as a service. The WebBoard icon does not appear on the Desktop.

Note

If you are installing WebBoard as an add-on application to WebSite or WebSite Professional, both WebBoard and the web server must be running either as desktop applications or as system services. You cannot mix the run modes.

---

16. Enter the email settings that WebBoard uses to send welcome and notification messages (see Figure 3-8):

Figure 3-8 WebBoard Email Settings

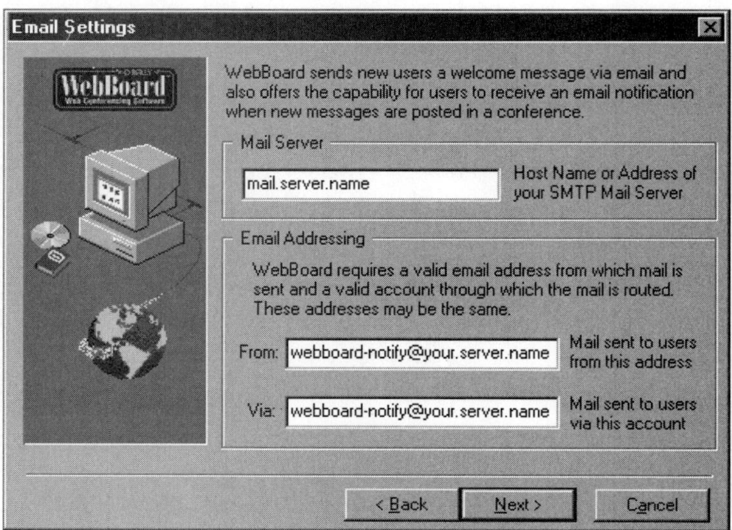

Mail server

The hostname or address of your SMTP mail server.

From address

The email address that appears in the return address or the From field on emails sent to WebBoard users.

Via account

The email account (address) used to send WebBoard email. This name appears in the To field, and all recipients (WebBoard users) are listed in the blind carbon copy (Bcc) field.

17. Setup next asks if you want backup copies made of all files replaced during installation. We recommend you answer yes, in case you need to recover the original files at any point. All actions taken by WebBoard's Setup program are recorded in the WebBoard installation log.

Note

In addition to the general backup directory, Setup renames the WebBoard 1.0 *Confs, HTML, Images,* and *System* directories to *Confs10, HTML10, Images10,* and *System10,* thus maintaining the original 1.0 files should you need to revert to that version or otherwise retrieve a specific file, such as a customized HTML or image file. These directories are retained in the WebBoard installation directory.

18. If you answered yes in Step 17, you must select the location for the backed-up files.

19. For either the WebBoard internal server or one of the WebSite servers, choose the authentication mode by which users log in to WebBoard:

    - Basic Authentication requires a login name and password each time.
    - Cookie Authentication lets a user have his or her password remembered between sessions.

20. If Setup does not find a WebBoard database file (*WEBBOARD.MDB*), it asks for WebBoard system administrator account information (for details, see Step 17 in "Performing a New Installation"). Otherwise, the WebBoard system administrator is user #1 or the first user with security level of 999 from the WebBoard 1.0 database. You can later change the identity of the system administrator, as described in Chapter 6. Note too, that if you had more than one administrator (security level 999) in WebBoard 1.0, you must reassign those administrators as managers to their respective boards after finishing the installation. See Chapter 5 for more information.

21. Setup installs the software on your PC. The program displays progress indicators and tells you which files are being installed. Setup also adds information to your Windows Registry and builds the program group or Start menu folder.

22. Setup then displays the WebBoard Release Notes for you to read. Click Next to continue.

23. When setup is complete, choose one of three options for continuing, as described on the final screen displayed to you:

    - Start WebBoard now. This option is available only if you installed WebBoard under Windows 95 or as a desktop application under NT. When you click Finish, WebBoard starts.
    - Start WebBoard as an NT service. This option is available if setup was successful and you installed WebBoard as a service. After you click Finish, you must start WebBoard from Services in the NT Control Panel or restart your computer.
    - Restart your computer. This option appears only if Setup encountered files that were in use. To update those files, click Finish and restart your computer. If WebBoard is running as a service, it will start automatically. If WebBoard is running as a desktop application, it will start either when you log in or when you manually start it.

24. Before you begin testing WebBoard, please take a few moments to enroll your copy of the software. Enrolling WebBoard makes you eligible for product

announcements, special offers, and discounts on product upgrades. You can enroll online at WebBoard Central (*http://webboard.ora.com*).

You're now ready to begin testing the installation as described later in this chapter.

Note

If your previous installation had a Guest user, the upgrade process converts that account into a full user account with message posting privileges. You should delete the Guest user from WebBoard as described in Chapter 5. With Cookie Authentication, a guest login is always available from the welcome page. Setting up a guest login with Basic Authentication is described later in this chapter.

Taking WebBoard for a Test Drive

After finishing the installation, you must take WebBoard for a test drive to verify that it is installed and operating properly. The test drive has four parts:

- Making sure WebBoard starts properly
- Reaching WebBoard from the local computer
- Reaching WebBoard from a remote computer
- Verifying WebBoard's mappings (external web servers only)

Is WebBoard Running?

The first part of any test drive is to make sure the engine starts and stays running. If you installed WebBoard as a desktop application and asked Setup to start WebBoard when it finished, it should be running. The WebBoard icon—a small golden pushpin—should appear on your screen. The icon title indicates WebBoard's status as *idle* or *busy*. Note that under Windows 95 and Windows NT 4.0, WebBoard's icon is in the Tray portion of the Taskbar. To see its status in a pop-up label, move the mouse cursor over the WebBoard icon in the Tray. If you can see the icon on your screen, then WebBoard has passed the first test—it's running.

If you didn't ask Setup to start WebBoard and you installed WebBoard as a desktop application, you must start it now. Under Windows 95 or Windows NT 4.0, click WebBoard in the WebBoard program folder of the Start menu. Under Windows NT 3.51, double-click the WebBoard icon in the WebBoard program group. WebBoard should start and minimize to an icon on the desktop.

If you installed WebBoard as an NT service or selected an external web server other than WebSite or WebSite Professional (which can run as either services or applications), WebBoard's icon is hidden. You must start the WebBoard service by one of two means:

- Open Services from the Control Panel. Scroll through the list of services until you see WebBoard. Highlight WebBoard, and click Start. The status should now say Started, as shown in Figure 3-9. Click Close to continue.

Figure 3-9 Starting WebBoard as an NT Service

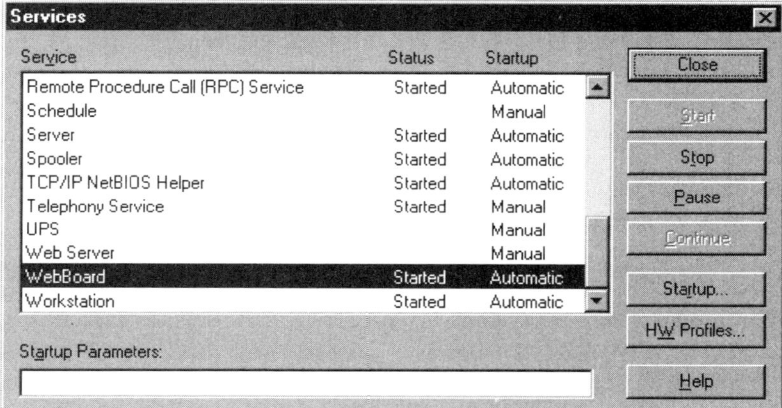

- Restart your system. WebBoard will start automatically as a system service each time you restart.

Note

If you are running WebBoard as a service under NT, make sure that WebBoard is set to *not* interact with the desktop (this option is available by clicking Startup in the Control Panel Services dialog box). If you are running WebBoard as a service with an external web server, *both* must be set to not interact with the desktop. Verify these settings before continuing.

If WebBoard does not start, check the error log (in the *logs* directory of WebBoard) for possible reasons.

Can You Reach WebBoard from the Local Computer?

The next phase of the test drive is to reach WebBoard with a web browser. The URL you use for WebBoard depends on which server you selected for running WebBoard, as listed in Table 3-1. Note that in every instance, the *your.server.name* part of the URL is the Fully Qualified Domain Name (FQDN) of your computer.

Table 3-1 WebBoard URL by web server type

Web Server	*WebBoard URL*
WebBoard internal web server, on port 80	http://your.server.name/
WebBoard internal web server, not on port 80 (for example, on port 8080)	http://your.server.name:port_number (example: http://myserver.com:8080)
WebSite or WebSite Professional	http://your.server.name/webboard/ $webb.exe
IIS, Peer Web Server, Personal Web Server	http://your.server.name/webboard/ webboard.dll
FastTrack	http://your.server.name/cgi-win/$webb.exe
Purveyor	http://your.server.name/scripts/webboard.dll
Other Windows CGI web servers	http://your.server.name/cgi-win/$webb.exe
Other ISAPI web servers	http://your.server.name/scripts/webboard.dll

With the appropriate URL for your web server from Table 3-1, complete the following steps:

1. Make sure WebBoard is running (as described in the preceding section).
2. If you are using an external web server with WebBoard, make sure it is running. You may also need to stop and restart the web server to update its configuration for use with WebBoard.
3. In the web browser's location or address field, enter the URL for WebBoard from Table 3-1, substituting *localhost* for your server's name, as shown for an installation using the WebBoard internal web server:

   ```
   http://localhost/
   ```

   Localhost is a generic address that causes the browser to look for a web server on the local computer. If the web server is not on the default port 80, make sure you include the port number.

   The WebBoard welcome page should appear in your browser, as shown in Figure 3-10.

   Note

   If you selected Basic Authentication during setup, WebBoard displays a Basic Authentication dialog box instead of the welcome page. See the section later in this chapter on setting up Basic Authentication so that users of your WebBoard see a similar welcome page.

Figure 3-10 WebBoard Welcome Page

4. Next, test WebBoard using the IP address. In the browser's location or address field, type in the WebBoard URL, substituting the IP address for the server's domain name, as shown for a WebBoard installation using the internal web server:

   `http://123.123.234.234/`

   The browser should display the page shown in Figure 3-10.

5. If your server's domain name is registered with DNS, test WebBoard using the domain name. In the browser's location or address field, type in the WebBoard URL using the server's domain name, as shown for a WebBoard installation using the internal web server:

   `http://your.server.name/`

   where *your.server.name* is the Fully Qualified Domain Name (FQDN) of your server, such as *www.myserver.com*. The browser should display the document shown in Figure 3-10.

Can You Reach WebBoard from Another Computer?

The next phase of the test drive is to reach WebBoard from a different computer, either one on your internal network or one connected to the Internet. This test is essentially the same as the previous one, only from a different location. It verifies that other people will be able to reach and participate in your web conferences. To complete this test, you must have access to another computer that has a working web browser.

To test WebBoard from another computer, follow these steps:

1. Make sure your WebBoard server is running.
2. If you are using an external web server with WebBoard, make sure it is running.
3. Start a web browser on the other computer.
4. Test WebBoard using the IP address. In the browser's location or address field, type in the WebBoard URL from Table 3-1, substituting the server's domain name with the IP address, as shown for a WebBoard installation using the internal web server:

   http://*123.123.234.234*/

   The browser should display the page shown in Figure 3-10.
5. If your server's domain name is registered with DNS, test WebBoard using the domain name. In the browser's location or address field, type in the WebBoard URL using the server's domain name, as shown for a WebBoard installation using the internal web server:

   `http://your.server.name/`

   where *your.server.name* is the Fully Qualified Domain Name (FQDN) of your server, such as *www.myserver.com*. The browser should display the document shown in Figure 3-10.

If you performed this test from a computer on your local network and it does not work, make sure WebBoard is running as well as the external web server, if appropriate. Next check the TCP/IP configuration of the computer and the network. If you continue to have difficulties, consult your network administrator.

If you conducted this test from a computer connected to the Internet and it failed, try again. Sometimes heavy traffic on the Internet can cause connections to timeout. If after several tries you still cannot reach the server, recheck the TCP/IP connections on both computers. Also make sure your server's name is a Fully Qualified Domain Name and that it is registered with DNS. If you continue to have difficulties, consult your Internet Service Provider.

Verifying WebBoard's Mappings

If the you were unable to reach WebBoard in the preceding tests and you are sure your TCP/IP setup is correct, the problem was most likely incorrect mappings. In general, however, WebBoard takes care of the mappings and you should not need to worry about them. During setup, WebBoard takes the information you provide about script and program file locations for your web server and tries to set up correct mappings. If the preceding tests worked, then it was successful. If they didn't work, you should take a few minutes to verify that the mapping is correct for your server type. Also, if you ever change the type of web server you use with WebBoard, you will want to refer to this section to make sure the mappings are correct for the new server.

Document and program or script mappings—sometimes referred to as *aliases*—are essential to how a web server finds information. In fact, every URL is an example of a mapped address: the path in the URL is completely different from the physical path of the source document for the URL.

For example, the home page URL for most web servers is *http://web.server.name/index.html*. The physical location for the *index.html* file may be much more complex, for example, *C:\WebSite\htdocs\index.html*. The same physical to URL space mapping is required for CGI programs and ISAPI scripts. Proper mapping is essential for a web server (and thus, WebBoard) to function. To understand more about mapping, we recommend you read your web server's documentation or see Chapter 9 of *Building Your Own WebSite* from O'Reilly & Associates.

Tip

You can easily avoid any problems with mapping by using WebBoard's built-in web server.

Table 3-2 shows the correct CGI or ISAPI script mappings for each type of external web server. The mapping column contains both the physical location of the WebBoard CGI program or ISAPI scripts (*$webb.exe,* and *webboard.dll* and *webboard.exe*, respectively) and the URL. Note that the drive letter *x* should be replaced by the letter of the actual drive. Also, the directory names may be different for your installation depending on the location of your web server and WebBoard.

Table 3-2 WebBoard external web server CGI or ISAPI mappings

Web Server	*CGI or ISAPI Script Location and Mapping*
WebSite, WebSite Professional	Directory: *x:\WebBoard\Scripts* URL: */webboard*
IIS, Peer Web Server, Personal Web Server	Directory: *x:\WebBoard\Scripts* URL: */webboard*
FastTrack	Directory: *x:\Netscape\Server\cgi-win* URL: *webboard*
Purveyor	Directory: *x:\Purveyor\Scripts* URL: */scripts*
Other Windows CGI web servers	Directory: *x:\web_server\cgi-win* URL: *cgi-win*
Other ISAPI web servers	Directory: *x:\web_server\Scripts* URL:*/scripts*

Table 3-3 shows the correct document mapping for WebBoard's images. The images are all stored in the *WebBoard\Images* directory. This directory must be mapped to the web server's document space, as listed in the table. Note that the drive letter *x* should be replaced by the letter of the actual drive. Also, the directory name may be different for your installation depending on the location of WebBoard.

Table 3-3 WebBoard external web server images mappings

Web Server	*WebBoard Images Location and Mapping*
WebSite, WebSite Professional	Directory: *x:\WebBoard\Images* URL: */wbimages*
IIS, Peer Web Server, Personal Web Server	Directory: *x:\WebBoard\Images* URL: */wbimages*
FastTrack	Directory: *x:\WebBoard\Images* URL: *wbimages*
Purveyor	Directory: *x:\WebBoard\Images* URL: */~wbimages*
Other Windows CGI web servers	Directory: *x:\WebBoard\Images* URL: */wbimages*
Other ISAPI web servers	Directory: *x:\WebBoard\Images* URL: */wbimages*

To change or review mappings for your particular web server, see its documentation. You may also want to check the online resources at WebBoard Central (described later in this chapter) for more detailed instructions.

Reviewing WebBoard's General Properties

During installation, WebBoard puts specific information in the Windows 95 or Windows NT Registry. Much of this configuration information is displayed—and can be changed—in WebBoard Properties, available from the Start menu folder or program group. We will cover WebBoard Properties in greater detail in Chapter 6, but for now, let's take a look at the most general information. You may need to make changes to the general setup at some point, and this section tells you how.

To view the general information, open WebBoard Properties from the WebBoard program group or Start menu folder. The General page is displayed, as shown in Figure 3-11.

Figure 3-11 WebBoard Properties General page

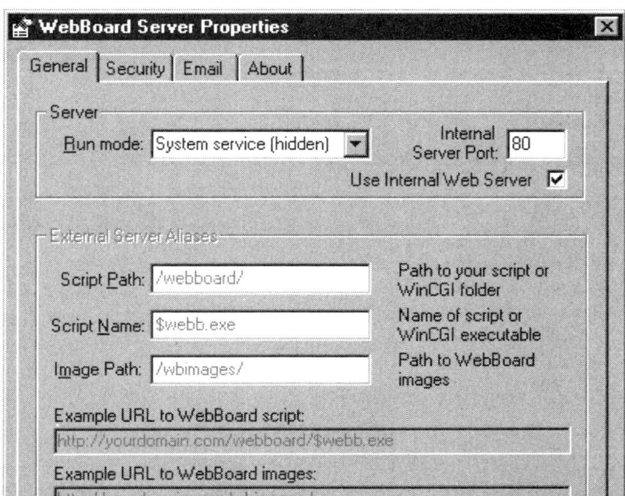

The top section of the General page includes general server information:

Run mode

Specifies how WebBoard will run the next time it is started. If you want to change WebBoard's mode from a desktop application to a service, you must first select a new run mode and then restart WebBoard. If you are running WebBoard with an external web server, both programs must have the same run mode.

WebBoard has three run modes:

Application (minimized)

login or manual start with the WebBoard icon on the desktop (Windows NT 3.51) or in the Taskbar (Windows 95 or NT 4.0)

Application (tray)

login or manual start with the WebBoard icon in the Tray (Windows 95 and NT 4.0 only)

System service (hidden)

continuously running with no icon visible. Technically, a true system service is only a Windows NT option. WebBoard runs as "service" under Windows 95 in that it will continue to run when no one is logged in to the computer. You still select system service as the run mode, but must start WebBoard manually or by placing it in your startup folder. If you are running under Windows 95, we recommend you experiment with WebBoard as an application first before switching to a service, unless you are familiar with running another application (such as WebSite) as a service under Windows 95.

Internal server port
Tells the built-in WebBoard web server what port number to use. The normal (TCP/IP) port is 80. If you are running another web server as well as the WebBoard web server, you will have to make this a different port number. Port 8080 is usually the second choice. You will have to include any port number other than 80 in the WebBoard URL.

Use internal web server
Specifies whether or not WebBoard will use the built-in web server.

The remainder of this page covers items specific to using an external web server with WebBoard:

Script path
Identifies the URL path to the Windows CGI or ISAPI script location. This path is used in building the URL for reaching WebBoard and in WebBoard HTML files that include links to other WebBoard documents. This value is determined during setup, based on the type of web server and location of the Windows CGI or ISAPI script directory you provided. If you change either of these items for WebBoard, you may also need to update the value in this field. See Table 3-1 and Table 3-2 for specific information. Note that you cannot change the value of this field when the internal web server is selected.

Script name
Identifies the name of the Windows CGI program or ISAPI script for running WebBoard. This name is used in building the URL for reaching WebBoard. This value is determined during setup, based on the type of web server you selected. If you change the web server type, you may also need to update the value in this field. See Table 3-1 for specific information. Note that you cannot change the value of this field when the internal web server is selected.

Image path
Identifies the URL path to the WebBoard images location. This path is used for sourcing images into WebBoard HTML documents. This value is determined during setup, based on the type of web server you selected. If you change the web server type, you may also need to update the value in this field. See Table 3-3 for specific information. Note that you cannot change the value of this field when the internal web server is selected.

Example URL to WebBoard script

Displays a sample URL for reaching WebBoard using the type of web server specified and the script path and name values from the preceding fields. See Table 3-1 for more information.

Example URL to WebBoard images

Displays a sample URL for reaching WebBoard's images based on the proper mapping, as specified in the image path field above. See Table 3-3 for more information.

Note

When you make a change to WebBoard Properties, you must either click Apply or OK for the changes to take place. When WebBoard's configuration is updated, you will hear the computer beep. If WebBoard is not running, you will not hear a beep, but the configuration is in effect the next time you start the program. If you change the script or image information, you may also need to stop and restart your web server and WebBoard.

Setting Up Basic Authentication

Both the WebBoard internal web server and the WebSite servers let you choose one of two authentication modes: Basic Authentication or Cookie Authentication. The differences between these two modes is discussed in Chapter 2. If you selected Basic Authentication, this section tells you how to set up a friendly login page for your users. It is similar to the login (or welcome) page presented to users on Cookie-based WebBoards, but does not include a username and password dialog box (see Figure 3-10). Rather, it includes three buttons: one for new users, one for existing users, and one for guest users, as shown in Figure 3-12.

The HTML file for the Basic Authentication login page is called *enter.html*. WebBoard installs this file in the *WebBoard* directory, not in the *WebBoard\Html* directory. Setting up this page differs according to which web server is being used, as described here:

Under WebSite or WebSite Professional

Copy *enter.html* to the web server's document root directory. The default document root directory for WebSite and WebSite Pro is *\WebSite\htdocs*. Then create a link from some other web page (for example, *index.html*) to *enter.html*. By clicking on this link, users will receive the WebBoard login page for Basic Authentication.

Under WebBoard's internal web server

This is a bit trickier and requires that you have another web server running from which *enter.html* can point to WebBoard's server. First, complete the procedure just listed. Then edit *enter.html* to change the WebBoard URLs to

Figure 3-12 Basic Authentication login page, *enter.html*

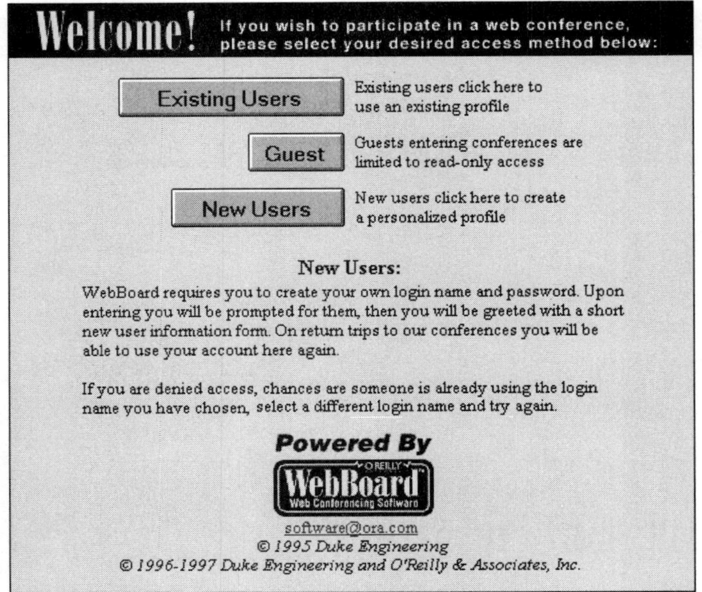

use the correct port. For example, if WebSite were running on port 80 and WebBoard on port 8080, you would need to add port 8080 to each of the WebBoard URLs. You must also make sure you have the correct document mapping set up so that */wbimages* points to *WebBoard\Images*. This mapping is necessary to correctly display the images in *enter.html*.

By default (and for security reasons), WebBoard does not configure a guest user for Basic Authentication even though *enter.html* has a Guest button. A guest can read messages but not post them or participate in chat. However, you can allow or disallow guest users under Basic Authentication, as described here:

To allow guest users

In the *WebBoard\Scripts* copy *$webb.exe* to *guest.exe*. This script causes WebBoard to make available only a limited feature set whenever a user clicks the Guest button on the login page.

To disallow guest users

Remove the Guest button from *enter.html*. This section is clearly labeled in the file and is displayed as follows:

```
<!-- To disallow Guest Users, remove this <TR> block -->
<tr>
<td align=right>
<form action="/webboard/guest.exe" method="get">
<input type="submit" value="Guest">
</form>
```

```
</td>
<td valign=top>
<font face="Arial,Helv" size="-1">
Guests entering conferences are
<br>
limited to read-only access
</font>
</td>
</tr>
<!-- To disallow Guest Users, remove the above <TR> block -->
```

For more information on logging in with Basic Authentication, see the discussion in Chapter 9.

Running WebBoard as a Service

You can elect to run WebBoard as a service rather than a desktop application under Windows 95 or Windows NT. The advantage of running WebBoard as a service is that it runs even when no one is logged on to the computer, a helpful feature if you run your server 24 hours a day and don't want to leave an open account on an unattended computer. In addition, running WebBoard as a service allows it to restart automatically when the operating system reboots.

Note

You can run WebBoard as a desktop application or service only if you are using WebBoard's built-in web server or one of the WebSite servers. The other external web servers all run as services and require that WebBoard also run as a service.

To change WebBoard from a desktop application to a system service requires only a few quick steps. All the information the operating system needs is in place—you simply have to shut down WebBoard as an application, make one change in WebBoard Properties, and start it up again as a service as described in these steps:

1. Close WebBoard if it is running.
2. Open WebBoard Properties and display the General page.
3. From the Run Mode pulldown list, select System service.
4. Close WebBoard Properties.
5. Under Windows 95, start WebBoard from the WebBoard Start menu folder. WebBoard is now running as a service.
6. Under Windows NT, you must complete some additional steps. From the Windows NT Control Panel, open Services.

7. Scroll through the listed services until you come to WebBoard, as shown in Figure 3-13.

Figure 3-13 Windows NT Services

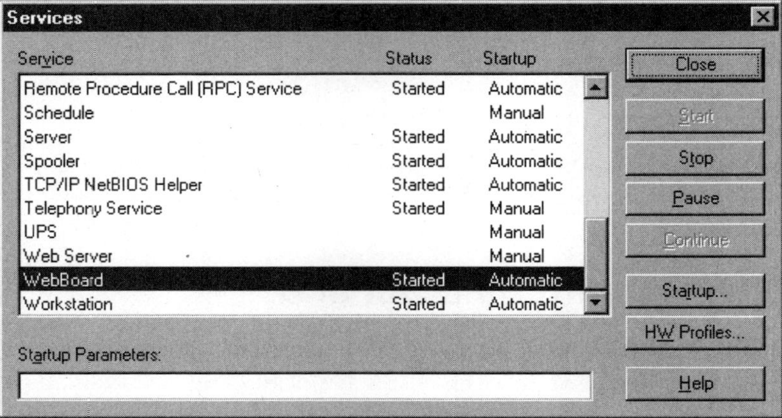

8. Highlight WebBoard and click Start. Services starts WebBoard.
9. Verify that WebBoard is set to not interact with the desktop. Click Startup on the Services dialog box and confirm that the checkbox is unchecked.

Note

To return WebBoard to a desktop application, simply stop the service, reset the Run mode in WebBoard Properties, and start WebBoard as an application.

For More Help

Several sources of help are available to WebBoard users, including the following:

- This book, *Building Your Own Web Conferences,* and the WebBoard user's guide, *Using WebBoard 2.0*
- WebBoard Online Help
- WebBoard Central (*http://webboard.ora.com/*) and O'Reilly Software Online (*http://software.ora.com/*)
- WebBoard Technical Support

Getting the Most Out of the Books

Building Your Own Web Conferences provides comprehensive instructions for installing, administering, and using WebBoard. This book takes a task-oriented approach, presenting as much procedural material as possible in a real-life, hands-on manner. The numerous tutorials give you an opportunity to practice the skills you need for building and maintaining a successful web conferencing system. We encourage you to work through the tutorials and apply the steps to your own specific web.

In addition, we've included scenarios for how your WebBoard can be made practical and useful to others. Helpful hints, ideas for using WebBoard, and notes for avoiding difficulties are scattered throughout the book. Special *WebBoard in Action* sections give you a first-hand look at how other WebBoard users are getting the most out of their web conferencing systems. And don't overlook the appendixes, which include valuable reference and troubleshooting material. For example, if you're having problems with WebBoard, first consult Appendix B, ***Troubleshooting Tips***.

An indispensable resource for your WebBoard end users, *Using WebBoard 2.0* takes the material included in Section 4 of this book and places it in a handy booklet. Your users can learn about WebBoard's many capabilities—without ringing your help desk (or home!) number. Step-by-step instructions and real-life examples will encourage them to explore WebBoard's basic and advanced features and understand how to get around successfully during their WebBoard sessions. *Using WebBoard 2.0* is available only from O'Reilly & Associates. Visit WebBoard Central (*http://webboard.ora.com*) or call O'Reilly Customer Service at (707) 829-0515 or (800) 998-9938 for more information.

Tip

If you would like to read more about web servers in general, we recommend another book from O'Reilly's Build Your Own series: *Building Your Own WebSite*, by Susan B. Peck and Stephen Arrants.

Using Online Help

WebBoard comes with complete online help available through either a menu item or a hyperlink. The WebBoard online help gives definitions and specific procedures regarding the current application. You can also modify WebBoard help (which are HTML files) to provide specific information to your users. Section 3 describes editing these files.

Checking Out Web Resources

You should also regularly consult the Web-based resources for news and information on WebBoard and other O'Reilly software products. WebBoard Central is the official O'Reilly Software site dedicated to supporting WebBoard. WebBoard Central provides product information, troubleshooting help, advice for particular implementations of WebBoard, ideas for new uses of WebBoard, sample HTML files, helpful utility programs, and opportunities to interact with the technical support staff and other WebBoard users through WebBoard conferences. In addition, WebBoard's Knowledge Base includes answers to many questions you may have about WebBoard.

Reaching WebBoard Central is simple: point your browser at *http://webboard.ora.com/*. While you are there, if you haven't already enrolled your copy of WebBoard, we encourage you to do so. Enrolling WebBoard makes you eligible for product announcements, special offers, and discounts on product upgrades.

We also recommend you visit O'Reilly Software's umbrella Web site, O'Reilly Software Online (*http://software.ora.com*). From this page you can learn about other O'Reilly products such as WebSite, WebSite Professional, and PolyForm, as well as general news about O'Reilly's doings.

Contacting Technical Support

If you've thoroughly investigated all the other sources for help and still need assistance, O'Reilly & Associates provides technical support on a per-incident basis or through annual technical support contracts. For per-incident support, call (707) 829-0515 between 7:00 A.M. and 5:00 P.M. (Pacific Time); please have your credit card ready. For more information or to set up an annual tech support contract, call O'Reilly Customer Service at (800) 998-9938 or send email to *webboard@ora.com*. Technical support options are also described at O'Reilly Software Online.

II

Managing WebBoard

Now it's time to start your own web conferences. Setting up and managing various conference types is described in Chapter 4, *Managing Conferences*. Chapter 5, *Managing Users*, provides details on understanding user types and step-by-step instructions for adding, deleting, and editing users. Use Chapter 6, *Advanced Management*, to create virtual boards, change WebBoard's configuration, track activity, and manage the WebBoard database.

4

Managing Conferences

Once WebBoard is up and running, you are ready to develop your online conference system. Conferences are made up of topics and messages. When you create a conference, you establish the main subject matter that is developed when users post new topics and messages. For example, the conference Office Equipment may have topics such as Repairing Copy Machines, Purchasing New Equipment, and so forth. As the WebBoard system administrator or manager, you need to add at least one conference in which your users can participate. WebBoard supports four different types of conferences: public, moderated, private, and read-only, as discussed in the next section, "Understanding Conference Types." You can also decide if this conference will be enhanced by the Chat feature of WebBoard, in which conference users can carry on real-time discussions.

This chapter walks you through the steps of setting up and managing WebBoard conferences. You will learn how to set up and add conferences, determine conference status (such as public or private), choose options to manage your conferences effectively, edit conference settings, and delete conferences. Also, you will learn how to use Chat settings and Chat Spots. The information in this chapter is given from the perspective of the WebBoard system administrator, although a WebBoard manager can also carry out these tasks. For more information on users' privileges, please see Chapter 5, *Managing Users*.

Understanding Conference Types

The conferences you set up are the backbone of your WebBoard—and user participation is key to a successful conference. Give some thought to the first few conferences you create, keeping in mind both the needs of your organization and what will generate the most user interaction and interest. For example, if your WebBoard is for developing your organization's human resource policies, you could create separate conferences on benefits, healthcare providers, vacation policy, performance evaluations, or salary. Since some of these topics may contain sensitive information, you may want to designate some conferences as private (closed), others as read-only, as described in the next section.

If you plan to use WebBoard for technical support, you may want to create a conference for general user questions and other conferences for more advanced topics. Often these conferences benefit from the postings of other users, so you will want to make them public. Or you may decide to moderate the conferences, to keep misinformation about your products out of the conference.

You can add new conferences at any time. If one conference gets too large or seems to splinter, then break it into two conferences. If you ship a new product, you may want to start a new conference. You may also find it useful to have a suggestion box conference for users to post ideas about your WebBoard and site in general. A suggestion box conference lets your WebBoard users have a structured way of giving input to the conferences.

Depending on the volume of users you anticipate, you may want to err on the side of having too few conferences rather than too many. Fewer conferences make navigation between them easier, but may make them less focused. Keeping close track of conferences and determining when to add a new one is a primary responsibility of the WebBoard system administrator or manager.

Note

The version of WebBoard included with this book allows you to have two virtual boards and up to 10 conferences per virtual board. The XL (extended license) version supports unlimited conferences and up to 255 virtual boards. For information on upgrading to WebBoard XL, see Appendix A.

Once your WebBoard is in business, you should check the content of postings from time to time, with an eye toward helping your users carry on more productive and satisfying sessions. You should especially look at the process from a user's perspective, by becoming a user yourself. Read messages often, post regularly, experience what your users do. For more information on using WebBoard (rather than just managing or customizing it), see Section 4, *Using WebBoard*. Chapter 9, *WebBoard Basics,* in particular will help you become familiar with navigation.

The following sections describe the different types of conferences you can select for your WebBoard.

Public Conferences

Public WebBoard conferences are open to all WebBoard users. Participants can read all posted messages, can post messages to the conference, respond privately to a posted message, and otherwise freely participate in conversation and collaboration through WebBoard. In a public conference there is no restriction on who can see messages, and all messages that are posted appear immediately. The only restriction in public conferences is on guest users, who can only read but not post messages (types of users are described in Chapter 5, *Managing Users*).

Moderated Conferences

A moderated conference allows a selected WebBoard user to exercise editorial control over what messages are posted in a conference. Users in a moderated conference can post messages (both to new and existing topics), but the moderator decides whether to post the message, discuss the matter with the user personally, or request that the user rephrase the message. The WebBoard system administrator or a WebBoard manager can moderate a conference or assign another user to be a moderator.

Private Conferences

A private (closed) conference is limited to specific WebBoard users. For example, an upcoming product release might be a good subject for a private conference whose audience includes product engineers, marketing specialists, and other team members. WebBoard lets them communicate and collaborate freely, yet the subject is not open to unwelcome eyes. In fact, users who are excluded from private conferences won't even see the name of a private conference in the Conferences list. The system administrator, manager, or moderator can select the list of users, as discussed later in this chapter in the section "Selecting Users for Private Conferences." (Also see the section "Setting up Virtual Boards" in Chapter 6, *Advanced Management.*)

Read-only Conferences

A read-only conference is open for reading by anyone, but only the WebBoard system administrator, conference manager, or moderator can post messages to it. Read-only conferences are a good way to distribute one-way information, such as memos, newsletters, and bulletins that come from a central source to be read by many people. You might, for instance, use a read-only conference to post new policies developed by your human resources department, a list of upcoming events, or to post a list of bug fixes to a product undergoing initial development.

Adding Conferences

It's simple to add conferences to your WebBoard. You can use either the Add Conference Wizard, which walks you through each step, or fill out the Add Conference form. The wizard provides detailed instructions while the form lets you create a new conference quickly. Both methods are available from the Administrator or Manager menu under More on WebBoard's menubar.

This section takes you through the steps of adding a conference. As you work through the following step-by-step instructions, you can customize each conference according to your needs. We recommend you use the wizard until you are comfortable with the conference settings; then you can choose to add conferences either with or without the wizard. You must have a JavaScript-enabled browser (Netscape 2.0 or higher, or Microsoft Internet Explorer 3.0 or higher) to use the wizard.

Note

If you decide not to use the Add Conference Wizard, click Add Conference without Wizard from the Administrator or Manager menu. You will be presented with a form that includes the same options described in the following steps. Complete the information according to the directions in each section of the form.

Step 1: Starting the Add Conference Wizard

The first step is to start the Add Conference Wizard. To do so, follow these steps:

1. From the WebBoard menubar, select More. The More Options menu opens.
2. Click Administrator. The System Administrator menu appears. Select Add Conference with Wizard.
3. The Add Conference Wizard opens, as shown in Figure 4-1.

Note

You may need to resize the wizard window to see the entire step. This is a JavaScript and browser idiosyncrasy.

---

4. Type in a brief name for the new conference. The name appears in the Conferences list and conference profile. You are limited to 255 characters. HTML and WebBoard tags are accepted.
5. Click Next to continue. The Conference Description window opens.

Figure 4-1 Add Conference Wizard

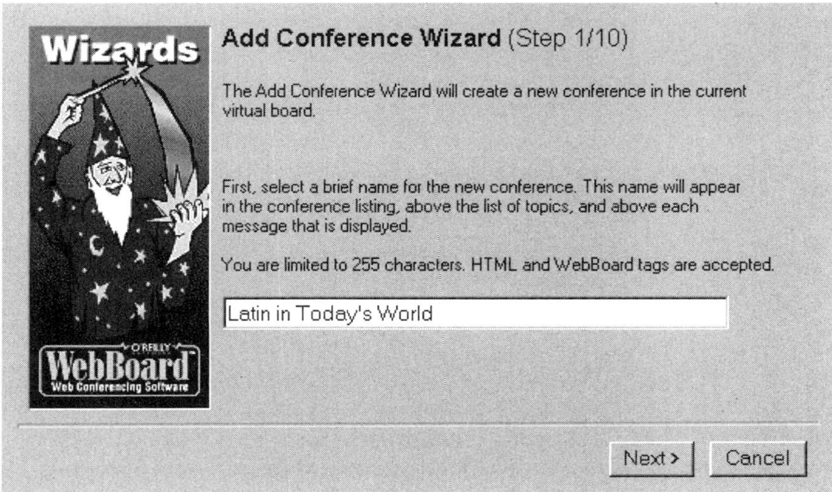

Step 2: Entering the Conference Description

Each conference may have a description to give the user more detailed information about the conference. The description is included with the conference profile, which is available from Profiles on the WebBoard menubar. A conference description is optional.

To create a description for the conference, follow these steps:

1. Type in a conference description. You are limited to 255 characters. HTML and WebBoard tags are accepted. (See Chapter 7 for more information on WebBoard tags.) For example, a description for the conference Great Local Books could be "The best literature available in our library and bookstore."
2. Click Next to continue. The Moderator window opens.

Step 3: Choosing the Conference Moderator(s)

In the Moderator window, choose the conference moderator(s), if any, for this conference. Moderators have full power to manage conferences and messages. Conference moderators verify messages before they are posted. They can also edit, retrieve from the archive database, and delete messages. The role of the moderator is discussed more in Chapter 5.

To add one or more moderators for this conference, follow these steps:

1. Select the moderator(s) for this conference from the list displayed. To select more than one moderator, press the Control key while clicking. The default option is Not Moderated.
2. Click Next to continue. The Archive window opens.

Step 4: Setting up Message Archiving

Your conferences will be more manageable if the number of messages displayed is kept to a reasonable size. You can accomplish this by having WebBoard archive messages over a certain number for each conference. For example, to have only 25 messages displayed at a time, set the number to be archived to 25. Archived messages are removed from the active database and may be retrieved at a later time. You can also set the length of time to leave messages in a conference. For example, if you set the length at two weeks, messages older than 14 days are removed from the active database. The oldest messages are stored first. System administrators, conference managers, and moderators can retrieve archived messages.

Note

For information on message retrieval, see "Retrieving Archived Conference Messages," later in this chapter.

You can set the two archiving options from this window, as shown in Figure 4-2:

- how *many* messages are to remain in your active database
- how *long* messages are to remain in your active database

To set the archiving options, follow these steps:

1. Enter a number in the Number of Messages field. To choose no message archiving, enter zero.
2. Enter a number in the Number of Days field. To choose no time limit, enter zero.
3. Click Next to continue. The first settings window opens.

Step 5: Setting Conference Restrictions

The first of two conference settings windows lets you establish certain restrictions, if desired. Sometimes you will want to screen, or verify, the postings of your users before they appear on WebBoard. From this window, you can choose to have messages automatically posted to conferences or else verified by a manager or

Figure 4-2 Archiving Conference Wizard

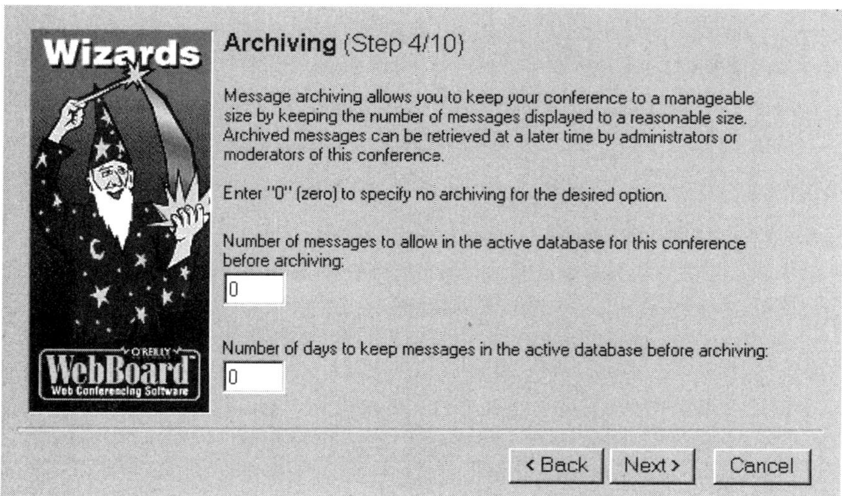
Wizards
Archiving (Step 4/10)
Message archiving allows you to keep your conference to a manageable size by keeping the number of messages displayed to a reasonable size. Archived messages can be retrieved at a later time by administrators or moderators of this conference.
Enter "0" (zero) to specify no archiving for the desired option.
Number of messages to allow in the active database for this conference before archiving:
0
Number of days to keep messages in the active database before archiving:
0
O'REILLY
WebBoard
Web Conferencing Software
< Back
Next >
Cancel

moderator. You can also choose whether you want this conference to be private and/or read-only.

Note

If you have not selected a conference moderator, the conference messages will be automatically verified. To select a moderator, click Back until the Moderator window appears (see Step 3, above). However, a moderator is not required unless you want messages verified.

To set the conference restrictions, follow these steps:

1. Select one of two options for message verification:
   - To automatically verify all new messages, leave checked the Automatically verify new posts checkbox. Selecting this option allows all messages to be immediately posted to conferences without prior verification by a manager or moderator. To verify a message, click the red checkmark.
   - To verify all new messages before they appear to other users in a conference, uncheck the Automatically verify new posts checkbox. Selecting this option requires that a manager or moderator verify a message before it appears to other users in a conference.
2. To restrict the conference to particular users, check the Private checkbox. To select users for a private conference, see "Selecting Users for Private Conferences" later in this chapter.

3. To specify a read-only conference, check the Read-only conference checkbox. Only system administrators, managers, and moderators can post to this conference.
4. Click Next to continue. The second settings window opens.

Step 6: Enabling Spell-Checking and Dynamic Loading

The second settings window provides you with opportunities to enable spell-checking and enhance performance on your WebBoard.

The spell-checking feature lets your users confirm the spelling in their messages when they post messages. The internal WebBoard spell-checker analyses the message and identifies possible misspellings as hyperlinks. When the user clicks on the misspelled word, WebBoard displays a list of suggested words from which the user can choose. WebBoard system administrators, managers, and moderators can add words to the dictionary from this same form. In addition, you can edit the custom dictionary with any text editor. WebBoard's custom dictionary is stored in *\webboard\system\custom.dic*.

By WebBoard is configured for maximum performance with dynamic loading. This saves memory and starts WebBoard a bit faster by only loading messages when they are requested by the user. Conference data is cached on the server side, so that it is loaded in cache (memory) only as needed. You can choose not to dynamically load a busy conference so that it will load all its messages on startup. This slightly reduces the load time for the first user of that conference. Unless you experience a problem, we recommend the default setting.

To enable these two features, follow these steps:

1. To enable spell-checking, check the Allow spell-checking checkbox.
2. To dynamically load conferences, check the Dynamically loaded conference checkbox. Leave this checkbox unchecked if you expect this to be a very active conference.
3. Click Next to continue. The Active Links & Images window opens.

Step 7: Allowing Active Links and Images

From this window, you can choose to allow active links and images in this conference. If you enable this feature, URLs included in messages become active links. For example, typing *http://webboard.ora.com* in a message creates an active link to WebBoard Central. This feature enhances a conference discussion by allowing users to integrate outside resources in their postings.

Likewise, you can allow links to images to become active. For example, typing *http://mydomain.com/image.gif* in an image causes an inline image to appear in the message.

To allow active links and/or images, follow these steps:

1. To allow active links, check the Allow active images in messages checkbox.
2. To allow images, check the Allow images in messages checkbox.
3. Click Next to continue. The Chat Wizard window opens

Step 8: Specifying Chat and Chat settings

Enabling the Chat feature for a conference lets users have real-time interactive discussions about the conference. You can choose whether active links and images are allowed in your chat rooms. You can also maintain records of chat rooms by logging chat dialogue to disk. For example, you may want to record brainstorming sessions, group meetings, or possible security breaches.

Note

You should use logged chat sessions with discretion. If you log chat sessions, we recommend you advise your WebBoard users that these sessions are recorded.

To specify the Chat settings, follow these steps:

1. To enable Chat in this conference, check the Allow chat checkbox. To disable Chat in this conference, leave this box unchecked.
2. To allow active links, check the Allow active links in chat mode checkbox.
3. To allow active images, check the Allow active images in chat mode checkbox.
4. To keep a record of chat sessions, check the Log chat dialogue to disk checkbox.
5. Click Next to continue. The File Attachment window opens.

Step 9: Allowing File Attachments

Allowing users to add file attachments to messages makes WebBoard more dynamic as an information generator. Your users can attach files such as documents, multimedia, sound, and images when they post a message. From the File Attachment window, you specify the number of attachments for each message as well as the size limit of any attached files. If most of your WebBoard users are using browsers that do not support file attachments, you should not choose this option.

> **Note**
>
> You must be using WebBoard's internal web server or a web server that supports HTTP file uploading. Both WebSite and Website Professional from O'Reilly & Associates supports this type of file uploading. Check your web server's documentation if you are unclear about the type of file uploading it supports.

To specify file attachment settings, follow these steps:

1. To enable file attachments, check the Allow file attachments checkbox.
2. To limit the number of attachments, enter that number into the Number of attachments allowed per message field. Enter 0 (zero) for no limit, or a number between 1 and 255 to set a limit.
3. To limit the size of file attachments, enter a number into the Size of file attachments per attachment field. Enter 0 (zero) for no limit, or a number greater than zero to set a limit (in bytes).
4. Click Finish. The Add Conference Wizard window opens, with a summary of all the options listed, as shown in Figure 4-3.

Figure 4-3 Add Conference Wizard summary

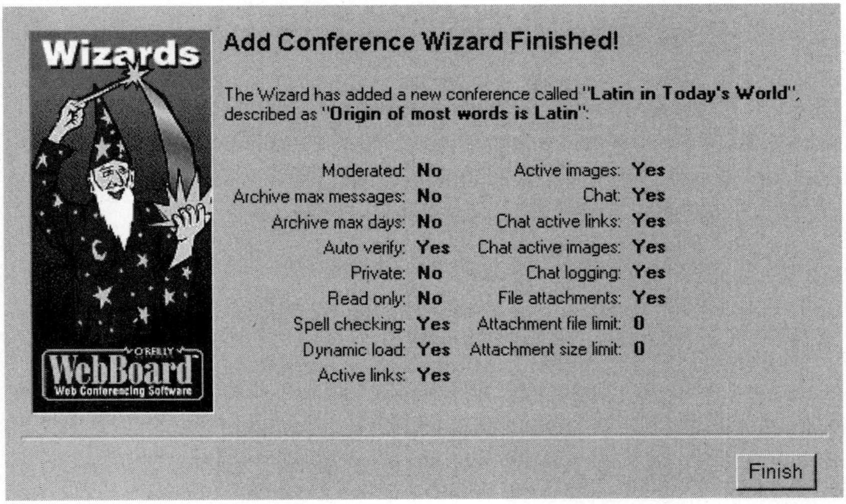

5. Verify the conference settings on this page.
6. Click Finish to exit the Wizard. If you need to change the settings, edit the conference as described in the following section.

Editing Conferences

From time to time, you may need to change a conference's settings. For example, you may want to modify the conference description, add or remove moderators, enable or disable Chat or Chat Spots, limit the size of attached files, and so forth.

Note

To modify a conference's settings, you must have WebBoard system administrator or manager privileges. Moderators can also edit any conference for which they are responsible.

To edit a conference, follow these steps:

1. From the WebBoard menubar, select More.
2. Click Administrator or Manager. The System Administrator or Manager menu opens.
3. Click Manage Conferences in the Management section. The Manage Conferences list opens, as shown in Figure 4-4.

Figure 4-4 Manage Conferences list

System Administrator Menu

Manage Conferences

Click on the conference name to view its profile, or select an action to perform on that conference.

Action	Conference	Created By	Message Count
Edit Delete Users Archive	Botany	Beverly Scherf	78
Edit Delete Users Archive	Cooking	Susan Becker	95
Edit Delete Users Archive	Family connections	Beverly Scherf	53
Edit Delete Users Archive	Fitness & Health	Susan Becker	67
Edit Delete Users Archive	Great Local Eateries	Beverly Scherf	86
Edit Delete Users Archive	Latin in Today's World	beverly S	93

This window lists each conference with a set of available actions (Edit, Delete, Users, Archive), the conference name, the conference creator, and the message count (of posted messages to that conference). The message count tells you how active a conference is.

4. In the Action column, click Edit, to the left of the conference name you want to edit. The Edit Conference form opens, listing the current settings.

5. On this form, change the following information as desired (see the section "Adding Conferences" for more detailed explanations):

   Conference name
   Use a brief name for the conference. This is a required field.

   Conference description
   Use a brief description for the conference. This provides information about the conference and appears in the conference profile.

   Moderators
   Specified moderators have full access to the conference and have power to manage conferences and messages. To select more than one moderator, press the Control key while clicking.

   Archiving
   Message archiving saves space in your active database. Archived messages can be retrieved by system administrators, managers, or moderators of the conference. You can enter information for two options: (1) the number of messages to allow in the active database for this conference before archiving. If you do not want archiving, enter zero; (2) the number of days to keep messages in the active database before archiving. If you want to have messages remain in the conference up to a certain time period, enter the number of days. To have them remain indefinitely, enter zero.

   Settings
   Automatically verify new posts. Leave this option unchecked if you want all new messages to be verified by a conference moderator or manager before they appear to other users. If you want automatic verification of all new messages, leave this unchecked.

   Private conference. Check this to limit conference participants (see "Selecting Users for Private Conferences" later in this chapter).

   Read-only conference. Check this if you want users to limit postings in this conference. Only system administrators, conference managers. and moderators can post messages to this conference.

   Allow spell-checking. Check this to enable spell-checking. Users can verify spelling in messages with the internal WebBoard spell-checker.

   Dynamically loaded conference. Check this to have WebBoard load conference data into cache only when it is needed, resulting in less memory consumption. If you expect this conference to be very active, leave this option unchecked so the conference is not dynamically loaded.

Active Links & Images. Change these options, if desired: (1) to allow active links in messages. Check this to allow links typed in messages to automatically turn into active links. Leave this unchecked if you do not want active links in this conference; (2) Allow active images in messages. Check this to allow image locations typed in messages to automatically turn into inline images. When a user types in the location, the location will appear as the image. Leave this unchecked if you do not want active images in this conference.

Chat settings

Check Allow Chat to enable real-time chat. You can specify the following options for chat:

Allow active links in chat mode. Check this to enable users to include active links in their chat messages.

Allow active images in chat mode. Check this to enable users to include inline images in their chat messages.

Log chat dialogue to disk. Check this to save chat dialogue in the active database.

Chat spots

The Chat Spots feature lets you display HTML documents (such as ads or informational messages) during chat sessions. If you enable Chat, you can use Chat Spots with the following options (discussed in detail later in this chapter in the section "Including Chat Spots"):

Turn chat spots. Click Off if you do not want Chat Spots.

On: Sequential. Click this for Chat Spots to appear sequentially. You need to specify how often sequential Chat Spots will appear, from 1 to 255 messages.

On: Random. Click this for Chat spots to appear randomly.

Disk path of HTML files named 1.HTML through 255.HTML. Enter the path name to the directory where Chat Spot HTML files are stored.

File Attachments

Check Allow file attachments to enable file attachments for conference messages. If you enable file attachments, you have two options:

Number of attachments allowed per message. Specify between 1 and 255 file attachments per message. Enter zero for no limit.

Size of file attachments allowed per attachment. Specify a number greater than zero to set a limit (in bytes) for the file size per attached message. Enter 0 (zero) for no limit.

6. Click Save when you complete your edits. A message indicates that your edits for that conference have been saved.

Selecting Users for Private Conferences

Occasionally you may want to add or remove users to or from private conferences. Perhaps some of the current members are no longer involved in the project, or you've had a new team member join the project. As the WebBoard system administrator, manager, or moderator, you can select which users can participate in conferences.

> **Note**
>
> Even if a conference is not identified as private, once you select users as described below, the conference becomes private. You do not need to edit the conference restrictions settings to make it a private conference.

To select conference users, follow these steps:

1. From the WebBoard menubar, select More.
2. Click Administrator. The System Administrator menu opens.
3. Click Manage Conferences from the Management section. The Manage Conferences list opens.
4. In the Action column, click Users to the left of the conference name. The Select Users form opens, as shown in Figure 4-5.
5. To add users to a conference, select the users' name(s) from the Without Access list. To specify more than one user, press the Control key as you make your selections. Click Add. The users are added to the conference.
6. To remove users from a conference, select the users' name(s) from the With Access list. To specify more than one user, press the Control key as you make your selections. Click Remove. The users are removed from the conference.

Retrieving Archived Conference Messages

Occasionally, you may want to retrieve an archived message to post again to one of your conferences. Archived messages include those deleted by the message poster (or by the WebBoard system administrator, manager, or moderator) or archived automatically. The Archived Messages window displays messages that have been deleted or archived in conferences.

Figure 4-5 Select Users form

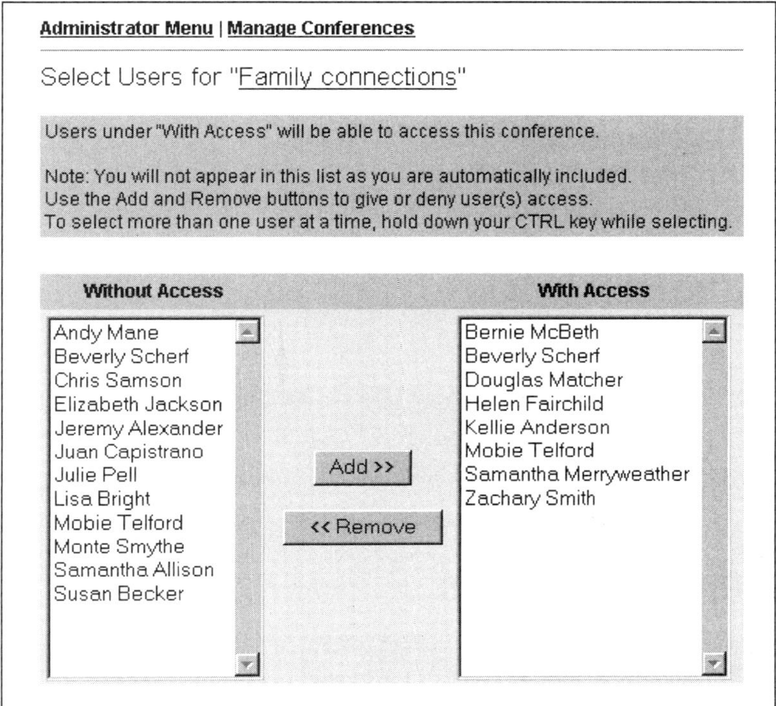

Note

When a message is retrieved, it is removed from the archive database and added to the conference as a new topic.

To retrieve an archived message, follow these steps:

1. From the WebBoard menubar, select More.
2. Click Administrator. The System Administrator menu opens.
3. Click Manage Conferences from the Management section. The Manage Conferences list opens.
4. In the Action column, click Archive, to the left of the conference name that contains the message you want to retrieve. The Archived Message list opens, showing all the archived messages in that conference, as shown in Figure 4-6.
5. Locate the archived message you want to retrieve. To view the contents of a message, click the message topic.
6. To retrieve the message, click Retrieve. A message indicates that the message has been retrieved. The message is immediately posted as a new topic in that conference.

Figure 4-6 Archived Messages list

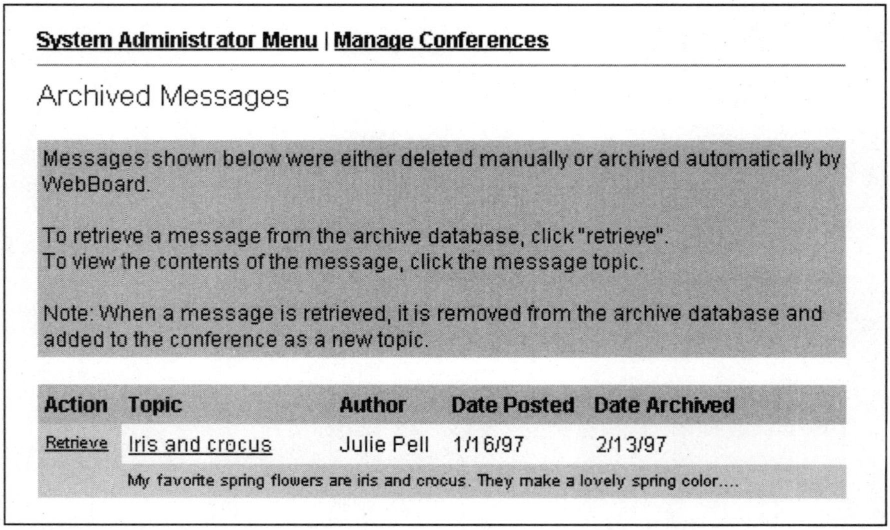

System Administrator Menu | Manage Conferences

Archived Messages

Messages shown below were either deleted manually or archived automatically by WebBoard.

To retrieve a message from the archive database, click "retrieve".
To view the contents of the message, click the message topic.

Note: When a message is retrieved, it is removed from the archive database and added to the conference as a new topic.

Action	Topic	Author	Date Posted	Date Archived
Retrieve	Iris and crocus	Julie Pell	1/16/97	2/13/97
	My favorite spring flowers are iris and crocus. They make a lovely spring color....			

Moderating Conferences

You may identify a moderated conference as moderated when you add or edit conferences. A moderated conference allows a moderator to monitor, or exercise editorial control over what messages are posted in a conference. A moderator can verify, add, delete, and edit messages in a conference. Users in a moderated conference can post messages (both to new and existing topics), but the moderator decides whether to post the message, discuss the matter with the user personally, or request that the user rephrase the message.

You should consider these issues when setting up a moderated conference:

- Moderated conferences help keep the discussion on track. If you have users who tend to get off track, or you have a very specific goal in the conference, a moderator keeps the users and messages focused.
- Moderated conferences provide an impartial review of messages. This means that the moderator should be someone who has the authority—both in your eyes and in the eyes of the conference participants—to ask contributors for clarity, focus, or revisions to a proposed posting, or to deny the posting altogether. A wise moderator uses these tools carefully, so that all legitimate sides of an issue get a hearing. An overly directive moderator will chase users away from a conference.
- The moderator should be known to conference participants. One way to accomplish this would be through the conference profile or an introductory

topic and message. describing the moderator, the conference purpose, and any guidelines for postings. The clearer this information is up front, the fewer problems the moderator will encounter.

- The moderator must have easy access to WebBoard, whether over the Internet or on an internal network. The moderator should also have the time (and desire) to commit to the conference. Reviewing new messages regularly and posting and rejecting them are essential for a healthy WebBoard conference. Users will not return to a conference that never changes.
- Moderated conferences can also be private or closed. This means that only certain users can participate in the conference. The moderator controls who can participate and must add each eligible user manually.

Users post messages to moderated conferences just as they would to any public or private conference. However, the moderator must first verify them before they are posted.

To verify conference messages, follow these steps:

1. From the Conferences list, locate each unverified message. Unverified messages have a red checkmark to the right of the message.
2. To verify the message without reading it, click the red checkmark.
3. To read the message first, click on it in the Conferences list. The message displays in the message window. You can edit the message, delete it, or click Post to post it to the conference.

Including Chat Spots

During chat sessions, WebBoard can insert HTML documents at regular or random intervals to display information to chat participants. The information displayed may be ads for products or services, informational pieces about the topic, or just interesting tips and tidbits. HTML documents displayed during chat are called Chat Spots. You can have up to 255 different HTML documents that display randomly or at regular intervals during a chat session.

For businesses, Chat Spots provide a means of advertising (for your own business or others). Perhaps you can trade Chat Spot time for discounts with your ISP or other vendors. Some chat participants may also want to advertise their companies and ask you to display their logos during chat (it's up to you whether you charge them or not). If your board is for a civic group or nonprofit organization, Chat Spots are great for getting out information on events, hot topics, or sponsors. On an intranet, Chat Spots can remind employees of policies, meetings, and opportunities within the company.

Chat Spots can be any kind of HTML document. They can contain text, images, links to other locations, and other multimedia elements, such as sound or animation. You will probably want to limit the size of the files or how often they are displayed so that users do not become annoyed with any (real or perceived) performance degradation or the notion of "too many ads, not enough talk." The HTML documents must reside on the WebBoard computer or on a computer in the same network as WebBoard. To have Chat Spots, you must create your own HTML files or have the sponsors supply their own HTML files.

Chat Spots can be included in any conference that has Chat enabled. The rest of this section covers creating and managing Chat Spots.

Setting up Chat Spots

The WebBoard System Administrator can configure any conference to have Chat Spots. A manager can set up Chat Spots for any conference on his or her virtual board; a moderator can set up Chat Spots for only his or her own conference(s). Currently you can set up Chat Spots only by editing an existing conference; later versions of WebBoard may provide other methods. Note that the Chat feature must also be enabled for the conference.

To set up Chat Spots, follow these steps (if you are currently editing this conference, skip to Step 5):

1. From the WebBoard menubar, select More. The More Options menu opens.
2. Click Administrator (or Manager or Moderator). The System Administrator menu opens for both administrators and managers. For moderators, the Manage Conference list appears, as in Step 3.
3. Click Manage Conferences from the Management section. The Manage Conferences list appears, with each conference available for you to edit.
4. Locate the conference you want to configure for Chat Spots, and click Edit from the Action column to the left of the conference name. The Edit Conference form opens.
5. Scroll through the Edit Conference form to the Chat Settings. Verify that Chat is enabled. If it is not, click the checkbox to enable it.
6. In the Chat Spots section (immediately following Chat Settings, as shown in Figure 4-7), turn on chat spots to run sequentially or randomly by clicking the appropriate radio button. The Sequential setting displays the Chat Spots in order by filename while Random setting displays the spots in no apparent order. See the next section for more information on filenames.
7. If you selected Sequential in Step 6, enter the number of chat messages to occur between Chat Spots. You can vary this number depending on how busy

Figure 4-7 Chat Spot section of Edit Conference form

Chat Spots

Chat Spots allow for sequential or random display of HTML files during chat. For more information on chat spots, click here.

Turn chat spots: ◉ Off ○ On: Sequential ○ On: Random

If chat spots are on, the following additional options can be changed:

If *Sequential*, specify how often a spot will appear. After [10] messages (1-255)

Disk path of HTML files named 1.HTML through 255.HTML:

[ ]

(i.e. c:\webboard\spots\cooking)

the conference is or how many different spots you have. For example, you might make the number higher for a very busy chat room so that Chat Spots don't interrupt the conversations or lower if you have many Chat Spots for this conference. You can enter any number between 1–255.

8. In the textbox field, enter the full directory pathname to the Chat Spot HTML files for this conference. For example, if this conference is about book reviews, the directory might be called *C:\WebBoard\Spots\Books*. Note that the directory name does not include any filenames (see the next section for details). The Chat Spot directory can be on the WebBoard computer's local hard drive(s) or on any mapped drive in your local network. For example, a WebBoard manager may want to keep all the Chat Spot directories for his or her conferences on his or her own computer in the network rather than on the WebBoard computer. If you want to share Chat Spot files among several conferences, you must use the same directory name for each conference (for example, *C:\WebBoard\Spots*).
9. Scroll to the end of the form and click Save to save the changes. WebBoard displays a message indicating that your edits are saved.

Managing Chat Spot HTML Files

Configuring the conference to display Chat Spots is only half the task. The other half is to create and manage the HTML files used in Chat Spots. As noted before, these files can contain any HTML elements: HTML tags, images, links to other pages, audio, or even Java applets. You should be sensitive to your users' connections when creating Chat Spots since large documents may slow down the discussion. However, you can display effective ads or information with well-designed and executed HTML.

The following list includes requirements and guidelines for creating and managing your Chat Spot HTML files:

- HTML files for Chat Spots are organized on a per conference basis. That is, the HTML files used as Chat Spots for a conference may be stored in a separate directory from other conferences' Chat Spots. See Step 8 in the preceding section for instructions on specifying this directory.
- HTML files must be named sequentially in the format *X.HTML*. The first Chat Spot must be named *1.HTML,* while the second is named *2.HTML,* and so on to *255.HTML* (the maximum number of Chat Spots per conference).
- If you selected Sequential display in Step 6 above, WebBoard displays Chat Spots in the order of filename: *1.HTML, 2.HTML, 3.HTML, 4.HTML,* and so on. If you selected Random display, WebBoard chooses the order from among the available files.
- If you delete an HTML file, you must rename the others to fill in the numeric gap. For example, if you have 10 Chat Spot files named *1.HTML* to *10.HTML* and remove *6.HTML,* you must rename *7.HTML* to *6.HTML, 8.HTML* to *7.HTML, 9.HTML* to *8.HTML,* and *10.HTML* to *9.HTML*. Unless there is a compelling reason to keep Chat Spots in order, we recommend you simply rename the last file to fill the gap.
- If you are using WebBoard's internal web server, all images included in Chat Spot HTML files must reside in the *Images* subdirectory of the main WebBoard directory. Otherwise, the server will not find the images. The URL path for this directory is */wbimages/,* which you must use in all references to images. For example, to display your company's logo in a Chat Spot, put the image file in the *Images* directory and include the following tag in the HTML file <img src=''/wbimages/logo.gif'', where *logo.gif* is the company's image.

> **Note**
>
> You may want to create a subdirectory in the WebBoard *Images* directory to keep Chat Spot images separate from the standard WebBoard images. You may even want to create subdirectories within that directory to better organize your files on a per conference basis. However, all images used in Chat Spots *must* be under the WebBoard *Images* directory and you must include the full path name (beginning with */wbimages/*) in the HREF.

- If you are using any other web server, you may call images from any correctly mapped location. See your web server's documentation for details.
- You can create HTML files for Chat Spots using any HTML editor (such as HomeSite) or any text editor (such as Notepad). If you want more information

on creating HTML files, we recommend *HTML: The Definitive Guide,* by Chuck Musciano and Bill Kennedy, published by O'Reilly & Associates.

- Always test your HTML files before adding them to your public WebBoard. Make sure they display correctly, the links work properly, and the coding does not cause errors. Some HTML editors have diagnostic tools, but the best test for Chat Spot HTML files is to view them in a live (albeit test!) Chat session.

Deleting Conferences

From time to time, you may want to delete a conference for some reason—lack of interest, completed project, or subject covered in other conferences. The WebBoard system administrator, manager, or moderator can delete conferences.

Warning

Once you delete a conference, you cannot retrieve it or its messages. You may want to first archive messages as described earlier in this chapter before deleting the entire conference.

To delete a conference, follow these steps:

1. From the WebBoard menubar, select More.
2. Click Administrator. The System Administrator menu opens.
3. Click Manage Conferences from the Management section. The Manage Conferences list opens.
4. In the Action column, click Delete, to the left of the conference you want to delete.

WebBoard prompts you to confirm the deletion. If you are sure you want to delete this conference, click Yes. To cancel this action, click No, and the conference will not be deleted.

WebBoard in Action: Kinetix, a Division of Autodesk®

Kinetix™ develops and delivers affordable content creation tools for professionals such as film and video producers, video/computer game developers, web content developers, architects, engineers, and designers. The leader in PC-based 3D modeling and animation tools, Kinetix provides a full range of products for the application development process, from 2D and 3D creation to assembly and delivery. With headquarters in San Francisco, Kinetix is a division of Autodesk® Inc., the fourth largest PC software company in the world, with three million customers in 130 countries.

As webmaster, Steve Wiggs put WebBoard's virtual board capability to work managing the content of Kinetix's public web site. Steve shared with us how he is using WebBoard on their intranet to help make his job more efficient and his work more effective.

I use WebBoard's conferencing system to manage the incoming web requests within Kinetix. Previously, this was all done via email. The email system was somewhat of a burden, as I had to create a filing system, a reply mechanism, a system for saving and one for prioritizing.

"WebBoard 2.0 provides a great medium for exchanging data. The data is centralized (so I can delegate, if needed), and it is prioritized so others can see where their jobs stand in the big picture.

"Some web postings are very complicated and require face-to-face discussion. These aren't the majority, though. I've discovered that 80 percent of postings are very simple and fall into four categories related to building and maintaining our web site: Additions, Changes, Deletions, and Problems.

"So, I set up an internal WebBoard server to manage the information/communication flow. The following example shows how well the WebBoard conferencing system works to manage and organize these tasks:

Additions.

A member of a product development team asked to get a new form on the Web. He's new to the Web (and to this process) and is pressured by time. Here's how it went. He posted a message to the Addition conference requesting a new form and attached the text for the form, as shown in the following figure. The webmaster picked up the attached text and created the new form. So the webmaster posted a reply to the team member saying that he had completed the script for the form, and asking the team member to verify that the form was working, and then send it back to him.

(continued)

(continued from previous page)

Figure 4-8 Addition conference for requests

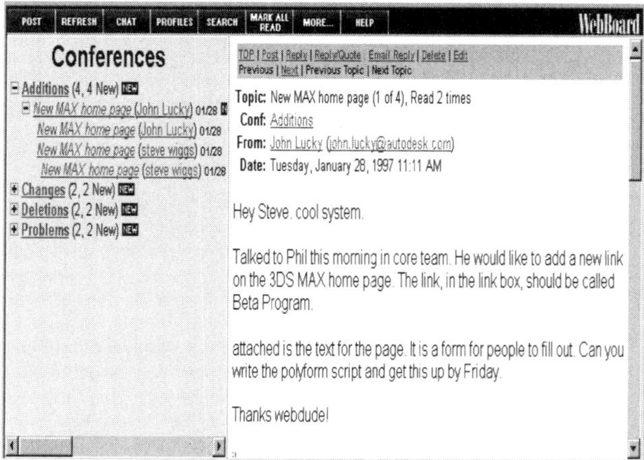

Problems.

The team member picks up the attached form, but is confused because he thinks the form isn't working. He returns to WebBoard and shares his concern with the webmaster by posting a message to the Problem conference. In reality, the job was simply postponed as noted in the webmaster's reply, shown below.

Figure 4-9 Problem conference for difficulties

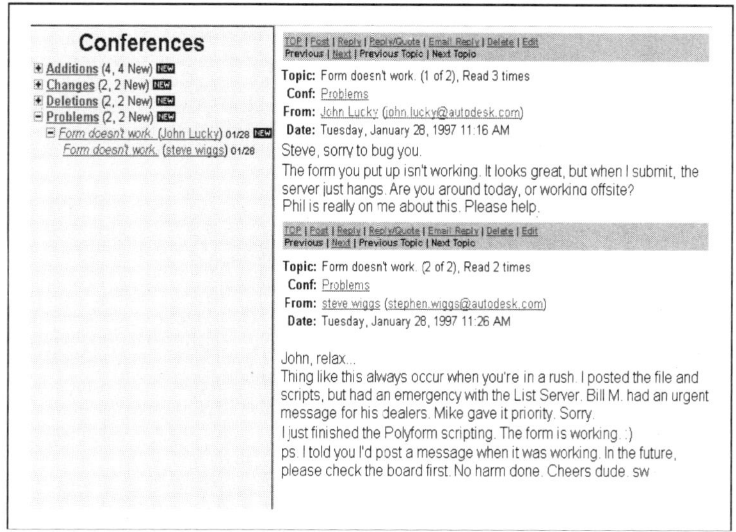

(continued)

(continued from previous page)

Deletions.

With his new form working, the team member remembers that an older version of the process was still present on the site. The team member posts a message in the Deletion conference requesting the webmaster remove it, as shown below.

Figure 4-10 Deletion conference for removal

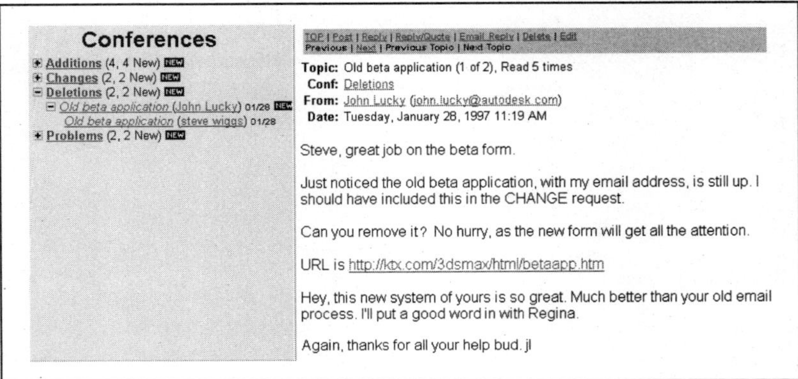

"This example illustrates a simple exchange of information. The job is tracked through time. And the end result is success."

Steve continues. "In my job, this situation occurs three to eight times a day. Sometimes tasks are as simple as this one, and other times they are a bit more complicated. I will be setting up similar WebBoards on our World Wide Web server to manage the following tasks that are currently handled (poorly, I might add) using email:

- communication with the webmaster
- ftp problems
- typos and bad links
- suggestions
- want a link to your site
- product support
- product user forums
- image and art contests

"WebBoard 2.0 has greatly improved the process for me and my peers—it has made the process more automated, more fun, and in general, a better experience."

Kinetix products are sold through dealers and distributors worldwide. Visit Kinetix on the World Wide Web at http://www.ktx.com, or contact the company at 800.879.4233.

Steve Wiggs, Kinetix Webmaster, can be reached at: ktxwebmaster@ktx.com or at swiz@worldnet.att.net

Autodesk, the Autodesk logo, and 3D Studio are registered trademarks, and 3D Studio MAX, ktx.com and Kinetix are trademarks, of Autodesk, Inc.

5

Managing Users

Once you've set up your WebBoard conferences, you need users to participate in the conferences and suggest ideas for new conferences. WebBoard lets you set up different types of users, for different purposes. For the most part, your users will be able to read and post messages. However, you may decide to give some users special privileges to moderate conferences or to manage users and conferences. If you are hosting WebBoard for other people, you may want to give them moderator or manager privileges. Or, if your WebBoard is running on an intranet, you may want to let each department choose a moderator or manager.

You should know that WebBoard maintains its own user login name and password database, which is distinct from the web server's or the operating system's user database. Users can self-register and create their own login names and passwords when they log in for the first time. Or, the system administrator or manager can add users to the WebBoard database.

In addition, WebBoard can be set up to use either users' real names or login names to identify them in WebBoard postings and user profiles. You may want to use login names to ensure some amount of privacy or anonymity for your users. If not, users can maintain some anonymity by making up an additional, fictitious WebBoard name.

This chapter first discusses the different user types. Then it covers instructions for adding users, editing their profiles, searching for users, viewing lists of users and their WebBoard habits, and deleting users.

Understanding User Types

There are five types of WebBoard users, each with a different level of privileges and security. In descending order, these are the system administrator, manager, moderator, user, and guest. The WebBoard system administrator has complete control over the entire WebBoard system, including all virtual boards, conferences, and users. The manager has control over an entire virtual board and can add or delete conferences and users on that board. The moderator has control over specific conferences on a virtual board. Users can read and post messages while guests can only read messages. Figure 5-1 shows the logic of this structure, so that you can see the overall user and security hierarchy.

To illustrate how you might implement WebBoard management, let's look at a medium-sized software company that provides customer service and technical support. The main board is used by the customer service department, and the WebBoard system administrator creates a new virtual board for technical support (creating virtual boards is covered in Chapter 6) and appoints managers over each of the two boards, in this case, the respective department heads. The managers create conferences for each of their boards and assign moderators over specific conferences.

The customer service department maintains moderated conferences for its customers to post questions regarding new products, price, availability, and shipping dates. The department manager moderates a read-only conference to publish official information for customers. The department also has internal conferences for staff who want to track down specific questions and other service-relevant information. These internal conferences are private, limited to department staff. As a result, employees save time, direct attention to more high-priority concerns, and reduce the backlogs that otherwise occur.

The technical support department uses private conferences for the staff to keep track of software bugs and customers' questions. A moderator maintains a read-only knowledge base conference for users to access. Tech support uses the Chat feature internally while they answer telephone queries, so that they can collaborate online with co-workers to solve user problems. With WebBoard's conferencing system, management stays in sync with customer interests and concerns, and consequently provides better service.

The following sections describe each type of WebBoard user.

Figure 5-1 WebBoard user hierarchy

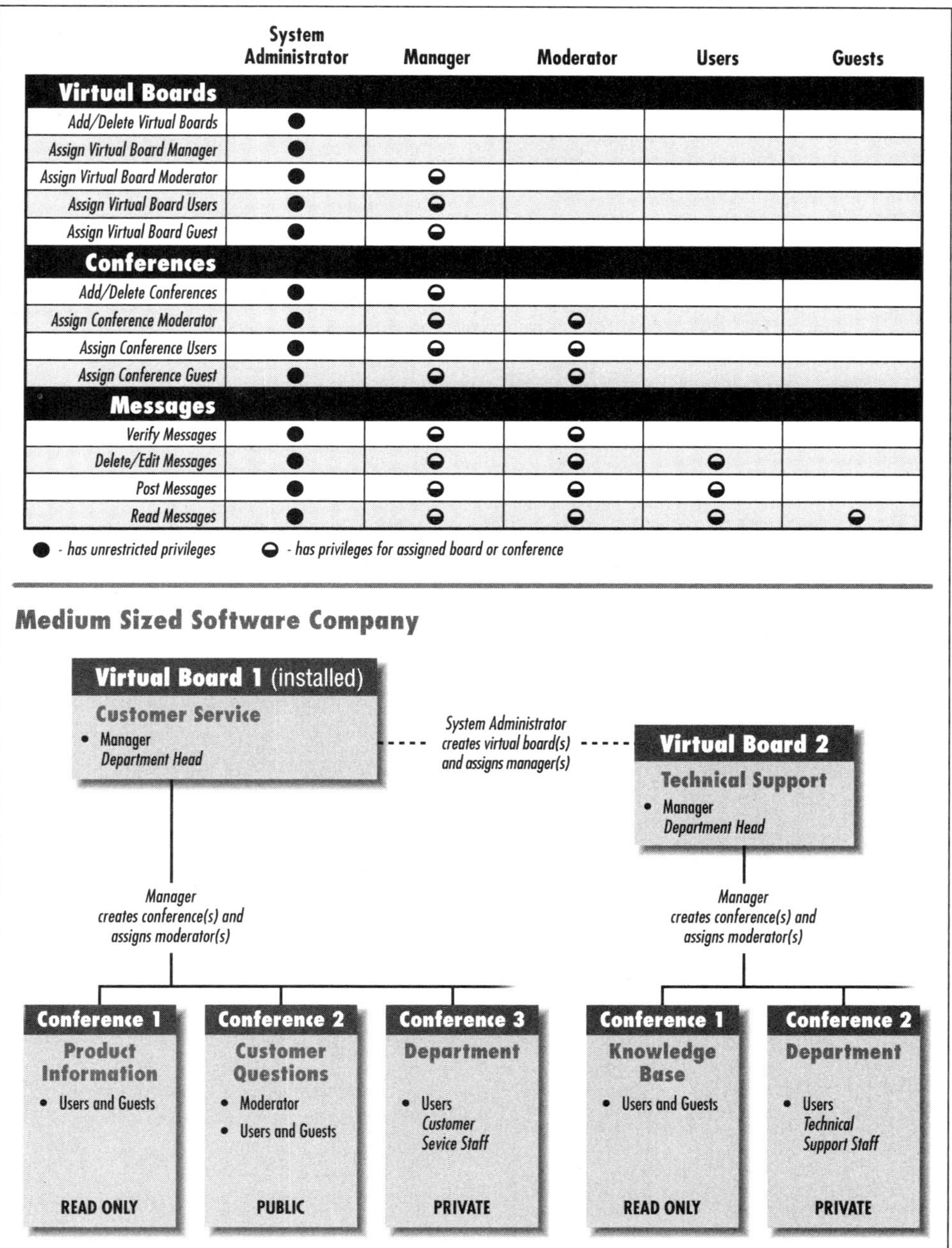

	System Administrator	Manager	Moderator	Users	Guests
Virtual Boards					
Add/Delete Virtual Boards	●				
Assign Virtual Board Manager	●				
Assign Virtual Board Moderator	●	◒			
Assign Virtual Board Users	●	◒			
Assign Virtual Board Guest	●	◒			
Conferences					
Add/Delete Conferences	●	◒			
Assign Conference Moderator	●	◒	◒		
Assign Conference Users	●	◒	◒		
Assign Conference Guest	●	◒	◒		
Messages					
Verify Messages	●	◒	◒		
Delete/Edit Messages	●	◒	◒	◒	
Post Messages	●	◒	◒	◒	
Read Messages	●	◒	◒	◒	◒

● - has unrestricted privileges ◒ - has privileges for assigned board or conference

Note

The version of WebBoard included with this book allows you to have two virtual boards and 10 conferences per board. The XL (extended license) version supports unlimited conferences and up to 255 virtual boards. For information on upgrading to WebBoard XL, see Appendix A.

WebBoard System Administrator

The WebBoard system administrator oversees the entire WebBoard system. The system administrator can add virtual boards, compact the database, add, delete, and edit users, as well as add, edit, and delete conferences, and change conference settings. The system administrator can assign one or more managers over virtual boards and one or more moderators of conferences. The system administrator is established during WebBoard installation.

Note

In earlier versions of WebBoard, the system administrator was called simply, the administrator.

Manager

The system administrator assigns managers to oversee an entire virtual board. They can add, edit, and delete conferences, as well as add, edit, or remove users in conferences. In addition, the manager can set the number of messages to keep in a conference as well as the length of time for messages to remain in the active database. Managers can also assign moderators to specific conferences. The system administrator assigns a manager when creating a virtual board (see Chapter 6).

Note

WebBoard 2.0 introduces the manager, a user level not present in earlier versions of WebBoard.

Moderator

Moderators are assigned to oversee conferences by the system administrator or manager. They have full management control over the conference with the power to edit and delete conferences, as well as add or delete users from the conference. They can also assign more moderators to their conferences. Moderators control the messages posted in their conferences. They can verify, edit, and delete messages in conferences—approving or rejecting messages based on the guidelines established for the conference. They can determine whether or not to archive messages in their conferences. A moderator can be a manager or a user. Often a participant in a WebBoard site is a user in most conferences, and a moderator in perhaps one or two.

User

Users are the most common WebBoard participants. Users can log in, read messages, post or mail replies, switch between conferences, participate in Chat, and otherwise participate as described in Section 4, *Using WebBoard*. Users can participate in moderated conferences, but contributions are screened (verified) by the moderator. They can read any read-only conferences, and they can participate in private conferences if they are on the list of allowed participants. The system administrator, manager, or moderator can select users for each conference, as discussed in Chapter 4. Users can self-register or be added by the system administrator or manager.

Guest

Guests can read any public, read-only, or moderated conferences, but they cannot post messages to the conferences. Guest accounts give occasional readers of your WebBoard a mechanism through which they can read and browse, without actually having to set up an account. The Guest account is automatic if your WebBoard is using Cookie Authentication. If your WebBoard uses Basic Authentication, see Chapter 6 for instructions on setting up guest privileges.

Adding New Users

Although users can self-register when they first come to your WebBoard, you can also add new users directly. For example, you may want to add users if your WebBoard is on an intranet. You can use either the Add User Wizard, which walks you through the necessary information, or fill out the Add User form. The wizard provides detailed instructions while the form lets you add a new user quickly. Both methods are available from the Administrator or Manager menu under More.

To add new users, you are required to enter their login name, user (real) name, password, and email address in the appropriate fields (marked with the red dots). Users enter their login name and password when they log in to WebBoard, as described in Chapter 9. Note that the type of security you select (Cookie or Basic Authentication) determines how the users log in and whether or not they must enter their password each time; again, Chapter 9 discusses this topic in detail.

Login names may also be used to identify users when they post messages. Real names identify who the user actually is and may also be used in message postings.

New users that you add can edit their user profiles later, to enter personal information such as their home page, hobbies, signature, and the default settings of frames and Full topic modes (discussed in the next section "Editing User Profiles").

This section walks you through the steps to add users. We recommend that you use the wizard until you are comfortable with the user information. You must have a JavaScript-enabled browser to use the wizard.

Note

If you choose not to use the wizard, click Add User without Wizard from the Administrator or Manager menu. You will be presented with a form with fields to complete.

To add a user with the Add Users Wizard, follow these steps:

1. From the WebBoard menubar, select More. The More Options menu opens.
2. Click Administrator. The System Administrator menu opens.
3. Click Add Users with Wizard from the Management section. The Add Users Wizard window opens. Click Next to continue.
4. Enter the required information in each field, shown in Figure 5-2. To add more than one user, click the Add another checkbox.

Figure 5-2 Add Users Wizard

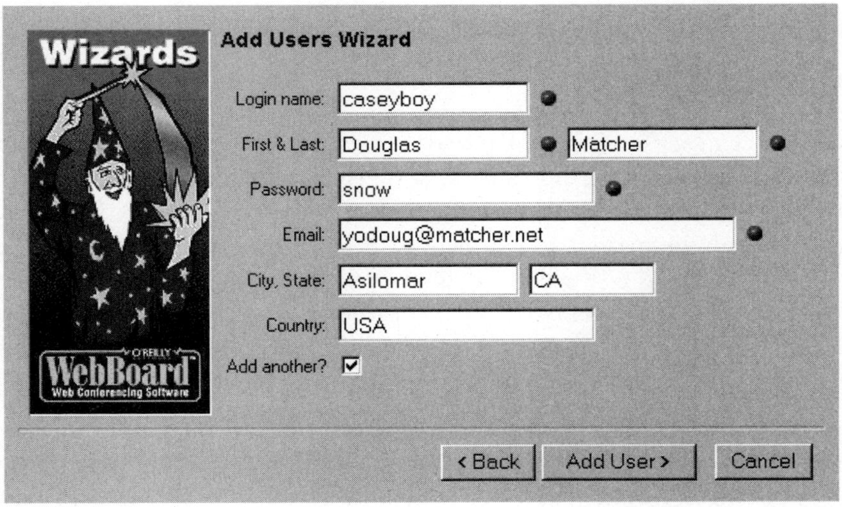

If you enter an existing login name, an alert window appears. The Add Users window reopens so that you can make the necessary corrections to add that user.

5. Click Add User. When you finish adding users, the Add Users Wizard window opens with summary information of the last user you add, as shown in Figure 5-3. Note that a NEW icon appears by each new user's name in various WebBoard user listings.

Figure 5-3 Add Users Wizard summary

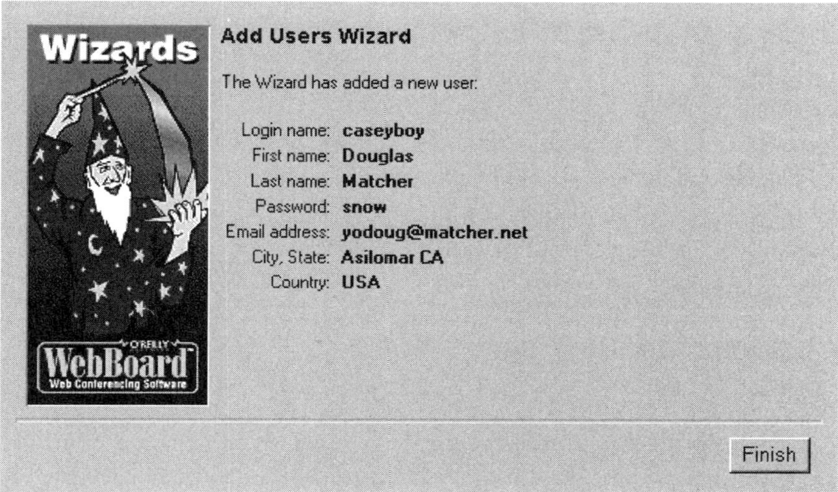

Note

WebBoard users can complete and edit the Home Page, Hobbies, Signature, and Window Layout fields from their users' profile (see the next section, "Editing User Profiles").

Editing User Profiles

As the WebBoard system administrator or virtual board manager, you can edit your own or any other user's profile. To edit your own profile, simply select Profiles from the WebBoard menubar and click Change your personal profile. To change another user's profile, you must first locate the user's profile and then make changes.

The process described below is written from the perspective of the system administrator; however, managers can also edit user profiles by selecting Manager from the More Options menu and then starting at Step 3.

To edit another user's profile, follow these steps:

1. From the WebBoard menubar, select More. The More Options menu opens.
2. Click Administrator. The System Administrator menu opens.

3. From the Management section, click Manage Users. The Search Users form opens (see Figure 5-4 in the section "Searching for Users"). Using this form you have a variety of ways to search for a user.
4. Once you have found the user whose profile you want to edit, click Edit (under the Action column to the left of the name).
5. Make the necessary edits to the user's profile. When you have completed these, click Save. The user profile indicates that your edits have been saved for that user.

Searching for Users

Sometimes you will want to find out more about certain WebBoard users. You have a variety of options to search for a user. You can search by selecting:

- the first letter of the user's first name
- all users by first or last name
- any letter(s) contained in the user's first or last name

Figure 5-4 shows WebBoard's Search Users form. Each name you see listed in the search results is a hyperlink, which takes you to the personal profile for that user. Users who have logged in today for the first time are marked with a NEW icon.

Tip

It's easiest to use the First Name option with the hyperlinked letter. However, if you don't know how to spell a user's name, use the last name option and simply enter a string that includes some of the letters in the last name.

To search for a WebBoard user by *first name:*

1. From the WebBoard menubar, select More. The More Options menu opens.
2. Click Search Users. The Search Users form opens.
   - If you know the spelling of the user's first name, click the hyperlinked letter that corresponds to the first letter of the user's first name. For example, your search is for Zachary Smith. You can find him fastest by choosing the First Name radio button and clicking the hyperlink *Z*, since you know there are a lot of Smiths on your WebBoard. A list displays each user whose first name begins with that letter.
   - If you do not know the spelling of the user's first name, but know some of the letters in it, enter the letters (a string) in the Search textbox and click Search. For example, you haven't noticed any postings recently by Jeremy Smith, but don't know if the correct spelling is Geremy or Jeremy. So you

Figure 5-4 Search Users form

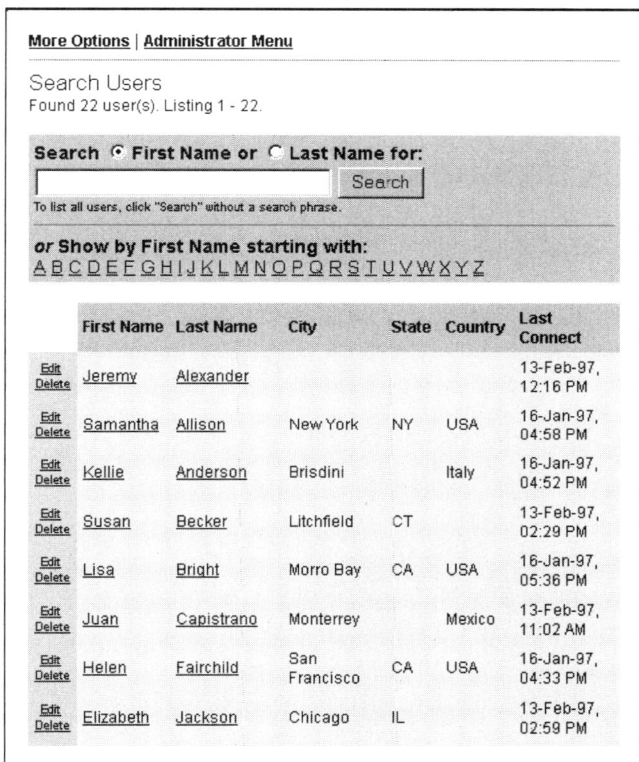

More Options | Administrator Menu

Search Users
Found 22 user(s). Listing 1 - 22.

Search ◉ **First Name or** ○ **Last Name for:** [Search]
To list all users, click "Search" without a search phrase.

***or* Show by First Name starting with:**
A B C D E F G H I J K L M N O P Q R S T U V W X Y Z

	First Name	Last Name	City	State	Country	Last Connect
Edit Delete	Jeremy	Alexander				13-Feb-97, 12:16 PM
Edit Delete	Samantha	Allison	New York	NY	USA	16-Jan-97, 04:58 PM
Edit Delete	Kellie	Anderson	Brisdini		Italy	16-Jan-97, 04:52 PM
Edit Delete	Susan	Becker	Litchfield	CT		13-Feb-97, 02:29 PM
Edit Delete	Lisa	Bright	Morro Bay	CA	USA	16-Jan-97, 05:36 PM
Edit Delete	Juan	Capistrano	Monterrey		Mexico	13-Feb-97, 11:02 AM
Edit Delete	Helen	Fairchild	San Francisco	CA	USA	16-Jan-97, 04:33 PM
Edit Delete	Elizabeth	Jackson	Chicago	IL		13-Feb-97, 02:59 PM

can enter *eremy* in the Search textbox. A list displays each user whose first name contains those letters.

To search for a WebBoard user by *last name:*

1. From the WebBoard menubar, select More. The More Options menu opens.
2. Click Search Users. The Search Users form opens.
   - If you know the spelling of the user's last name, click the Last Name radio button. Enter the letter(s) in the search textbox and click Search. A list displays all the users whose last name contains those letters.
   - If you do not know the spelling of the user's last name, but know some of the letters in it, click the Last Name radio button. Enter the letters (a string) in the Search textbox and click Search. For example, you want to find the user whose name is Monte Smythe, but you can't remember how to spell it. After you click the Last Name radio button, you can enter *Sm* in the Search textbox. A list displays each user whose last name contains those letters.

To search for *all users:*

1. From the WebBoard menubar, select More. The More Options menu opens.
2. Click Search Users. The Search Users form opens.
   - To list all users by *first* name, click the First Name radio button. Do not put any letters in the Search textbox. Click Search. A list of all the users' first names is displayed.
   - To list all users by *last* name, click the Last Name radio button. Do not put any letters in the Search textbox. Click Search. A list of all the users' last names is displayed.

Note

You can search for users in the current virtual board only. Cross-board searches for users are not possible.

Viewing User Lists

You can view your WebBoard users from a main list, and from the two top 10 lists. WebBoard makes it easy for you to track the top 10 users of your WebBoard, with statistics on the number of times they log in to WebBoard and the number of messages they post. This information can be a way of identifying key customers, opinion leaders, and valuable resources among your WebBoard participants. Any WebBoard user can see these lists by following the procedures described next.

Note

Users are shown for the current board. If you have virtual boards, you must be in the specific board to see its users. Creating separate virtual boards is an easy way to have different sets of users. Chapter 6 describes creating virtual boards.

All Users

In addition to the top 10 lists, WebBoard can show you everyone who has ever logged into your WebBoard. This list lets you track participants in your current WebBoard, whether they are customers, potential customers, colleagues, or just interested parties. You can display the user list by first name or a character in the name. New users to your system have a NEW icon next to their names.

To see a list of all WebBoard users, follow these steps:

1. From the WebBoard menubar, select More. The More Options menu opens.
2. Click Search Users. The Search Users form appears.

3. From the Search Users form, you have two options:
   - search by first name
   - search by last name
4. To search all users by first name, leave the First Name radio button selected. To search all users by last name, select the Last Name radio button. Do not enter any information in the textbox field.
5. Click Search. An alphabetized list with the first name (or last name) of your WebBoard users is displayed.

Top 10 Users

You can also see the Top 10 Users, who are determined by the number of times they've logged in to your WebBoard. Thus, the Top 10 Users may be avid readers, but never post any messages.

To see the Top 10 Users list, follow these steps:

1. From the WebBoard menubar, select More. The More Options menu opens.
2. Click Top 10 Users. The Top 10 Users list appears, listing their names and their total.
3. To return to the More Options menu, click More Options.

Top 10 Posters

You can also see the Top 10 Posters to learn who is contributing the most heavily to your WebBoard. Although volume doesn't guarantee quality, knowing who is posting messages helps you identify who is a regular participant of your conferences.

To see a list of the Top 10 Posters, follow these steps:

1. From the WebBoard menubar, select More. The More Options menu opens.
2. Click Top 10 Posters. The Top 10 Message Posters list appears, listing their name and their total posts.
3. To return to the More Options menu, click More Options.

Deleting Users

Occasionally you will need to delete a user. If your are running WebBoard on an intranet, you may need to delete users who leave the company. You may also need to delete disruptive users. Inactivity is another reason to delete users (although another mechanism exists for automatically deleting inactive users, as described in Chapter 6, *Advanced Management*).

The process described next is written from the perspective of the system administrator. A manager can complete this task by selecting Manager from the More Options menu.

To delete a user, follow these steps:

1. From the WebBoard menubar, select More. The More Options menu opens.
2. Click Administrator. The System Administrator menu opens.
3. From the Management section, click Manage Users. The Search Users form opens (see Figure 5-4).
4. Click the hyperlink letter of the user's first name. A list of users with that first letter appears.
5. Click Delete from the Action column to the left of the user's name. WebBoard asks you if you want to delete that user.
6. Click Yes if you want to delete that user. Click No if you don't want to delete that user. If you click Yes, a message displays that user has been deleted. If you click No, you return to the Search window.

6

Advanced Management

Chapters 4 and 5 have covered the basics of running your WebBoard. You understand how conferences work and the relationships between conferences, topics, and messages. You know how to add, manage, and delete conferences. You also understand the relationships between users with different privileges—from the system administrator to a guest user—and know how to add, manage, and delete users. By and large, 80 percent of your administrative time with WebBoard will be spent in those two areas: conference and user management.

However, the remaining 20 percent of your administrative time will deal with advanced issues such as creating and managing virtual boards. Other advanced management tasks include configuring the web server, compacting the database, changing authentication modes, setting email properties, and updating system administration data.

Another important area of advanced WebBoard management is understanding the various tracking data WebBoard provides. Several logs and a real-time statistics generator let you know what is happening on your WebBoard.

Finally, you may want to perform some WebBoard administrative tasks automatically. The WBUtil program lets you schedule certain activities to take place at times you designate.

All these advanced management tasks are covered in this chapter. As you become more familiar with WebBoard, you will want to explore these advanced features.

Creating Virtual Boards

WebBoard lets you set up multiple separate and unique boards, with only one copy of WebBoard running. Each board is called a *virtual board*. During installation, WebBoard created the first virtual board (virtual board number 1). As the WebBoard system administrator, you can create 254 additional boards. Each virtual board has its own WebBoard menubar and set of conferences, topics, and messages. The user data of each board is specific and distinct to that board, segregated in WebBoard's user database.

Note

The version of WebBoard included with this book allows you to set up two virtual boards with 10 conferences per board. The XL (extended license) version of WebBoard supports up to 255 virtual boards and unlimited conferences. To upgrade to WebBoard XL, see Appendix A or visit WebBoard Central at *http://webboard.ora.com*.

You can use virtual boards for different product lines, different departments, or to provide individual WebBoards to your clients. For example, to generate revenue you can sell separate virtual boards to different companies or organizations. Each company can use its own board to provide conferences specific to its site localities, products, employees, and customers. Companies can have each board dedicated to updates, questions, known problems, and their solutions for specific products. In addition, companies can have links to other virtual boards.

The following sections show you how to work with virtual boards. For simplicity, let's assume this is the first virtual board you are creating after initially installing and setting up WebBoard. Each WebBoard has a number. The first board is number 1. Thus, the first virtual board you add can be number 2 (or higher, up to 255). Individuals wanting more than two virtual boards can purchase WebBoard XL, which provides up to 255 virtual boards and unlimited conferences. As you add virtual boards to your site, keep track of the number of the board and its purpose (or client's name) for easy administration.

Notice that you can create private (closed) virtual boards. For each private board that a the system administrator sets up, he or she needs to include users with unique logins who can participate in the private board. For example, user Mobie Telford has the login MT for all public boards. However, for private board number 3, the system administrator assigns Mobie Telford the login MT3. For private board number 4, the login is MT4, and so forth. Separate login names create a security measure, thereby ensuring that those on public boards cannot access private boards.

Understanding Virtual Boards

Virtual boards are separate and distinct WebBoards with their own conferences and users. For example, you can have individual virtual boards set up for different businesses operating from completely independent locations. For each virtual board, the WebBoard system administrator can select a manager to have full control over the board, conferences, and users. The board manager can then select moderator(s) over specific conferences on that board. Figure 6-1 illustrates how WebBoard manages virtual boards.

Figure 6-1 Virtual board management

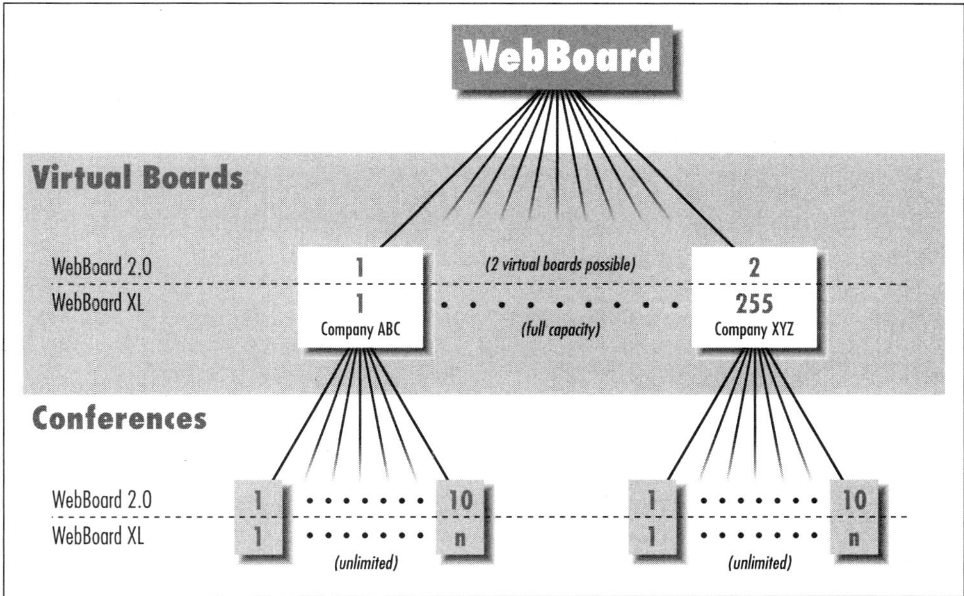

You can reach a specific virtual board by including the virtual board identifier (which is a ~ followed by the board number) in any WebBoard URL. For example,

```
/webboard/$webb.exe/~2/
```

takes you to virtual board number 2.

WebBoard remembers the last virtual board a user visits. In fact, users will return to the last virtual board they visited when they log in again. If users try to reach a virtual board that does not exist, WebBoard returns them to the last board they visited. Likewise, if unauthorized users try to access a private virtual board, they will return to the last virtual board they visited.

You can use the WebBoard tag `<WB-BOARD>` in files located in *\Webboard\Html* to display the virtual board number, if desired. See Chapter 7 for instructions on how to use these tags.

Adding a New Virtual Board

WebBoard allows you two methods for adding more boards—the Add Virtual Board Wizard which walks you through the necessary information, or the Add Virtual Board form. The wizard provides detailed instructions, while the form provides a quicker means of adding a board. Both methods are available from the System Administrator menu under More.

If you are using the XL version of WebBoard, you can create a total of 255 boards in exactly the same process described next. Be sure to keep a record of each virtual board's number, purpose, and function.

This section takes you through the steps to add virtual boards. We recommend that you use the wizard until you are comfortable with the process.

To set up a virtual board, follow these steps:

1. From the WebBoard menubar, select More. The More Options menu opens.
2. Click Administrator. The System Administrator menu opens.
3. From the Management section, click Add Virtual Board with Wizard. The Virtual Board Wizard window opens (as shown in Figure 6-2).

Figure 6-2 Virtual Board Wizard

Step 1: Choosing the Virtual Board's Number

1. From the Virtual Board Wizard window, click the board ID field to display and select a unique ID for this new board (from number 2 to 255). You won't

be able to overwrite an existing board—only available numbers are displayed for new board numbers.

2. Click Next to continue. The Security window opens.

Step 2: Choosing the Virtual Board's Security Type

1. From the Security window (see Figure 6-3), specify whether or not this board is public or private. Check the Closed board checkbox if you want this to be a private (closed) board; this will restrict the board to specific users that you assign to the board. To add users to this board, use the Add Users Wizard (see the section "Selecting Users for Private Conferences" in Chapter 4).

Figure 6-3 Virtual Board Wizard Security window

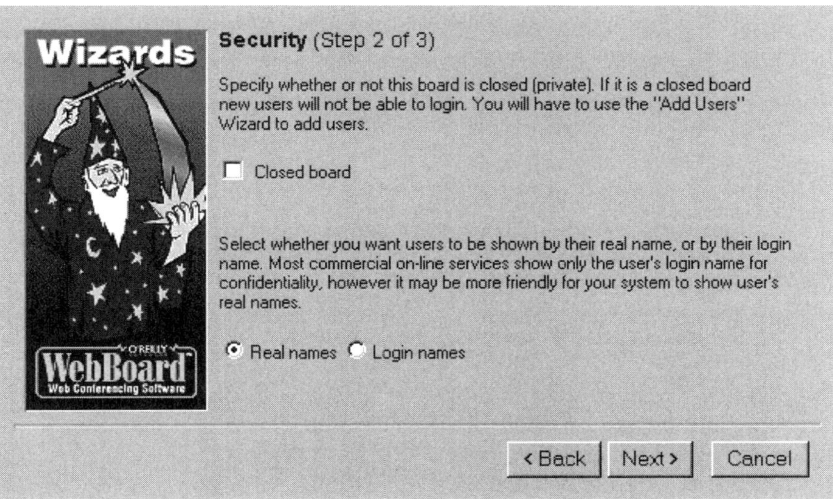

2. Choose whether you want users shown by their real name or by their login name. The default is real names. Most commercial online services (CompuServe, America OnLine, the Microsoft Network) show only the users' login name, for confidentiality; however, it may be more friendly for your system to show users' real names.

3. Click Next to continue. The Managers window opens.

Step 3: Choosing the Virtual Board's Manager(s)

1. From the Managers window, scroll to select manager(s) for this board. The manager(s) you select will have full access to this board and have the power

to manage conferences, messages, and users. To specify more than one manager, press the Control key while making your selections.

2. Click Create to add this virtual board. The Virtual Board Wizard Finished window lists a summary of the board ID, security, manager (s), and path. Be sure to keep a record of this board and its purpose.
3. Click Finish to exit.

You can add managers to the first virtual board (the WebBoard you installed) by editing it, as described in the next section.

Editing a Virtual Board

From time to time, you may want to modify a virtual board. For example, you may have changes in personnel and want to add more, or different, managers to a particular board. Or you may decide that your users would like their real names listed, rather than their login names. You can change the specifications of an existing virtual board by editing the virtual board.

Note

You must currently be logged in to the virtual board you want to edit.

To edit the current virtual board, follow these steps:

1. Make sure you are logged in to the virtual board you wish to edit.
2. From the WebBoard menubar, select More. The More Options menu opens. Click Administrator. The System Administrator menu opens.
3. From the Management menu, click Edit Virtual Board. The Edit Virtual Board *x* (where *x* is the number of the board) window opens.
4. Modify the following security specifications, if desired:
   - Closed (private) board
   - Users' real names/Login names
5. Modify selections for manager(s), if desired, from the list of names. You can add managers to the first virtual board (the WebBoard you installed) here.
6. Click Save to save the changes you have made to this board. A message indicates that your edits to this board have been saved.

Deleting a Virtual Board

You may decide to delete a virtual board for a variety of reasons. For example, you created one for a particular product that you were developing, and the product is completed now. Or perhaps, you think your users are responding more to the conferences on another virtual board. In any case, you can delete a virtual board by using Delete Virtual board. Be sure to keep in mind that all the conferences and messages contained in that board will be irreversibly deleted.

Warning

You cannot reverse the action of deleting a virtual board. The board and all its conferences will be permanently deleted. Keep in mind that the "real" virtual board (the WebBoard you installed) is virtual board number 1. *Do not delete virtual board number 1.*

To delete the current virtual board, follow these steps:

1. Make sure you are logged in to the virtual board you wish to delete.
2. From the WebBoard menubar, select More. The More Options menu opens. Click Administrator. The System Administrator menu opens.
3. From the Management section, click Delete Virtual Board. The Delete Virtual Board *x* window opens, where *x* is the number of the board.
4. If you are certain that you want to delete this board, click Yes. The virtual board, all its conferences, and all the messages within the conferences will be permanently deleted. WebBoard tells you this virtual board has been deleted. If you do not want to delete this board, click No.

Changing WebBoard Properties & Settings

WebBoard has a variety of general properties and settings that affect the overall operation of WebBoard. Most of these settings you supplied during installation, such as the authentication mode and email information. At some point, you may need to change these general settings. WebBoard has two places where you change properties and settings: the WebBoard Properties and the System Administrator menu.

WebBoard Properties is the program's property sheet. Under Windows NT 3.51, this is an icon in the WebBoard program group. You can also open the property sheet by selecting Properties from WebBoard's Control menu (visible when you maximize the WebBoard icon). Under Windows NT 4.0 or Windows 95, the Properties are listed in the WebBoard folder on the Start menu. You can also open the property sheet by selecting Properties from WebBoard's context menu (right-click on the WebBoard icon), by double-clicking on the WebBoard icon in the system tray, or from the Control menu.

You can also change many of WebBoard's settings from the browser-based System Administrator menu. This menu is available to WebBoard system administrators from the More Options menu.

This section takes a task-oriented approach for changing WebBoard's properties and settings from either the WebBoard Properties or the System Administrator menu, as appropriate to the task.

Setting the Authentication Mode

WebBoard provides two different authentication modes: Basic Authentication and Cookie Authentication.

- Basic Authentication is available only through the internal WebBoard web server or O'Reilly Software's WebSite and WebSite Professional servers, and is supported by most web browsers. During login, an authentication dialog prompts the user for a name and password. Users can still self-register but cannot have WebBoard remember their login information. If you choose to use Basic Authentication, we highly recommend that you test it thoroughly so you can see what your users may encounter before they use it.
- Cookie Authentication gives users the option to log in to WebBoard without entering their password for six months. Cookie Authentication is supported by all web servers and most web browsers. It is easier to use, but requires that users accept Cookies being downloaded to their local systems.

The authentication mode is set from the Security tab of WebBoard Properties, as shown in Figure 6-4. Your current authentication mode setting is displayed.

To set the authentication mode, follow these steps:

1. Open the WebBoard Properties and select the Security tab.
2. Click Basic Authentication to require users to enter their name and password during each login.
3. Click Cookie Authentication to display the option Remember my password option on the authentication window, so that they needn't reenter their password during each login for six months.
4. Click Apply, then click OK.

Changing Email Settings

WebBoard email messages are sent notify existing users of newly posted messages, if they have selected email notification. WebBoard sends email by putting the users' addresses on the blind carbon copy (BCC) line of the message to hide the names of the other recipients receiving notifications. Messages require a valid recipient in the To field, or the mail server will reject them. In the Subject field, the token <*where*> is replaced by the actual conference or topic name.

Figure 6-4 Security tab

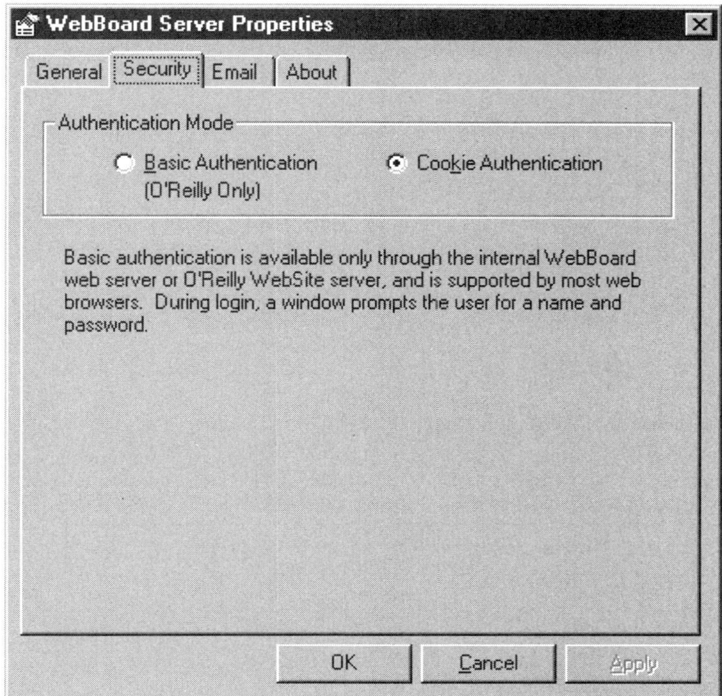

Figure 6-5 shows the Email tab of WebBoard Properties, with the current email information filled in as supplied during installation.

To change email settings, follow these steps:

1. Open WebBoard Properties and select the Email tab.
2. Enter the host name or address of your SMTP mail server in the Mail Server field. This is the server that you use for sending mail.
3. Set the time of day when email notifications and new user welcome messages are sent out in the Notification hour field. The default time is 1:00 pm.
4. Enter the full name of the sender of the message in the From field. For example, *mycompany@domain.name*.
5. Enter the full name of the system administrator in the To field.
6. Click Apply, then click OK.

Compacting the Database

Compacting the database improves performance and saves disk space. You can manually compact the database from the System Administrator menu, as described

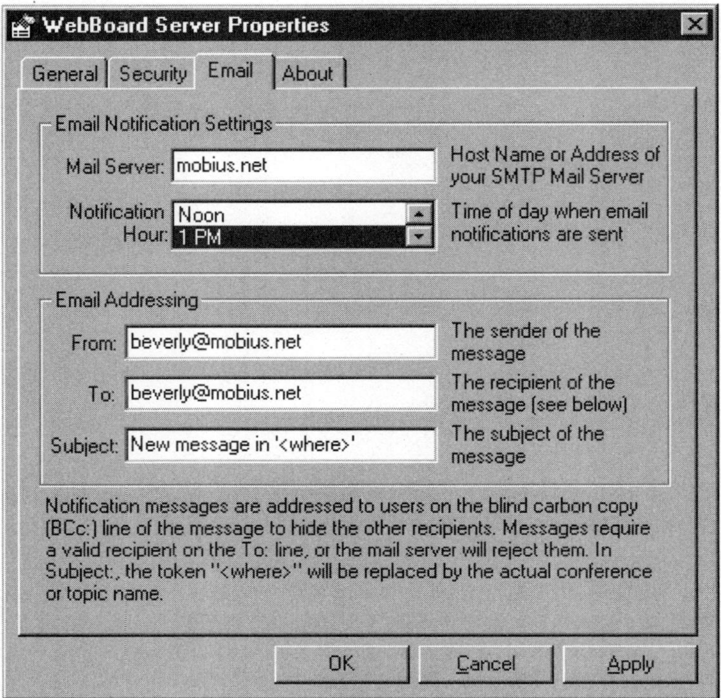

Figure 6-5 Email tab

in this section. You can also use *WBUtil* to compact your database, as discussed later in this chapter. While you compact the database, WebBoard pauses.

> **Note**
>
> WebBoard automatically compacts the database daily at 4:00 a.m.

To compact the database from the System Administrator menu, follow these steps:

1. From the WebBoard menubar, select More. The More Options menu opens.
2. Click Administrator. The System Administrator menu opens.
3. From the System Settings section, click Go Compact Database.

Resetting System Counters

Occasionally you may want to reset some of WebBoard's counters. For example, you may have moved WebBoard to a new computer or changed the web server used with WebBoard. Or you may find that the number of topics in the active database is too many or too few. By resetting WebBoard's counters, you can alter how Webboard works. All system counters are available from the WebBoard System Administrator menu.

To reset system counters, follow these steps:

1. From the WebBoard menubar, select More. The More Options menu opens.
2. Click Administrator. The System Administrator menu opens. Scroll to the Settings section as shown in Figure 6-6.

Figure 6-6 System Administrator menu settings

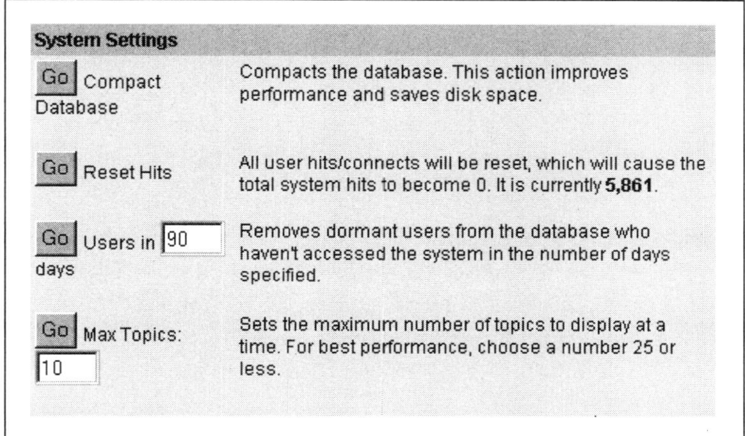

3. To reset hits to zero, click Go Reset Hits from the System Settings section. All user hits/connects will be reset which causes the total system hits to become 0 (zero). You can use this if you have moved WebBoard to another server.
4. You can specify the number of days before users are considered inactive. Enter a number in the Days field. Click Go. For example, if you specify 30, users who have not logged in to WebBoard for more than 30 days will be deleted. The default is 90 days. It is an optimal choice to remove inactive users from your database. While you delete inactive users, WebBoard pauses.
5. To set the maximum number of topics to display at one time, enter the number in the Max Topics field. Click Go. This function lets you specify the maximum number of topics to display in the Conferences list at one time in a conference. The default is 20. For best performance, choose a number of 25 or less.

Changing Internal Web Server Settings

If you are using WebBoard's internal web server, you may need to change some of the settings such as the location of the attachments (uploads) directory or the server's name. You can change the internal web server settings menu from the System Administrator menu.

Note

You can also change some web server settings from the General tab of the WebBoard property sheet. This tab is described in Chapter 3.

To change internal web server settings, follow these steps:

1. From the WebBoard menubar, select More. The More Options menu opens.
2. Click Administrator. The System Administrator menu opens.
3. Scroll to the System Settings section, and select from the following options:

Server Active

To turn the internal server on or off. Click Yes to turn on the internal server, or click No to turn off the internal server. Click Change after you make your selection. A message alerts you as to the change you made. You must restart WebBoard for this change to take effect.

Port Number

To assign the port number for your server. Click Change after you change the port number. The default is set to port 80. Most web servers are set to this port; however, if you have another web server running on this computer, you may want to change the port number to 8080. Note that you will have to include any port number except 80 in the WebBoard URL. The system administrator should ensure that no two servers are set to the same port.You must restart WebBoard for this change to take effect.

Server Administrator

To enter the complete email address of WebBoard's system administrator. Note that this email address appears on error messages and other system notices. You can change the address here by entering a new one in the Server Admin field. Click Change when you finish.

Server Name

To specify the server name. The server name is the domain name assigned to your WebBoard. Click Change after you enter the information.

Images Folder

To specify the directory for storing images. The images contained in this folder are the WebBoard images, such as the powered by WebBoard logo, chat smileys, navigational buttons, and so forth. Click Change after you enter the location.

Attachment Folder

To specify the upload directory for storing message attachments. Be sure to allow enough disk space for these files. Click Change after you enter the location.

Content Types

To specify server content types. Content types determine what types of files WebBoard will recognize. By scrolling through the textbox, you see that WebBoard supports a variety of types from text to jpeg to audio. If you add more content types, they must be separated by commas, for example, `html=text/html,htm=text/html`. Click Change after you enter your specifications.

Tracking WebBoard Activity

WebBoard's logs provide a wealth of useful information about individual activities, errors, and installation data. The WebBoard URL *~stats* gives you a quick status report of WebBoard. The following sections describe how to use these resources.

Reviewing WebBoard's Logs

Collecting information about WebBoard is the job of the WebBoard logs. You can use this information to analyze traffic, performance, problems, and configuration changes. The logs are an important source of information for managing WebBoard, providing statistics for users, debugging error messages, and diagnosing problems. If your WebBoard is quite active, you can remove the logs and WebBoard will recreate them.

At any given time, the system administrator can move or delete log files. If WebBoard detects that you have moved or deleted a log file, it will recreate the log even if WebBoard is running. This section describes WebBoard's five logs; *WEBBOARD.LOG, ERROR.LOG, MAIL.LOG, UPLOADS.LOG,* and the *CHAT#.LOG*. All the logs provide diagnostic information or confirm an action, with the exception of the Chat log, which simply stores information in a file. The logs are all ASCII text files that can be read with any text editor.

WebBoard provides the following logs:

WebBoard Log

The *WEBBOARD.LOG* records every action that occurs on WebBoard. Check this log for general trends and information about WebBoard. The WebBoard log displays each action as a single line of text:

```
1/10 10:38a WebBoard Server 2.0 started
```

This line in the log indicates when WebBoard was started. Other lines record when users logged in and what pages they viewed.

Error Log

The *ERROR.LOG* records any error occurring on WebBoard, with an error number and a description. If you are having problems with WebBoard, check the error log first. If you are unable to solve the problem, check the troubleshooting appendix in this book or check the resources at WebBoard Central (*http://webboard.ora.com*). The Error log displays each error message as a single line of text:

```
01/10/97,13:38,2.0,1/10 01:38p (220) Chris Duke ERROR #5: CHAT_
Dialog(): Invalid procedure call,CHAT
```

Mail Log

The *MAIL.LOG* records the mail activities performed by WebBoard. *WBMail* sends out email notification and new user welcome messages. If *WBMail* encounters any internal errors or errors communicating with the mail server, diagnostic information is recorded to this file. The Mail log displays each action as a single line of text:

```
1/10/97,1:00:07 PM,2.0.6,Connecting to mail server.
```

Uploads Log

The *UPLOADS.LOG* records any upload activity (that is, file attachments). The attachment filename, description, and time of the file attachment are listed, as well as the user who uploaded the file. The Uploads log displays each upload as a single line of text:

```
1/29/97 7:15:30 PM 06adman.doc by Beverly Scherf <beverly@mobius.net>
(advanced management)
```

Chat Log

The *CHAT#.LOG* records a separate log file of all the dialogue that occurs in each of WebBoard's chat rooms (if you have enabled the Chat feature and Chat Logging). Each chat room has a unique ID (which is the same ID as the conference for the chat). Separate chat logs are kept for each chat room; for example, *CHAT5.LOG* would be the Chat log file for chat room #5. The Chat log displays each chat message as a single line of text:

```
1/10,12:26p,4,1,1,"Is ANYONE here?",0
```

Note

You should log chat sessions with discretion. If you log chat sessions, we recommend you advise your WebBoard users that these sessions are recorded.

Checking Current Activity with *~stats*

In addition to the logs, WebBoard keeps a set of internal statistics of its activity. You can see these statistics at any time by using the *~stats* URL, a special WebBoard URL. When you request this URL with a browser, the server responds with a summary of server activity. Figure 6-7 shows a statistics report for WebBoard.

Figure 6-7 WebBoard Statistics via *~stats*

```
WebBoard Statistics for mobius.net

O'Reilly WebBoard 2.0
WebBoard Client/CGI version is WebBoardInternal/2.0
Web Server version is WebBoard/2.0
Operating system is Windows NT 4.0.1381

WebBoard Server first started on Wednesday, 12-February-97 17:51:4
WebBoard Server last started on Friday, 14-February-97 14:46:10

Total requests:                5,854
Total number of Users:         2285
Total number of conferences:   114
Total number of Messages:      704
Total number of Topics:        448
Messages posted today:         85
New users today:               18
```

You can request the statistics URL directly by typing in your browser *http://localhost/~stats,* if you are using WebBoard's internal server, or *http://localhost/webboard/$webb.exe/~stats,* if you are using an external web server.

You can also include the *~stats* URL as a link in any HTML document. For example, the anchor tag

```
<A HREF="http://localhost/webboard/$webb.exe/~stats">statistics
report</a>
```

would display the Statistics page. We recommend you use the full path for this URL. Since some of the information in the statistics report may be sensitive, you should limit access to this URL.

Managing the WebBoard Database with *WBUtil*

The WebBoard Utility *(WBUtil)* is a command-line program that lets you automate certain system maintenance tasks, such as removing inactive users from the database and compacting the database. *WBUtil* works from the command prompt and can also be used for regularly scheduled maintenance through the Windows NT Scheduler service or a Windows 95 System Agent (available in the Windows 95 Plus! package.) Refer to your operating system's documentation for instructions on using the Scheduler service or System Agent.

Note

WBUtil automatically pauses the WebBoard server. You should remember what effect this will have on your users when you are performing system maintenance with WebBoard.

The syntax for *WBUtil* is as follows:

```
WBUtil arguments <options>
```

where the arguments and options allow you to perform the following administrative tasks:

`WBUtil USERS <DAYS>`
: This command sends a message to the WebBoard server to remove all users from the WebBoard database who have not logged in for the number of days specified by `<DAYS>`. The action pauses WebBoard. Cleaning the database of inactive users saves disk space and improves performance. You can also perform this task from the System Administrator menu.

`WBUtil COMPACT`
: This command sends a message to the WebBoard server to compact the databases, a function that improves database performance and saves disk space. The action pauses WebBoard. As you change data in a database, the database file can become fragmented and use more disk space than necessary. Compacting your database defragments the database file, usually making it smaller and thereby improving performance. However, WebBoard automatically compacts the database daily at 4:00 a.m. You can also perform this task from the System Administrator menu.

WebBoard in Action: Children with Diabetes

Jeff Hitchcock, the editor of Children with Diabetes, a site dedicated to providing information to families of children diagnosed with diabetes, had used WebBoard 1.0 and has now moved his conferencing system to WebBoard 2.0. He spoke with us about his site and how WebBoard has enhanced it and made his job of administration easier.

The Children with Diabetes site is very active with 70,000 hits per week, and 6500 user sessions. Of these, Chat accounts for 35,000 hits per week, or half my user activity. I'm enthusiastic about WebBoard 2.0, since the look and feel is very crisp and contemporary in terms of the Web. It's nicer looking than WebBoard 1.0, and the navigation area at the top of the client window really simplifies getting around.

"I did a survey on my site, and most users indicated that they wanted me to keep all the messages in the conferences available for their reference. However, our conference system has become quite large. But WebBoard 2.0's new navigation makes this easy.

"Overall, I notice that the performance of WebBoard 2.0 is much faster. I also found the system administrator features were easy to use. Even though I prefer the non-wizard mode for my tasks, it's simple to carry out administrative tasks. I also like the security capabilities to do Cookie-based boards. The memory footprint in WebBoard 2.0 is smaller—this is very attractive to smaller providers.

"Most of my WebBoard users visit the Parents of Children with Diabetes site. I've created the following conferences so that my visitors will readily find and share the information they need:

- Parents of Children with Diabetes
- Kids with Diabetes
- Teens with Diabetes
- Diabetes Products
- Camp Reunions
- Grandparents of Children with Diabetes
- Adults with Diabetes
- Pumpers

"Visitors to my site like the easy navigation, since the information is managed in an effortless way for them. They also like the look and feel of the new Chat feature.

"WebBoard 2.0 is a superb product. I haven't seen anything on the market as nice and feature-rich."

Since so many users on Jeff's site wanted to retrieve older messages, we recommended that he set up an "Archived" conference, where he could keep older messages stored in his archived database. If no new messages on a topic are posted in a month's time, he can archive the topic to this conference. Users can then search this conference for particular messages and Jeff can retrieve requested messages. This process will save him disk space in his active database as well as time.

You can visit Jeff's site at http://www.castleweb.com/diabetes.

III

Tailoring WebBoard

Once you've created conferences and found activity is increasing, you'll want to review this section for help with fine-tuning the look and feel of your WebBoard. Read Chapter 7, *Customizing WebBoard Pages*, to understand how to modify WebBoard's HTML, help and text files. Enhancing navigation and adding variable information is also discussed in Chapter 7. Take a look at Chapter 8, *WebBoard File Reference*, to see descriptions of the HTML files used in WebBoard. These reference pages describe the purpose of each HTML file as well as notes about exceptions, JavaScript, and examples.

7

Customizing WebBoard Pages

Unlike most applications' user interfaces, which are coded into the program's executable, WebBoard's user interface is almost completely composed of HTML files. With an HTML editor and a basic understanding of some special WebBoard HTML tags, you can easily change the look and feel of WebBoard's user interface. For example, you may want to personalize your WebBoard by adding a name or logo to the Welcome page. Or you may want to provide more feedback, such as what number visitor a user is to your WebBoard on a particular day. If your board serves foreign language users, you can also translate the HTML files. All these changes and more are part of customizing your WebBoard.

WebBoard gives you great flexibility in changing the content and appearance of your site. In addition to editing the HTML, you can use WebBoard-specific tags for adding dynamic information to pages, such as the date or the visiting user's name. Special WebBoard URLs aid navigation by taking users to specific tasks or locations in WebBoard. WebBoard's help files are also HTML files and can be changed as necessary to meet your users' needs. In addition, you can change the text files WebBoard sends as email to new users and to notify users of new messages posted to a conference.

As you become familiar with the WebBoard HTML files, tags, URLs, help files, and text files, you'll find many other ways to enhance your WebBoard. Your imagination is the only limiting factor. This chapter describes the ways you can modify

WebBoard's files; Chapter 8 serves as an annotated reference list of all the WebBoard files.

Editing WebBoard's HTML, Help, and Text Files

The standard WebBoard look is pleasant and unobtrusive. But let's say you wanted to add more pizzazz and dress it up a bit. Your company's logo on the Welcome page might be a good place to start. Or perhaps your boss can't stand light yellow and wants all the backgrounds to wear the official corporate color—bright blue. If you are trying to wean users away from an online service, you might want to change *Conferences* to *Forums* throughout. All these ideas and more are easy to implement by changing a few items in WebBoard's HTML files.

WebBoard's help files are also HTML files. The appropriate help file is called by WebBoard whenever a user clicks a Help button or link. If your WebBoard serves an international community or if you are using WebBoard to teach a foreign language to your students, you may want to add instructions specific to your site or translate the help text.

When a new user joins your WebBoard, he or she is sent a message by email describing how to use your WebBoard. The email includes the user's login name and password (a handy feature that will save the WebBoard system administrator lots of questions about forgotten passwords!). When users select email notification for postings made to specific conferences, WebBoard once a day sends them email informing them of new messages in the conference. Both of these notifications are text files, named *welcome.txt* and *notify.txt*, respectively. You can modify these files to provide more specific information about your organization or the email address of a contact person.

This section discusses some general guidelines and tips for editing the WebBoard HTML, text, and help files, such as where they are located and some recommended editors. It then covers some specific items you should be careful about when working with these files, such as the WebBoard-specific tags. We recommend you read this section before making changes to any WebBoard files.

General Guidelines and Tips

The following guidelines and tips will make your editing chores easier:

- WebBoard's HTML, help, and text files reside in the *\WebBoard\Html* directory and subdirectories, *Chat, Help,* and *Wizards*. Note that if you installed WebBoard into a directory other than *WebBoard*, *Html* is a subdirectory of that directory. Do not move these files from this directory or WebBoard will not function properly.

- Images included in the WebBoard HTML files reside in the *\WebBoard\Images* directory. This directory is mapped to the URL */wbimages/*. You can change the default images called by the WebBoard files simply by replacing those files with new image files. Make sure the names you use for the new images are the same as the original files or that you change the names of the images called in the HTML file.

- Before you make any changes to a WebBoard file, make a backup copy of it. In fact, you might want to make a backup of the entire *Html* directory in case you need to recover a file.

- Chapter 8, *WebBoard File Reference,* lists all the HTML and text files, with brief descriptions and any specific caveats about their contents.

- When you create a virtual board (see Chapter 6), WebBoard still uses the default HTML, help, and text files from the *Html* directory. You can maintain a custom set of these files (any or all of them) by copying the desired files to the virtual board's numbered subdirectory in the *Html* directory. For example, when virtual board 2 was created, a subdirectory named *2* was also created in the *Html* directory. To customize the text notification files and the introductory message users receive, copy *welcome.txt, notify.txt,* and *intro.html* to the subdirectory *2* and edit them as necessary.

Note

The version of WebBoard included with this book allows you to have two virtual boards and 10 conferences per board. WebBoard 2.0 XL is an extended license version of the software that supports up to 255 virtual boards and unlimited conferences. For more information on upgrading to the XL version, please see Appendix A.

- Many of WebBoard's HTML files contain WebBoard-specific elements and JavaScript routines. The WebBoard custom HTML tags, variable tags, and URLs are described in the following sections. JavaScript routines are embedded between `<script language="JavaScript">` and `</script>` tags. *Be especially careful when editing files that contain JavaScript routines.* If you inadvertently change a JavaScript routine, WebBoard may not function correctly. Before starting, always make backup copies of all files you plan to edit. For an example of a file with a JavaScript routine, see *chatrooms.html.*

- WYSIWYG HTML or visual editors do not properly display WebBoard's custom HTML tags. For example, the FrontPage editor or Netscape's Navigator Gold editor will not show the custom tags WebBoard uses. For that reason, we recommend you use an HTML editor that shows the actual source with all tags. A plain text editor (such as Notepad) is also a wise choice.

- One of our favorite HTML editors for WebBoard is HomeSite 2.0 or higher by Nick Bradbury of Bradbury Software. HomeSite lets you edit the source directly with all standard and custom HTML tags visible and then lets you view it using its built-in viewer or Microsoft's Internet Explorer. Another useful feature of HomeSite is the ability to make global changes to multiple files. For example, if you want to change all the white backgrounds to purple, a single command will make that edit in all files. For more information on HomeSite and other recommended editors, visit the Software Library at WebBoard Central (*http://webboard.ora.com*).

- For more information on HTML, we recommend *HTML: The Definitive Guide* by Chuck Musciano and Bill Kennedy, published by O'Reilly & Associates, available at *http://www.ora.com*.

WebBoard's Custom HTML Tags

WebBoard 2.0 supports five custom HTML tags. These tags are processed by the WebBoard server before the page is sent to the browser (remember that browsers are responsible for processing both standard and generally accepted HTML extensions). The WebBoard custom tags provide additional functionality to the display and content of WebBoard pages, as described here:

<LOOP> and </LOOP>

The `<LOOP>` tags enclose text, HTML, and WebBoard variable tags that are repeated as many times as necessary to display a list or table of dynamic information. In essence, the loop provides a template into which varying numbers of entries are poured. For example, the Conference Profile list includes a loop to display conference names consistently whether you have 3 conferences or 300. To give lists a different look and feel, you can change any of the information between the `<LOOP>` and `</LOOP>` tags. Example 7-1 shows the `<LOOP>` tags in *profmenu.html*, the source of the Conference Profile list, while Figure 7-1 shows the resulting page `<LOOP>` section of *profmenu.html*

Example 7-1 The <LOOP> section of *profmenu.html*

```
<!-- Start loop for list of conferences and check boxes -->
<!-- All HTML between the LOOP tags will be repeated for each
conference listed -->
<loop>
<tr>
<td bgcolor="#FFFFD9" valign=top>
<font face="Arial,Helv" size="-1">
<a href="/webboard/$webb.exe/confinfo?<wb-forumid>"><wb-forumname></
a>
</font>
</td>
<td bgcolor="#FFFFD9">
<font face="Arial,Helv" size="-1">
<wb-forumdescription>
</font>
```

Example 7-1 The <LOOP> section of *profmenu.html*

```
</td>
</tr>
</loop>
<!-- End loop -->
```

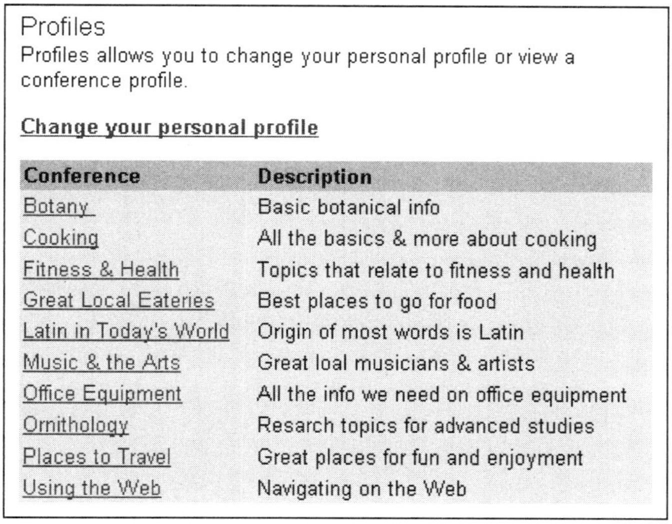

Figure 7-1 The Conference Profile LIst

Profiles

Profiles allows you to change your personal profile or view a conference profile.

Change your personal profile

Conference	Description
Botany	Basic botanical info
Cooking	All the basics & more about cooking
Fitness & Health	Topics that relate to fitness and health
Great Local Eateries	Best places to go for food
Latin in Today's World	Origin of most words is Latin
Music & the Arts	Great loal musicians & artists
Office Equipment	All the info we need on office equipment
Ornithology	Resarch topics for advanced studies
Places to Travel	Great places for fun and enjoyment
Using the Web	Navigating on the Web

<FRAMESOFF> and </FRAMESOFF>

The `<FRAMESOFF>` tags indicate material for users who choose to view WebBoard in the no frames mode. Each HTML file used by WebBoard has a `<FRAMESOFF>` section, which can contain text, HTML, and WebBoard special tags. You can customize the information within this section as necessary. Example 7-2 shows the `<FRAMESOFF>` section of *profmenu.html*, the source of the Conference Profile list.

Example 7-2 The <FRAMESOFF> section of *profmenu.html*

```
<framesoff>
<a href="/webboard/$webb.exe/menu"><b>Conferences Menu</b></a>

<a target="_help" href="/webboard/$webb.exe/help"><b>Help</b></a>
<hr size="0">
</framesoff>
```

<ADMIN> and </ADMIN>

The `<ADMIN>` tags indicate material for the WebBoard system administrator. WebBoard processes the information inside these tags and displays it only if the person viewing the page has system administrator privileges. The Administrator link from the More Options menu is an example of material shown only to the system administrator. You can customize the material between these tags and use the tags in other WebBoard files to display messages specific to the system administrator. Example 7-3 shows the <ADMIN> section of *more.html*, the More Options menu file.

<MANAGER> and </MANAGER>

The <MANAGER> tags indicate material for WebBoard managers. WebBoard processes the information inside these tags and displays it only if the person viewing the page has manager privileges. The Manager link from the More Options menu is an example of material shown only to managers. You can customize the material between these tags and use the tags in other WebBoard files to display messages specific to WebBoard managers. Example 7-3 shows the <MANAGER> section of *more.html*, the More Options menu file.

<MODERATOR> and </MODERATOR>

The <MODERATOR> tags indicate material for WebBoard moderators. WebBoard processes the information inside these tags and displays it only if the person viewing the page has moderator privileges. The Moderator link from the More Options menu is an example of material shown only to moderators. You can customize the material between these tags and use the tags in other WebBoard files to display messages specific to WebBoard moderators. Example 7-3 shows the <MODERATOR> section of *more.html*, the More Options menu file.

Example 7-3 The <ADMIN>, <MANAGER>, and <MODERATOR> sections of *more.html*

```
<admin>
<tr>
<td bgcolor="#93C9FF" width="30%">
<font face="Arial,Helv" size="-1">
<a href="/webboard/$webb.exe/admin"><b>Administrator</b></a>
</font>
</td>
<td bgcolor="#FFFFD9" valign=top>
<font face="Arial,Helv" size="-1">
Only accessible by the system administrator.
</font>
</td>
</tr>
</admin>
<manager>
<tr>
<td bgcolor="#93C9FF" width="30%">
<font face="Arial,Helv" size="-1">
<a href="/webboard/$webb.exe/admin"><b>Manager</b></a>
</font>
```

Example 7-3 The <ADMIN>, <MANAGER>, and <MODERATOR> sections of *more.html*

```
</td>
<td bgcolor="#FFFFD9" valign=top>
<font face="Arial,Helv" size="-1">
Only accessible by managers.
</font>
</td>
</tr>
</manager>
<moderator>
<tr>
<td bgcolor="#93C9FF" width="30%">
<font face="Arial,Helv" size="-1">
<a href="/webboard/$webb.exe/admin?conferences"><b>Moderator</b></a>
</font>
</td>
<td bgcolor="#FFFFD9" valign=top>
<font face="Arial,Helv" size="-1">
Only accessible by moderators.
</font>
</td>
</tr>
</moderator>
```

Note

Once you have enrolled your copy of WebBoard at WebBoard Central (*http://webboard.ora.com*), you may want to remove the <ADMIN> section from the *intro.html* page. Enrolling your copy of WebBoard ensures that you will receive information about product enhancements, news, and special offers.

Adding Variable Information with WebBoard Tags

As you've used WebBoard, you've noticed pages that include variable information. For example, the Welcome page (*intro.html*) includes the user's first name and the number of new messages you have. This variable information is added to WebBoard pages through special WebBoard tags.

Similar to HTML tags in appearance and use, WebBoard tags can be included in almost any WebBoard HTML, help, or text file. You can also put them in messages, conference profiles, and user profile information. WebBoard tags let you create dynamic pages that provide pertinent information for your users.

For example, to insert a WebBoard user's real first name in a conference profile description, include the tag <WB-FIRST> in the description:

```
Add your comments to this product discussion, <WB-FIRST>
```

To show a long version of the current date and time on the Messages Posted Today list, include the tags <WB-DATELONG> and <WB-TIME> in the file *msgtoday.html*:

```
The following messages were posted <WB-DATELONG> before <WB-TIME>:
```

When Meghan reads these pages, she sees the following:

```
Add your comments to this product discussion, Meghan
The following messages were posted Tuesday, March 18, 1997 before 5:57 pm:
```

WebBoard supports a large number of tags, which you can use in a variety of ways to create dynamic pages for your WebBoard. The following sections describe the WebBoard special tags.

Note

As you edit WebBoard's files, you'll notice many tags that are in the form <WB-*variable_name*>. Many of these tags are used by the WebBoard program; the ones available for general use are listed in the following sections.

Tags Related to the User

The following WebBoard tags provide information about the current user. Note that some information may not be available if the user did not provide it in his or her user profile.

Tag Name	*Replaced with*
`<WB-NAME>`	User's full real name (mixed case)
`<WB-NAMEU>`	User's full real name (all upper case)
`<WB-FIRST>`	User's first name (mixed case)
`<WB-FIRSTU>`	User's first name (all uppercase)
`<WB-LAST>`	User's last name (mixed case)
`<WB-LASTU>`	User's last name (all upper case)
`<WB-CITY>`	User's city name. This information is taken from the City/Town field of the user's personal profile.
`<WB-STATE>`	User's state name. This information is taken from the State/Province field of the user's personal profile.
`<WB-COUNTRY>`	User's country name. This information is taken from the Country field of the user's personal profile.
`<WB-EMAIL>`	User's email address
`<WB-USERID>`	User's WebBoard ID number
`<WB-FIRSTLOGIN>`	Date of user's first login in *MM/DD/YY* format (03/18/97)
`<WB-TOTALCONNECTS>`	Total number of connects (WebBoard requests) for the user

Tag Name	*Replaced with*
<WB-NAME>	User's full real name (mixed case)
<WB-BIO>	User's biographical information (interests, hobbies). This information is taken from the user's personal profile.
<WB-HOMEPAGE>	User's home page. This information is taken from the user's personal profile.
<WB-HOSTNAME>	Hostname of the location from which the user is reaching your WebBoard. Note that this information is available only if you are using an external web server and reverse DNS lookup is enabled for the server. See your web server's documentation for instructions on enabling this feature. WebBoard's internal web server does not support reverse DNS.
<WB-IPADDRESS>	The IP address of the location from which the user is reaching your WebBoard. This information is taken from the user's browser.

Tags Related to Users, Conferences, and Boards

These WebBoard tags provide information about the current user and his or her current WebBoard session.

Tag Name	*Replaced with*
<WB-NEWMSGS>	Number of new messages for the user; until a user marks messages as read (Mark Read from the menubar), messages are considered new.
<WB-POSTS>	Number of messages the user has posted
<WB-BOARD>	Name of the current virtual board the user is in

Tags Related to the Web Server

These WebBoard tags provide information about the web server—either internal or external—you are using with WebBoard.

Tag Name	*Replaced with*
<WB-SVRSOFTWARE>	Version/revision number of the web server software
<WB-SVRNAME>	Server's network hostname
<WB-SVRPORT>	Server's network port number, typically 80
<WB-SVRADMIN>	Email address of the web server's administrator

Tags Related to the System

These WebBoard tags provide information about the system on which WebBoard is running and about WebBoard.

Tag Name	*Replaced with*
<WB-HITS>	Number of WebBoard requests since WebBoard was last started
<WB-TOTALHITS>	Total number of WebBoard requests
<WB-DATE>	Current system date in *MM/DD/YY* format (03/18/97)
<WB-DATELONG>	Current system date in the format day of week, month, day, year (Tuesday, March 18, 1997)
<WB-TIME>	Current system time in 12-hour format (5:57 p.m.)
<WB-TIME24>	Current system time in 24-hour format (17:57)
<WB-USERS>	Total number of WebBoard users

Enhancing Navigation with WebBoard URLs

To reach WebBoard, you point your browser to the main WebBoard URL, either by typing it in directly or by clicking on a link. The path of the main WebBoard URL is either the server's domain name (if WebBoard is using the internal web server), or the server's domain name and the URL path */webboard/$webb.exe*. This URL takes you to the login page, from which you log in to WebBoard.

WebBoard supports many other URLs that extend this basic address and take the user directly to specific WebBoard locations. Many of these URLs are incorporated into the program to move users from location to location and feature to feature quickly, such as the Conferences list or Search form. The WebBoard URLs can also perform specific tasks such as marking a user's messages as read. These URL extensions have the same effect as clicking one of the selections on the menubar.

As you customize WebBoard's pages, you can use WebBoard URLs in HREF of an anchor tag (the tag that creates a hyperlink to another location) to move the user quickly to a new location or to accomplish a specific task. For example, it may be important for your users to know who else has visited WebBoard that day; perhaps the board is dedicated to a specific project and members need a quick way to determine who has checked new postings. You can add a link to the Welcome page (*intro.html*) to display the list of today's users:

```
<a href="webboard/$webb.exe/loginstoday">Today's users</a>
```

If you want the resulting page to display only in the Message window frame (on the right in the browser), you must add a target attribute to the HREF identifying the frame:

```
<a href="webboard/$webb.exe/loginstoday" target="messages">Today's users</
a>
```

The names of each frame are given in the *layout1.html* file (see Chapter 8).

These two examples assume that you are using an external server, which requires the extra path information */webboard/$webb.exe*. If you are using WebBoard's internal web server, do not include the path.

You can use WebBoard URLs in any WebBoard HTML or help files. The following list gives the WebBoard URLs and their actions.

Note

You must include the extra path information (*/webboard/$webb.exe/*) if you are using a server other than WebBoard's internal server.

WebBoard URL	*Location*
/~stats	Go to the WebBoard statistics summary (see Chapter 6 for details of this page)
/~#	Go to virtual board number #
/search	Go to the Search form.
/search?today	List new messages posted today.
/markread	Mark as read all messages in all conferences.
/markread?#	Mark as read all messages in conference number #; note that conferences are numbered in order of creation and retain that order even if a conference is deleted.
/list	Go to the Conferences list.
/top10posters	Go to the list of top 10 posters.
/top10users	Go to the list of top 10 users.
/loginstoday	Go to the list of today's users.
/userpeek?#	Go to the user profile for user number #.

WebBoard in Action: The CityNet

The CityNet began in Kansas City as a premiere online service with a proprietary dialup system providing local content for the entire metro area. As interest in the Internet grew, The CityNet moved to the World Wide Web and expanded its coverage to encompass 30 cities throughout the United States. We caught up with Scott Johnson, President of Data Supply Outlet, Inc., the company behind The CityNet. He shared with us how The CityNet has put WebBoard to work.

The goal of The CityNet is to provide information for local residents and visitors to cities served by The CityNet. On The CityNet's site, people can find anything from local events to classified ads. A partnership arrangement with local community papers hosts these papers' content and makes them part of the bigger picture offered by The CityNet. Since going to the Web at the end of 1996, The CityNet has experienced tremendous success in its designated markets by generating over 300,000 hits per month.

Scott Johnson says of the site's success, "So far we're not on anyone's search engine, but still our site is quite active, with over 12,000 hits a day. We are very excited about the future plans for The CityNet. One of the best traffic builders we had on our dialup system was online bulletin boards and chat. As we looked for a program that would suit our needs, we were very disappointed with what was available. As we watched WebBoard 2.0 take shape, we were encouraged not only by its features but also by its intuitiveness. Our visitors especially enjoy the chat features."

The following figure shows a typical chat session on The CityNet. Participants make good use of many Chat features including adding smileys to messages, varying the text, and whispering to others in the room. Note too, that The CityNet has customized the Chat menubar to include their logo.

Figure 7-2 The Comedy chat room

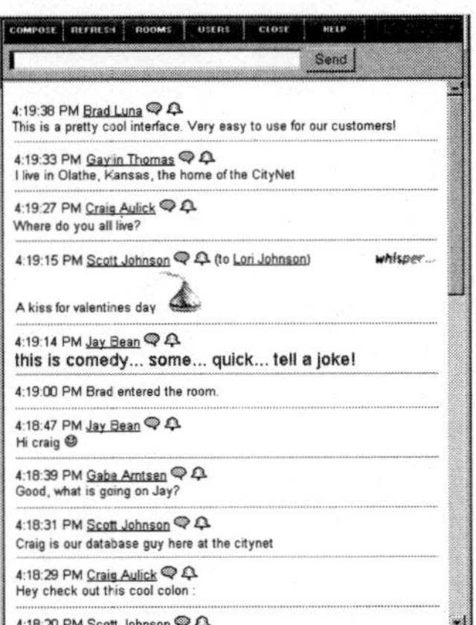

(continued)

(continued from previous page)

"Because we provide information on entertainment, sports, classifieds, and local news," Scott continues, "it was only natural that we have a forum for our users to meet and discuss the community topics at hand." WebBoard has provided that forum both with conferences and live chat.

Since our initial encounter with The CityNet, they have upgraded to WebBoard 2.0 XL and created 30 virtual boards—one for each city they serve. Within each virtual board, The CityNet has about nine conferences and plans to expand that as each city develops its own online "personality." These conferences attract everyone from teens to singles to people just looking for entertainment.

The CityNet conferences include:

- 20 and Loving It
- 30 Something
- 40 and Over
- Teens
- Comedy
- Local Politics
- Religion
- Sports

Scott noted that The CityNet crosses demographic barriers, and becomes a meeting place for people everywhere. The people who visit The CityNet are as varied as the community itself.

In commenting on WebBoard's features, Scott said, "WebBoard's email notification lets our users know when there is new information in a conference they are active in—it's great for us because it draws them back to our site to check the messages! Also, the frames mode format works wonderfully. Our users find WebBoard's Chat feature to be exceptional. In fact, this feature is the most heavily used on our site and it creates a strong sense of community."

The CityNet generates revenues by selling advertising in every city. WebBoard's Chat Spot feature has proven to be a gold mine for The CityNet. Companies like Cellular One, Gateway 2000, and a large chocolate manufacturer are advertising with Chat Spots. These companies' logos appear appear in the Chat window while people are engaged in chat sessions. The CityNet charges advertisers for this exposure and have so far generated some nice revenue, all while people are talking.

Scott ended our session by noting, "One of the largest benefits of WebBoard is that we can easily customize it to harmonize with our business. The user interface makes navigation really easy, so we want to retain the functionality of the product. In fact, WebBoard's functionality is what we see as one of the greatest draws to our system."

You can visit The CityNet at http://citynet.com.

8

WebBoard File Reference

As discussed in Chapter 7, most of WebBoard's user interface is controlled by HTML files, which you can customize to reflect the look and feel you want for your WebBoard and to provide more pertinent information to your users. In addition to the HTML files, WebBoard's text and help files are also easy to customize.

This chapter serves as a reference for the many HTML files used in WebBoard. Each file is listed (in alphabetical order by category) with a brief description of its purpose and any items you should note when editing the file. For example, many files contain JavaScript code, which should not be touched.

Often you may need to update more than one file to make sure the customizations you've made are reflected in all instances. As appropriate, we've cross-referenced files that work closely together. However, we cannot stress enough the need to *test any files you edit.* If you need more information on editing files, please refer to Chapter 7.

This chapter first covers the general HTML files. Next it covers the text files used to send email messages to users. The Chat HTML files are covered next, followed by the Wizard HTML files. The last section of this chapter covers the help files.

General HTML Files

WebBoard's general HTML files determine most of the program's user interface, from the login page to the conference profile list. These files reside in the WebBoard Html directory (typically *C:\WebBoard\Html*). You can edit these files to customize your pages as described in Chapter 7. This section lists each HTML file, its purpose, and any suggestions or caveats about making changes. The files are listed in alphabetical order.

Note

Before making changes to any WebBoard file, be sure to make a backup copy of it.

asknew.html

Purpose

This page appears under Cookie Authentication mode when a user logs in and either the password was incorrect or the login name is taken by another WebBoard user. The page redisplays the login name and password dialog for the user to try again with the correct password or a different login name.

Notes

This page does not appear if WebBoard is using Basic Authentication mode. Under this mode, if the user mistypes his or her password or the login name is already in use, WebBoard redisplays the Basic Authentication dialog box.

attach.html

Purpose

This page appears if a user has checked the Attach a File box when creating a new message and has pressed Post. Note that any preview options occur first, and the message is posted before the file attachment. The File Attachment page is a form for selecting the type of file, the location of the file on the local system, a description of the file, and whether or not additional files are to be uploaded.

Notes

- Not all browsers support file attachments. For example, Netscape Navigator 2.0 (and higher) supports file attachments, but Microsoft Internet Explorer does not. If a user's browser does not support file attachments, the Browse button on this page does not display.

- Not all web servers support file attachments (implemented via http file uploading). The WebBoard internal web server and O'Reilly Software's WebSite servers do; Microsoft IIS does not. If file attachments are not supported in your environment, we recommend you disable this feature for all your conferences (you can do so on the Edit Conferences form).
- This file contains two conditional pages that are sent when the number of attached files is exceeded or the size limit for attached files is exceeded.
- This file contains a <LOOP> section for reading in the list of categories and their images.
- You can change the default images by replacing the appropriate files in the *\WebBoard\Images* directory. The images are as follows: *fa_app-s.gif* (application), *fa_audio-s.gif* (audio), *fa_doc-s.gif* (document), *fa_image-s.gif* (image), *fa_misc-s.gif* (unknown), and *fa_mm-s.gif* (multimedia).
- You can also add categories or rename categories by editing the Board Attachments table of the WebBoard database (*Webboard.mdb*). However, unless you are familiar with Access databases, we recommend you do not edit the database directly. Future versions of WebBoard may include an interface for editing the database. If you do edit the database, *make a backup copy first*.

authfail.html

Purpose

This page appears if WebBoard is not able to complete a login or the user has canceled the login process. This page appears only if Basic Authentication mode is in use; it replaces the standard access denied message.

Notes

This file contains a *mailto* URL to the WebBoard system administrator using the tag <WB-SRVADM>. If you want queries directed to another address, replace the tag with the proper email address.

boardadd.html

Purpose

This page is the form for creating a virtual board without using the wizard. It appears when the WebBoard system administrator selects Create Virtual Board without Wizard from the Administrator menu.

Notes

This page is only displayed to users with system administrator privileges.

boardadded.html

Purpose

This page is a table summarizing the setup of a just-created virtual board. This page displays after the system administrator clicks Create on the Add Virtual Board page. This page includes a link to the new virtual board.

Notes

None.

boardclosed.html

Purpose

This page alerts users that the virtual board they are trying to reach is limited to a selected group of users. Such restricted virtual boards are called *private* or *closed*. The WebBoard system administrator and board manager(s) must manually add users to a closed board.

Notes

This page's default background is red. You may want to change the color.

boarddelete.html

Purpose

This warning page prevents the system administrator from inadvertently deleting the wrong virtual board. This page appears when the system administrator selects Delete Virtual Board from the Administrator menu. The two links on this page either complete or cancel the deletion.

Notes

This page contains two conditional pages that are sent when the selected board does not exist or after the deletion is completed to confirm the action.

boardedit.html

Purpose

This page is the form for editing an existing virtual board. It appears when the WebBoard system administrator selects Edit Virtual Board from the Administrator menu.

Notes

None.

chatrooms.html

Purpose

This page lists the available chat rooms (by conference name) and the number of users currently participating in the chat session. Each chat room name is a link that launches the Chat program. This page is updated every 60 seconds. Users see this page when they click Chat on the menubar.

Notes

- This HTML file contains sensitive WebBoard tags and JavaScript code; we highly recommend you do not edit it. If you must, make a backup copy first.
- This page contains two conditional sections, one of which replaces the <WB-RESULTS> tag in the body of the displayed page, depending on the current status of the Available Chat Rooms. If no chat rooms are available, <WB-RESULTS> is replaced with a message to that effect. If chat rooms are available, a listing of the rooms appears.
- The second conditional section includes a <LOOP> section that creates a list of available chat rooms and the number of current active users.
- The <LOOP> section also contains a call to the JavaScript code that launches Chat when a user clicks the chat room's name in the list.
- The JavaScript code is embedded in the main HTML portion of the page, enclosed in <SCRIPT> tags. *Do not edit the JavaScript!*

confadd.html

Purpose

This page is the form for adding a new conference without using the wizard. It appears when the WebBoard system administrator or a virtual board's manager selects Add Conference without Wizard from the Administrator or Manager's menu.

Notes

This form has checkboxes for a variety of conference settings, such as the conference type and whether or not file attachments are allowed. You can change the default settings by editing the HTML form tags. If a checkbox is checked (the setting is on), the HTML appears as

```
<input name="FieldName" checked type="checkbox">
```

If a checkbox is not checked (the setting is off), the HTML appears as

```
<input name="FieldName" type="checkbox">
```

To turn off a default setting, change `checked type` to `type`; to turn on a default setting, change `type` to `checked type`.

confadded.html

Purpose

This page is a table summarizing the setup of a just-added conference. This page appears after the system administrator or manager clicks Create on the Add Conference page. The page includes the conference's name and description.

Notes

None.

confarchive.html

Purpose

This page retrieves and displays a list of the archived and deleted messages for the current conference. This page appears to the system administrator, virtual board manager(s), and conference moderator(s) from the Archive command on the Manage Conferences page.

Notes

- This file includes a conditional section that appears when no messages are found in the conference archive.
- This page includes <ADMIN> and <MANAGER> sections that display links back to the appropriate menus. Because conference moderators can also view this page, you may want to add a link back to the More Options menu to be shown only to moderators (see *confmanage.html* for an example).
- This page also includes a <LOOP> section that displays the list of archived messages.

confdelete.html

Purpose

This warning page prevents the system administrator, manager, or moderator from inadvertently deleting a wrong conference. This page appears when the system administrator, manager, or moderator selects Delete from the Manage Conferences page. The two links on this page either complete or cancel the deletion.

Notes

This page contains two conditional pages that are sent (1) if the selected conference does not exist or (2) after the deletion is completed to confirm the action, respectively. The page also contains an <ADMIN> section with a link back to the Administrator menu.

confedit.html

Purpose

This page is the form for editing an existing conference. It appears when the system administrator, manager, or moderator selects Edit from the Manage Conferences page.

Notes

The page contains an <ADMIN> section with a link back to the Administrator menu.

confmanage.html

Purpose

This page lists each conference in the current board with detailed information on the creator and the number of messages in the conference. Each conference also has four actions: Edit, Delete, Users, Archive. This page appears to the system administrator, manager(s), and moderator(s) from the Manage Conferences menu item. Note that moderators see only conferences to which they are assigned.

Notes

This page contains <ADMIN>, <MANAGER>, and <MODERATOR> sections with links back to the appropriate menu. It also contains a <LOOP> section that displays the list of conferences.

confnotify.html

Purpose

This page lets users select the email notify option for one or more conferences. It displays a list of all conferences followed by a checkbox for selecting email notification. This page appears when users select Email Notify from the More Options menu.

Notes

This page contains a <LOOP> section that displays the list of conferences and a checkbox for each one.

confprofile.html

Purpose

This page displays the profile (or summary) information for the selected conference. It also includes links to post a message to the conference and to mark all messages in the conference as read. This page appears when the user clicks a conference name from the Profiles menu page (*profmenu.html*)

Notes

None.

confselect.html

Purpose

This error message appears when a user tries to post a message using the Post button when no conference is selected. Two typical cases are when no conferences exist and when no conference is expanded.

Notes

You may want to personalize this page by adding the WebBoard tag for the current user's name (<WB-FIRST>) or add a graphic such as your company's logo.

guest.html

Purpose

This error message appears when a guest user tries to use a feature that is not available to guest users. Typically this message appears when a guest tries to post a message. It includes a link to the New User Information form, to encourage the guest to become a registered user.

Notes

You may want to customize this page by adding text describing your WebBoard and the benefits of being a full user. You may also want to add a graphic, such as your company's logo.

intro.html

Purpose

This page welcomes users to your WebBoard. It appears immediately after a user successfully logs in. The page includes a brief welcome message and a link to a list of new (unread) messages (displayed via *msgsnew.html*).

Notes

- You may want to customize this page with information about your WebBoard, its purpose, and actions the user may take.
- This page includes the WebBoard tag for the system administrator's email address (<WB-SRVADMIN>). You may want to replace that with another email address (such as your support or marketing group's address) or make it an active *mailto* link.
- This page has an <ADMIN> section that includes information about enrolling your copy of WebBoard 2.0. We encourage you to enroll online at WebBoard Central (*http://webboard.ora.com*) today. Once you have enrolled, you may want to delete this section.

> **Note**
>
> Enrolling your copy of WebBoard is easy. Just click the link on this page for WebBoard Central. By enrolling your copy of WebBoard, you will be notified of product news, updates, and special offers.

layout1.html

Purpose

This page serves two purposes. First, it sets the default configuration for the frames layout used in WebBoard (size, name, borders, and so forth). Second, it includes an error message for users whose browsers do not support frames, telling them to upgrade to a frame-capable browser or to edit their user profile to not use frames. This page appears only if a user logs into WebBoard with a browser that does not support frames.

Notes

You may use the frame names when adding WebBoard URLs to HTML files (see Chapter 7). The HREF must contain the frame name as a target attribute. The three names are as follows: *toolbar* for the menubar; *topics* for the Conferences list (the frame on the left of the browser window); and *messages* for the message window (the frame on the right side of the browser window).

login.html

Purpose

This page is the standard login page when Cookie Authentication mode is selected. It includes buttons for Guests and New Users and a login dialog box for existing users. The dialog box includes a checkbox for remembering the user's password. This page appears anytime a user or guest points his or her browser at your WebBoard's URL.

Notes

- You may want to customize this page with information about your WebBoard, its purpose, and actions the user may take. You may also want to personalize it for your business or organization. If you do so, we ask that you leave the copyright notice in place.
- Do not modify the form action tag that submits the login information to WebBoard. Warning remarks in the file surround this tag.
- If you are using Basic Authentication, this page is not displayed; instead, *enter.html* is used. See the instructions in Chapter 5 for setting up Basic Authentication logins.

loginagain.html

Purpose

This page gives instructions to users who want to login as a different user on a WebBoard that uses Basic Authentication. The user must close his or her browser, restart it, point at the WebBoard URL again, and complete the login process as the different user. This procedure is necessary because browsers remember the Basic Authentication information collected during login. Cookie authentication does not require this procedure. This page appears only when the user selects Login as a Different User from the More Options menu.

Notes

None.

loginfailed.html

Purpose

This page informs the user that his or her login was not successful. It appears when a user has logged in under Cookie Authentication and the login was not completed. The typical causes are a mistyped password (or login name) or the login name belongs to another registered WebBoard user. The page includes a dialog box that lets the user retry to log in.

Notes

- You may want to customize this page to include more information about retrying the login. You may also want to personalize it for your business or organization. If you do so, we ask that you leave the copyright notice in place.
- Do not modify the form action tag that submits the login information to WebBoard. Warning remarks surround this tag.
- If you are using Basic Authentication, this page is not displayed.

loginsNow.html

Purpose

This page lists users currently logged into WebBoard or who have been logged in in the last hour. This page appears when a user clicks Current Users from the More Options menu. The page is updated every 60 seconds.

Notes

- The refresh rate for this page is set in the tag `<meta http-equiv="refresh" content="60;">`. To change the refresh rate, edit the value of the content attribute. For example, if your WebBoard is very busy, you may want to raise the rate.
- This page contains a <LOOP> section that displays the list of current users.

loginsToday.html

Purpose

This page lists users who have logged into WebBoard on the current day. This page appears when a user clicks Today's Users from the More Options menu. The list includes the time of each user's last login.

Notes

This page contains a <LOOP> section that displays the list of today's users.

manager.html

Purpose

This page is the Manager menu. It appears when a user with manager privileges clicks the Manager link on the More Options menu. The Manager menu includes a list of actions available to a manager such as adding conferences and users.

Notes

This file contains JavaScript code for calling the Add User and Add Conferences wizards; we highly recommend you do not edit it. If you must, make a backup copy of this file first.

markread.html

Purpose

This page lets users mark all messages as read in some or all conferences. The page displays a list of all conferences with a checkbox to indicate that the messages in that conference should be marked as read. A link also lets users update all conferences at once. This page appears when the user clicks Mark All Read from the menubar.

Notes

- This page contains two conditional sections, which define the pages WebBoard displays after messages are marked as read depending on whether single conferences or all conferences were updated.
- This file also includes a <LOOP> section that creates a list of conferences and a checkbox for each.

more.html

Purpose

This page is the More Options menu that appears when a user clicks More from the menubar. In addition to the options available to all users, special menu items are displayed only to the system administrator, managers, and moderators.

Notes

This file contains <ADMIN>, <MANAGER>, and <MODERATOR> sections that cause the Administrator, Manager, and Moderator menu items to appear on the menu, respectively.

msgdelete.html

Purpose

This confirmation page prevents a user from inadvertently deleting a message. This page appears when an authorized user (the message creator, system administrator, board manager, or conference moderator) selects Delete from the Message menu. The two links on this page either complete or cancel the deletion.

Notes

This page contains a conditional section that is sent if the selected message does not exist.

msgsearch.html

Purpose

This page is the Search form for locating specific messages. It appears when a user clicks Search on the menubar.

Notes

This page contains a conditional section that is sent if the selected message does not exist.

msgsearched.html

Purpose

This page displays the results of a search for messages. It appears after a user clicks Search on the Search Messages form.

Notes

This page contains three conditional sections, which replace the <WB-RESULTS> tag in the body of the displayed page. The first section is displayed if no results are found. The second section displays standard results. The third section displays detailed results of the search. Both the standard and detailed displays contain <LOOP> sections that format lists of the results.

msgsnew.html

Purpose

This page lists new messages (messages that have not been marked as read). It appears when a user clicks New Messages from the More Options menu or on one of several links that appear in WebBoard.

Notes

This page contains two conditional sections, which replace the <WB-RESULTS> tag in the body of the displayed page. The first section is displayed if no new messages exist. The second section displays the list of new messages. The second results contains a <LOOP> section that formats the list of messages.

msgtoday.html

Purpose

This page lists new messages posted since midnight. It appears when a user clicks Today's Messages from the More Options menu.

Notes

This page contains two conditional sections, which replace the <WB-RESULTS> tag in the body of the displayed page. The first section is displayed if no new messages exist. The second section displays the list of today's new messages. The second results contains a <LOOP> section that formats the list of messages.

msgview.html

Purpose

This page displays the contents of a message that has been archived or deleted. This page appears when the system administrator, manager, or moderator clicks a message's topic name from the Archived Messages list, which is displayed from the Archive action on the Manage Conferences page. A link on this page lets the viewer retrieve the message.

Notes

None.

newuser.html

Purpose

This page is the New User Information form, which new users must complete to register on WebBoard. This form appears when a user clicks New User from the login page (independent of Cookie or Basic Authentication).

Notes

This file includes several error messages that are returned to the new user if required fields are not completed, if the login name is already taken, or if the password was entered two different ways. These messages are displayed in red.

offline.html

Purpose

This page informs users that WebBoard is currently unavailable. This page appears when WebBoard is paused.

Notes

This page includes the WebBoard tag for the system administrator's email address (<WB-SRVADMIN>) in a *mailto* URL. You may want to replace that with another email address (such as your support or marketing group's address).

postmsg.html

Purpose

This page is the message-posting form displayed to users in no frames mode. It appears when a user clicks a link or menu item to post a new topic or reply to an existing topic. The text entry box is wider in the no frames mode.

Notes

This file contains several warning remarks. Please heed all warnings before editing this file.

This file also contains default settings for the message posting options, such as spell-checking and converting line breaks to HTML paragraph tags. You can change the default settings by editing the HTML form tags. If a checkbox is checked (the setting is on), the HTML appears as

```
<input name="FieldName" checked type="checkbox">
```

If a checkbox is not checked (the setting is off), the HTML appears as

```
<input name="FieldName" type="checkbox">
```

To turn off a default setting, change `checked type` to `type`; to turn on a default setting, change `type` to `checked type`.

postmsg-f.html

Purpose

This page is the message-posting form displayed to users in frames. It appears when a user clicks a link or menu item to post a new topic or reply to an existing topic. In the frames mode, the text entry box is narrower.

Notes

This file contains several warning remarks. Please heed all warnings before editing this file.

This file also contains default settings for the message posting options, such as spell-checking and converting line breaks to HTML paragraph tags. You can change the default settings by editing the HTML form tags. If a checkbox is checked (the setting is on), the HTML appears as

```
<input name="FieldName" checked type="checkbox">
```

If a checkbox is not checked (the setting is off), the HTML appears as

```
<input name="FieldName" type="checkbox">
```

To turn off a default setting, change `checked type` to `type`; to turn on a default setting, change `type` to `checked type`.

preview.html

Purpose

This page displays a message before it is posted, allowing the user to make changes before posting it to the conference. This page appears if either Preview message or Preview/Spell check are checked on the message-posting form.

Notes

This page includes instructions for returning to the message-posting form to make corrections by clicking Back on the browser. Some versions of Microsoft Internet Explorer (MSIE) do not have this feature properly implemented. If you know that most of your WebBoard visitors are using MSIE, you may want to edit the instructions to accurately describe the procedure. We recommend you test the procedure first, since browsers are being constantly updated.

profmenu.html

Purpose

This page lets a user view his or her own personal profile or any conference profile. This page appears when the user clicks Profiles from the menubar.

Notes

This file contains a <LOOP> section that displays a list of all conferences. Each conference name is a link to the conference's profile (see *confprofile.html*).

read.html

Purpose

This page displays a single message for reading. It includes the message and the Message menu for posting a new topic or replying to the current message. This page appears when the user selects a message to read and is not using the Full topic view (as set on his or her User Profile form).

Notes

- This file contains two conditional sections that return messages if the selected message is not found.
- This file also contains a <LOOP> section for displaying file attachments.

readFull.html

Purpose

This page displays multiple messages for reading. It includes all messages in the topic from the selected message to the end. Each message also has a Message menu for posting a new topic or replying to the current message. This page appears when the user selects a message to read and is using the Full topic view (as set on his or her User Profile form).

Notes

- This file contains two conditional sections that return messages if the selected message is not found.
- This file also contains a <LOOP> section for displaying file attachments.
- This file should not have closing </BODY> or </HTML> tags.

readonly.html

Purpose

This page informs the user that the conference he or she has selected is a read-only conference and does not allow replies or new posts, except by the WebBoard system administrator and conference manager(s).

Notes

None.

suggest.html

Purpose

This page suggests replacement words for words not found in WebBoard's dictionary. The system administrator, manager(s), and moderator(s) have the ability to add words to the dictionary from this page. This page appears when a user clicks a misspelled word while previewing a message. This page does not appear if spell-checking is not enabled.

Notes

- This file contains <ADMIN>, <MANAGER>, and <MODERATOR> sections that include the form input tags for adding words to the dictionary.
- This file also contains a <LOOP> section that displays the list of suggested replacement words.

sysadmin.html

Purpose

This page is the system administrator's menu. It appears when a user with system administrator privileges clicks the Administrator link on the More Options menu. The system administrator's menu includes a list of actions available to the WebBoard system administrator, such as adding and deleting virtual boards.

Notes

This file contains JavaScript code for calling the Create Virtual Board, Add User, and Add Conference wizards; we highly recommend you do not edit it. If you must, make a backup copy of this file first.

toolbar.html

Purpose

This page defines the WebBoard menubar, which is displayed in frames mode. In no frames mode, the menubar is defined in *topics.html.*

Notes

The buttons on the menubar are images, which you can change for your WebBoard. The image files reside in the *\WebBoard\Images* directory; their names begin with *tb-*. If you edit this file, we strongly recommend you back it up first.

top10posters.html

Purpose

This page lists the 10 most frequent posters to WebBoard. This page appears when a user clicks Top 10 Posters from the More Options menu. The list includes the number of posts each user has made.

Notes

This page contains a <LOOP> section that displays the list of top 10 posters.

top10users.html

Purpose

This page lists the 10 most frequent users to WebBoard by number of logins. This page appears when a user clicks Top 10 Users from the More Options menu. The list includes the number of logins each user has made.

Notes

This page contains a <LOOP> section that displays the list of top 10 users.

topics.html

Purpose

This page is the WebBoard Conferences list. It displays the list of WebBoard conferences, topics, and messages. In the no frames mode, this page supplies the menubar.

Notes

- This file contains a conditional section that displays a message if no conferences exist. The conditional section contains <ADMIN> tags that include a link to the Administrator menu for setting up conferences.
- The buttons on the menubar are images, which you can change for your WebBoard. The image files reside in the *\WebBoard\Images* directory; their names begin with *tb-*. If you edit this file, we strongly recommend you back it up first. Changes made to the menubar in this file only appear in no frames mode.

useradd.html

Purpose

This page is the form for adding a new user without using the wizard. It appears when the WebBoard system administrator or a Virtual Board's Manager selects Add a User without Wizard from the Administrator or Manager menu.

Notes

None.

useradded.html

Purpose

This page is a table summarizing the newly added user. This page displays after the system administrator or manager clicks Create on the Add User page.

Notes

None.

userdelete.html

Purpose

This warning page prevents the system administrator or manager from inadvertently deleting a user. This page appears when the system administrator or manager selects Delete from the Manage Users page. The two links on this page either complete or cancel the deletion.

Notes

This page contains two conditional pages that are sent (1) if the selected user does not exist or (2) after the deletion is completed to confirm the action, respectively.

userdone.html

Purpose

This page welcomes a new user with the user's ID number and a message to write down his or her login name and password. It also includes a link to the Conferences list. This page appears after a new user successfully registers on WebBoard.

Notes

You may want to customize this page to provide more information about your WebBoard.

useredit.html

Purpose

This page is the form for changing a user's profile. The system administrator or manager can work with this form for any user; an individual user can see this form only for his or her own user profile. This page appears when a user clicks the Personal Profile link from the Profiles menu or from the Manage Users page (available only to the system administrator or manager).

Notes

This file includes several error messages that are returned if required fields are not completed, the login name is already taken, the password was entered two different ways, or the frames mode is changed. These messages are displayed in red.

userlist.html

Purpose

This page is the search form for locating users by first or last name. This page appears when a user clicks Search Users from the More Options menu in a virtual board that is configured to use real names. The system administrator and manager(s) see the users' login names and can edit user profiles or delete users from the resulting page.

Notes

- This file contains <ADMIN> and <MANAGER> sections that display login names and provide edit/delete options.
- This file also contains a <LOOP> section that displays the results of the search.

userlist-l.html

Purpose

This page is the search form for locating users by login name. This page appears when a user clicks Search Users from the More Options menu in a virtual board that is configured to use login names. The system administrator and manager(s) see the users' real first and last names and can edit user profiles or delete users from the resulting page.

Notes

- This file contains <ADMIN> and <MANAGER> sections that display first and last names and provide edit/delete options.
- This file also contains a <LOOP> section that displays the results of the search.

user-profile.html

Purpose

This page displays the profile (or summary) information for a selected user. This page appears when a user clicks on any user's name that is a link (for example, in a message posting) in a virtual board that is configured to use first and last names. The system administrator and manager(s) also see the user's login name.

Notes

This file contains <ADMIN> and <MANAGER> sections that display the user's login name.

user-profile-l.html

Purpose

This page displays the profile (or summary) information for a selected user. This page appears when a user clicks on any user's name that is a link (for example, in a message posting) in a virtual board that is configured to use login names. The system administrator and manager(s) also see the user's real first and last names.

Notes

This file contains <ADMIN> and <MANAGER> sections that display the user's first and last name.

userselect.html

Purpose

This page lets the system administrator, manager(s), or moderator(s) select users for a private (closed) conference. The page has two list select boxes: one contains a list of all users and the other is a list of users with access to this conference. This page appears when the system administrator, manager, or moderator clicks Users from the Manage Conferences page.

Notes

This file contains an <ADMIN> section that includes a link back to the Administrator menu.

Text Files

WebBoard includes two text files that are used as email messages sent to users. These files reside in the *\WebBoard\Html* directory and have the filename extension *.txt*. You can edit these files to fit the needs of your WebBoard. These two files are described next.

notify.txt

Purpose

This message is sent to users who have requested email notification when new messages are posted to conferences. The message includes the name of the conference.

Notes

You can customize this message to identify your WebBoard or add other information. You may also want to change the default signature, which is *WebBoard Administrator,* or include other WebBoard variable tags.

welcome.txt

Purpose

This message is sent to each user who has registered on your WebBoard. It includes his or her login name and password as well as the URL for reaching your WebBoard.

Notes

You can customize this message to further identify your WebBoard or describe your company or organization. You may also want to change the default signature, which is *WebBoard Administrator,* or include other WebBoard variable tags.

Chat HTML Files

WebBoard's Chat feature is a JavaScript application that runs in a window launched from the browser. The user interface for Chat is determined by several HTML files, which also contain the JavaScript code. These files reside in the *\WebBoard\Html\Chat* directory. This section describes these files.

bar.html

Purpose

This page sets the basic display of the Chat window. It includes the Chat menubar, the message window, and the send button.

Notes

This file contains much of the JavaScript that Chat uses. Do not edit this file without first making a backup copy.

The buttons on the menubar are images, which you can change for your WebBoard. The image files reside in the *\WebBoard\Images\Chat* directory; their names begin with *tb-*.

create.html

Purpose

This page is the Compose Message window, used to create longer messages with various font attributes, including size and color.

Notes

This file contains JavaScript; do not edit this file without first making a backup copy.

dialog.html

Purpose

This page defines the frame layout of the chat window. The top frame is called RefreshBar while the lower frame is called Dialog. It is very similar to *layout1.html*.

Notes

None.

messages.html

Purpose

This page displays the messages posted during a Chat session.

Notes

This file contains JavaScript; do not edit this file without first making a backup copy.

off.html

Purpose

This page informs the user that Chat is not available to them. Either Chat is not enabled for that conference or the user is logged in as a guest. Guests cannot participate in Chat.

Notes

None.

rooms.html

Purpose

This page displays the Available Chat Rooms list in a separate window launched by Chat. The active rooms are preceded by (A) in the list. A user can switch to another room by selecting a name from this list. This page appears when a user clicks Rooms on the Chat menubar.

Notes

This file contains JavaScript; do not edit this file without first making a backup copy.

roomsLayout.html

Purpose

This page sets the page layout for the Available Chat Rooms list (see *rooms.html*).

Notes

None.

users.html

Purpose

This page displays the list of users participating in the current chat room. The Users list appears in a separate window launched by Chat. The list lets you see who is in the room and select one or more users to send a private, or Whispered, message to. This page appears when a user clicks Users on the Chat menubar.

Notes

This file contains JavaScript; do not edit this file without first making a backup copy.

usersLayout.html

Purpose

This page sets the page layout for the Users list (see *users.html*).

Notes

None.

Wizards HTML Files

WebBoard's wizards are JavaScript applications that run in a window launched from the browser. The user interface for the Create Virtual Board, Add Conference, and Add User wizards is determined by several HTML files, which also contain the JavaScript code. These files reside in the *\WebBoard\Html\Wizards* directory. This section describes these files.

AddBoard*.html

Purpose

The four AddBoard HTML pages make up the four pages of the Create Virtual Board wizard, available from the Administrator menu.

Notes

These files contain JavaScript as well as HTML codes and WebBoard tags. *Do not edit these files without making a backup copy.*

AddConference*.html

Purpose

The nine AddConference HTML pages make up the nine pages of the Add New Conference wizard, available from the Administrator menu and Manager menu.

Notes

These files contain JavaScript as well as HTML codes and WebBoard tags. *Do not edit these files without making a backup copy.*

AddUsers*.html

Purpose

The three AddUsers HTML pages make up the three pages of the Add New User wizard, available from the Administrator menu and Manager menu.

Notes

These files contain JavaScript as well as HTML codes and WebBoard tags. *Do not edit these files without making a backup copy.*

WebBoard Help Files

The WebBoard help files are also HTML files, which reside in the *\WebBoard\Html\Help* directory. The help files are self-explanatory and thus not discussed individually in this chapter; for example, *index.html* is the help index, *chat.html* is the help for Chat help, and *msgpost.html* is the help for posting a message.

You can edit them with any HTML or text editor. As with any WebBoard files, you should make a backup copy before editing the help files.

IV

Using WebBoard

If you want to quickly learn how to navigate around WebBoard, this section is for you. Chapter 9, *WebBoard Basics*, describes the user interface, login procedures, and basic steps to working with WebBoard. To become more involved in the WebBoard community, go to Chapter 10, *Participating in Conferences*, where you'll find an overview of how to post, send, edit, and delete messages. Descriptions of the More Options Menu start Chapter 11, *What's Happening on Your WebBoard?* Here you'll also learn how to use the Email Notification feature and find various users and messages. If you're ready to chat, take a look at Chapter 12, *Chatting in WebBoard*. This chapter gives you step-by-step instructions for sending and customizing messages, finding and paging other chat users, and navigating from one chat room to another.

9

WebBoard Basics

WebBoard gives you a way to exchange messages with others in a recorded format. You may have used online services such as America Online, or you may be familiar with bulletin board services. WebBoard is similar to that, but lets you have discussion forums and chat sessions on the Web. WebBoard makes it easy for you to communicate with others in your organization, business, or personal affairs with its online conferencing system.

This chapter walks you through all the steps you need to get started with WebBoard. First it gives an overview describing what you can expect to see and how to use WebBoard. Then it shows you how to establish an account, navigate, and find information. The next section gives a short overview of WebBoard.

A Quick Look at WebBoard

WebBoard has many features and options to make online communication a snap. WebBoard is arranged so that you can quickly navigate to get information. The main structural elements of WebBoard that you see are the Conferences list, menubar, and Message window. At a glance you see the main information on WebBoard in the Conferences list. The handy menubar makes it easy for you to use WebBoard's features. It's convenient for you to read WebBoard's information in the Message window. The next section describes these elements.

WebBoard's Three Activity Areas

This section gives you the big picture of the main areas of WebBoard. Figure 9-1 shows WebBoard's Main menu in the frames mode, from which you can see WebBoard's three activity areas:

- The *conference list* displays the conferences, topics, and messages (the left frame).
- The *menubar* has buttons for using WebBoard's commands and features (the top frame).
- The *message window* is the working area where information and forms are displayed. For example, the message window is where you read and post messages, complete user profile information, and execute searches (the right frame).

Figure 9-1 WebBoard's Main menu in frames mode

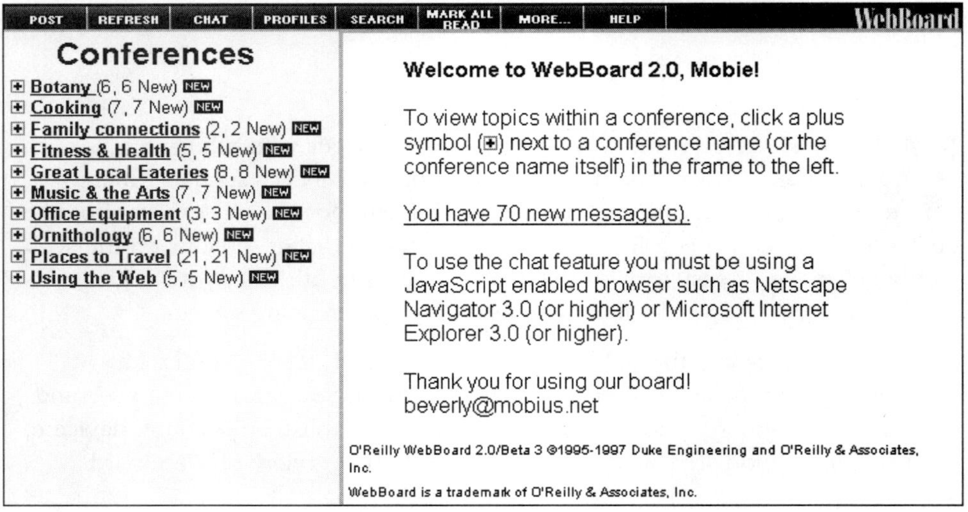

If you are using the frames mode when you use WebBoard, you see all three areas at the same time in your browser. If you are using the non-frames mode, the menubar is always present and either the conference list or message window is displayed, depending on your current activity. Working with these areas is explained in much more detail in the rest of the chapter.

What's the Difference Between Conferences, Topics, and Messages?

WebBoard's well-designed user interface makes it a breeze for you to participate in conferences. You can choose from a variety of methods to post messages: the WebBoard menubar, the Message window menu, or the conference profile. Your WebBoard conferences are simple to use and navigate. As a WebBoard user, you can post topics and reply to messages in the conferences your manager has set up.

As a WebBoard user, you will want to know some basic information before you start participating in conferences and chat sessions. Once through this overview, not only will you be able to use WebBoard, but you'll also know some tricks on how to get the most out of it for your needs.

WebBoard conferences are arranged, or threaded, in a logical hierarchy with three basic levels. You might liken this hierarchy to the structure of a book, with each conference being similar to the book's title. A topic is the equivalent to the chapter's title, while its messages contain the actual content. Each conference has at least one topic, and each topic contains at least one message, but can have dozens or hundreds more. Multiple conferences are similar to many books on a bookshelf. Figure 9-2 illustrates this relationship. In essence, conferences are the most general, while messages are the most specific.

Figure 9-2 Conferences, topics, and messages

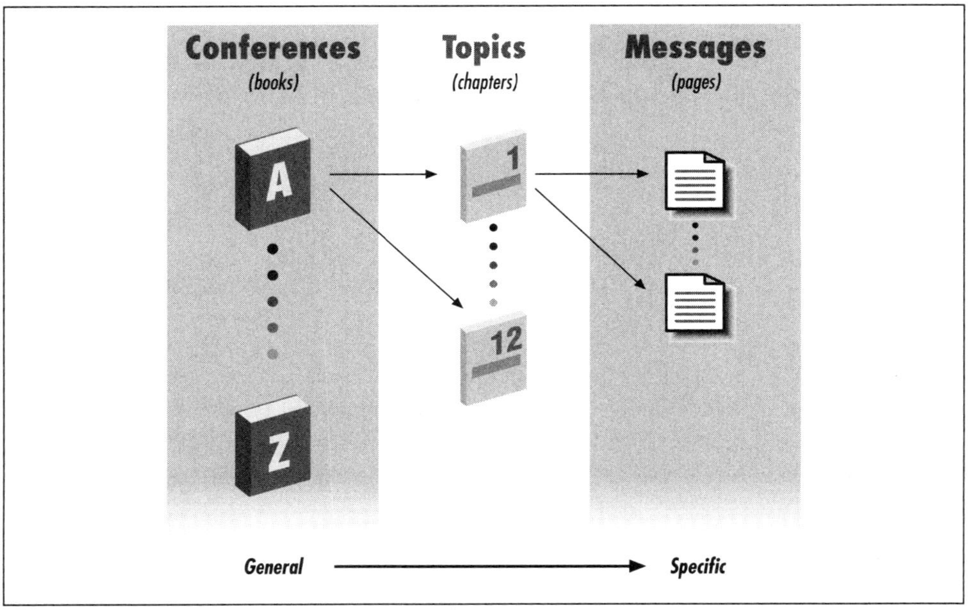

WebBoard conferences are set up by the WebBoard manager. You can post and reply to topics and messages in the conferences, in essence helping to write the books. Keep in mind that topics should be relevant to the conference and messages should be specific to each topic. You can start a new topic in a conference any time you want to change the subject. As your conference develops with more topics, it begins to resemble a book on a particular subject. This is even more apparent when messages appear in the Full topic view, which allows you to read and scroll through several messages in a topic at a time. This feature is discussed in the section "Editing Your User Profile" later in this chapter.

The WebBoard hierarchy provides a means for you to track information in a logical and simple fashion—you can zero in on a subject that interests you For example, if you have a conference on Great Local Eateries, you could look under the topic Breakfast Spots to find a good place for your early morning java and scones. Or say you want to find a great restaurant for dinner. Simply scroll through the topics until you find one that sounds interesting. Because of WebBoard's message structure, it's simple to quickly locate the information you want. Consequently, you can avoid any unnecessary searches through the entire list of conferences and topics.

A Word about Browsers

Some of WebBoard's features such as frames, file attachments, Cookie Authentication, and Chat have certain browser requirements. We recommend you use a JavaScript-enabled browser such as Netscape Navigator 3.0 or higher or Microsoft Internet Explorer 3.0 or higher. Note that Internet Explorer 3.0 does not support file attachments.

If your browser does not support frames, you have the option to change this default setting in your user profile (described later in this chapter). As browsers develop there may be changes on how they work. Check WebBoard Central (*http://webboard.ora.com*) to see new information on browsers.

Logging in to WebBoard

To enter WebBoard, you must log in by supplying a login name and password. Depending on how WebBoard's security is set up, you will be presented with one of two login methods. The Basic Authentication method is less common and is described in the sidebar titled "Logging in with Basic Authentication."

The Cookie Authentication method is more common and is described in the following procedural sections. When you come to a WebBoard with Cookie Authentication, you will see a Welcome page like the one shown in Figure 9-3.

Figure 9-3 Welcome page

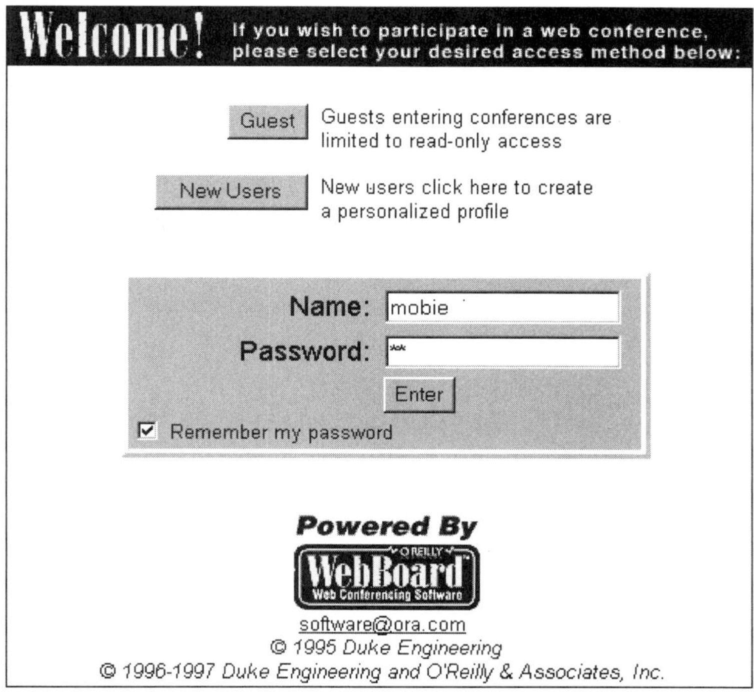

From this page, you can log in as a Guest, a New User, or an Existing User, as described briefly below; detailed instructions are covered in the following sections.

As a guest

To log in to WebBoard as a guest, click Guest to just look around WebBoard and read the conferences. You will not be able to participate as a user.

As a new user

To log in to WebBoard as a new user, click New Users to enter WebBoard for the first time and register yourself as a WebBoard user. WebBoard opens the New User Information page for you to complete.

As an existing WebBoard user

To log in to WebBoard as an existing user, enter your login name and password in the two textbox fields. To have WebBoard remember your password for six months, check the Remember My Password box. This option is available if the WebBoard system administrator set up this WebBoard with Cookie Authentication.

Logging in as a Guest

If you just want to browse WebBoard, you may want to log in as a guest so that you can look around. If you log in as a guest, you can view the conferences but not participate in them. You cannot post messages or join a Chat session. When you select Guest at the WebBoard login page, as shown in Figure 9-3, the Conferences list opens and you can navigate to the different conferences.

Logging in as a New User

If you want to post messages in WebBoard, you must be a real user. The first time you log in, you need to choose a unique login name and a password. You must provide this information as well as your real name and email address to participate in WebBoard conferences or chat sessions.

Your login name and password are required each time you log in to WebBoard. You should avoid using your actual name for your login name. Your real name identifies you and your messages to other WebBoard users. As a new user, you make up your own login name and password to self-register. Note that some WebBoards may use your login name rather than your real name to identify you. You should be sure your login name is something easy to remember and would not be embarrassing or offensive.

To log in as a new user, follow these steps:

1. On the WebBoard login page (Figure 9-3), click New User. The New User Information form opens, as shown in Figure 9-4.
2. Follow the directions on this page and fill in the required blanks (marked with red dots). You can also add optional information about yourself that will be displayed in your personal profile for other WebBoard users to view. You can use up to 2,000 characters (equivalent to over three pages), and you can use HTML for your Hobbies and Signature. If you want to change this information later, you can edit your user profile (see the section "Editing Your User Profile" later in this chapter).

   Notice that the default setting for using WebBoard is frames, which enables you to view the Conferences list while you view and post messages. However, for this option you must be using a browser such as Netscape Navigator 3.0 (or higher) or Microsoft Internet Explorer 3.0 (or higher). If your browser does not support frames or you prefer to not use frames, select the No frames mode.
3. When you have completed entering information on this form, click Create. WebBoard's Welcome user page opens. The page identifies you as a new WebBoard user. From this form, you can link to the Conferences list, from which you can participate in conferences and chat sessions.

Figure 9-4 New User Information form

New User Information

Please fill out this form to create a new user profile for yourself.
Once this information is gathered you will not need to enter it again and you will be able to change it later

Use the button at the bottom of this page to continue when you are finished.
For security reasons it is best to keep your login name different from your real name.

A red dot ● indicates the field is required.
For help on each field, **click here**.

Login name: sam ●
First name: Samantha ●
Last name: Merryweather ●
Password: *** ●
Enter it twice *** ●
Email address: sam@merry.net ●
City/Town: Florence
State/Province:
Country: Italy

Note

Your browser may warn you that cookies are being sent whenever you log in. Click OK to accept the cookies. You can turn off these warnings in your browser if you like.

Logging in as an Existing User

As a registered WebBoard user, you may need to enter your name and password in the Name and Password textboxes each time you log in (see Figure 9-3). Click Enter when you complete this process. If you have checked Remember my password, it is unnecessary for you to enter your password again. If you misspell your name or password, WebBoard displays a page for you to try again. If you can't remember your login name or password, log in under a new name and then ask the WebBoard system administrator or manager for assistance.

Logging in with Basic Authentication

If the WebBoard system administrator has set up WebBoard to use Basic Authentication for logins, you will have to enter your login name and password each time you visit this WebBoard. Typically, a WebBoard using Basic Authentication has a login page similar to that shown in Figure 9-3, but with only three buttons: Existing Users, Guest, and New Users.

If you are a member of this WebBoard, click the Existing Users button. Your browser displays a Basic Authentication dialog box, similar to that shown below. Type in your login name and password, click OK, and you should be in. If you mistyped an entry or you are not a user, an authorization failed message is displayed and you can try again. You will have to enter your name and password each time you visit this WebBoard.

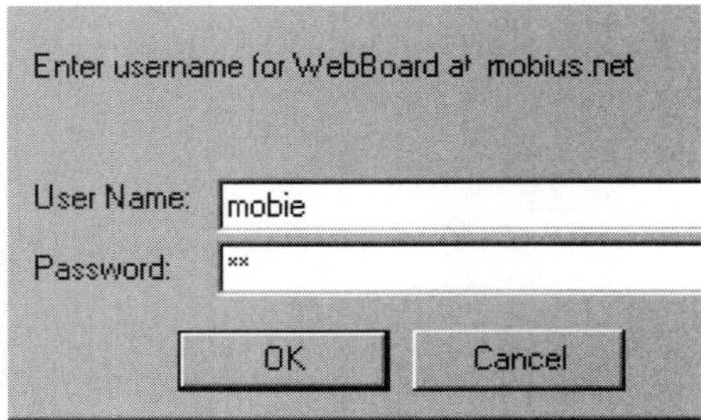

If you are a guest, click Guest. WebBoard displays the welcome page with the conference list. You may browse conferences and read messages but not post messages or participate in conferences.

If you are a new user, click New Users. WebBoard displays the New User Information form for you to complete, as described in the section "Logging in as a New User" in this chapter.

To log in as a different user, you must close your browser, restart it, and login to WebBoard again as a different existing user or a new user. Under Basic Authentication, the browser remembers your current login and password information and there is no way to clear it except to close the program.

If you have questions about the authentication method used by a WebBoard, contact the WebBoard system administrator. Also, if the authentication mode changes (from Basic to Cookie, for example), your login information remains the same.

Logging in as a Different User

Once you are a WebBoard user, you may want to log in to WebBoard as a different user, perhaps to use a different name for different conferences. A guest may also want to log in as a different user to establish a user account. For example, you may log in to WebBoard to browse and see a conference that interests you. By logging in as a different user, you can participate in the conference and chat. This option is available from More on WebBoard's menubar.

To log in as a different user, follow these steps:

1. From the WebBoard menubar, select More. The More Options menu opens, as shown in Figure 9-5.

Figure 9-5 More Options menu

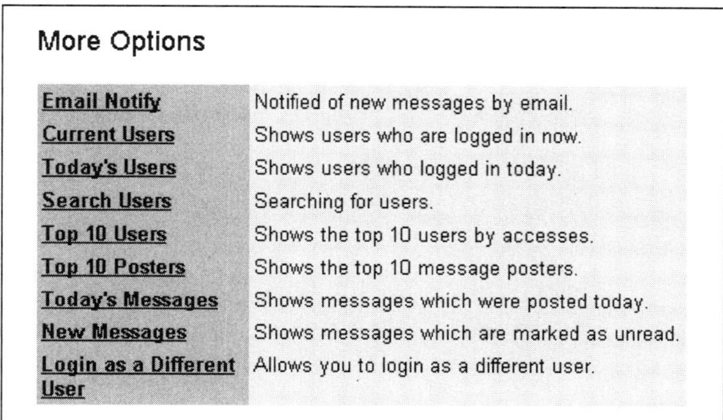

2. From the More Options menu, click Login as a Different User. The WebBoard Welcome page opens.
3. Choose to log in as a New user. The New User Information form opens, as shown earlier in Figure 9-3.
4. Complete the information on this page, as discussed in "Logging in as a New User" earlier in this chapter. Follow the directions on this form and fill in the required blanks (marked with red dots).

Editing Your User Profile

Your user profile is a way of letting other WebBoard participants know a little bit about you. When you first log in as a new user, WebBoard asks you to fill out a New User Information form, as described earlier in this chapter. This information (except for your login name and password) is then displayed whenever you or another WebBoard user clicks on your real name within WebBoard.

You can edit your user profile at any time. To do this, select Profiles from the WebBoard menubar and then link to change your personal profile. Your current profile is displayed in a form you can edit. You should keep your personal profile up to date, editing it for the following reasons:

- *To change your basic information*. For example, if you get a new job, a new preferred Internet address, take up a different hobby, or set up your own web site, you should update your profile.

- *To change your password.* For security reasons, you should change your password from time to time—often enough to protect against casual disuse, but not so often that you forget it. Note that you must enter the new password twice, for verification.
- *To change the Full topic view option.* By default, the Full topic view lets you see all the messages in a topic in a continuous flow so that you don't need to go back to the Conferences frame to open the reply messages to a topic. Just scroll through the messages. However, you may want to change the topic-viewing mode to display only one message at a time.

Note

You will see messages sequentially in Full topic view, starting with the message you select and those that follow it. So be sure to select the message you want to start with.

- *To change frames or non-frames mode.* If your browser does not support frames, you can use the non-frames mode.

Working with WebBoard

Before you start using WebBoard, you need to become familiar with its navigational aids. This section begins with an explanation of WebBoard's menubar and proceeds to discuss how to determine what conferences you are interested in, how to identify new messages, and how to search for messages.

Using the Menubar

You can navigate WebBoard quickly by using WebBoard's menubar, shown in Figure 9-6. This section describes each of the functions you can perform from the menubar.

Figure 9-6 WebBoard's menubar

POST | REFRESH | CHAT | PROFILES | SEARCH | MARK ALL READ | MORE... | HELP | WebBoard

Post

to post a new topic or message to the conference (note, you must select a conference before selecting this). The message appears as the first message in the new topic. The procedure for posting a message is covered in the section "Posting a Topic or Message" in Chapter 10, *Participating in Conferences.*

Refresh

updates your Conferences list to indicate any new activity. When you use Mark All Read, select Refresh to display new messages.

Chat

displays the Available Chat Rooms list, which includes links to all the chat rooms and how many active users are in each (see Chapter 12, *Chatting in WebBoard*). You can carry on real-time interactive discussion with other conference users in Chat. Note that the WebBoard system administrator may have disabled the Chat feature.

Profiles

provides you with the options to edit your user profile or to view conference profiles:

- To view or edit your personal profile, click Change your personal profile. The information on your User Profile form includes your name, the city you live in, your web page (if any), and a brief description of yourself. (You provided this information from the New Users Information form when you logged in to WebBoard.) You can also change the way WebBoard works for you in your profile, by choosing the Frames/No Frames and the Full topic view options. (Also, see the section "Editing Your User Profile" earlier in this chapter.)
- To view a conference profile, click the conference name. From this page, you can post a message to the conference and/or mark all messages read in the conference.

Search

opens the Message Search form which you can use to find specific content in topics and/or messages (see "Searching Messages" later in this chapter).

Mark All Read

allows you to mark messages as read in one or all conferences. Marking messages as read eliminates the NEW icon and the italics from new messages. WebBoard does not automatically update a message you have read; you must do it manually.

When you select Mark All Read, a page opens listing the conference names. Select the conferences that you want to have marked read. WebBoard instantly updates the information. To see the updated Conferences list, select Refresh from WebBoard's menubar. To update all conferences at once (for example, if you've been away from WebBoard for a period of time), select the Mark All Conferences Read hyperlink. You can also use the mark read feature for a particular conference from its conference profile.

More

opens the More Options menu from which you can link to the information described below. (For a full discussion of the options you can select from this menu please refer to Chapter 11, *What's Happening on Your WebBoard?*)

Current Users
lists the users who are currently logged on (updates every 60 seconds).

Today's Users
lists the names of people who have logged in today.

Search Users
displays a form for searching for users by first name or last name. You can search the names of everyone who has an active account. A hyperlink letter is available for selecting the first letter of the first name.

Top 10 Users
lists the top 10 users by the number of logins.

Top 10 Posters
lists the top 10 message posters.

Today's Messages
lists conferences that have messages posted today.

New Messages
lists all new messages that you have not read.

Login as a Different User
lets you to log in as a different user.

Help
displays Help for WebBoard features (see "Getting Online Help" later in this chapter).

Note

If you have been designated as a WebBoard manager or moderator by the system administrator, you will see more items on this menu. Please contact the WebBoard system administrator for more information.

Browsing Conferences

Before you participate in any conferences, take a few minutes to browse them. This way you not only get a good idea of what information is in WebBoard, but you also see how others are presenting information.

Remember that the information in WebBoard is set up like a book, in that the conferences correspond to book titles, topics to chapter titles, and messages to the content (see Figure 9-2).

The Conferences list displays all the conferences on this WebBoard (see Figure 9-7). An expansion box (+ icon) is to the left of each conference name that contains topics. The number in parentheses to the right of the conference name tells how many messages are in it. New messages in a conference are noted by a NEW icon displayed to the right of the conference name. To display the topics list for a conference, just click the conference name or the expansion box.

Figure 9-7 Conferences list

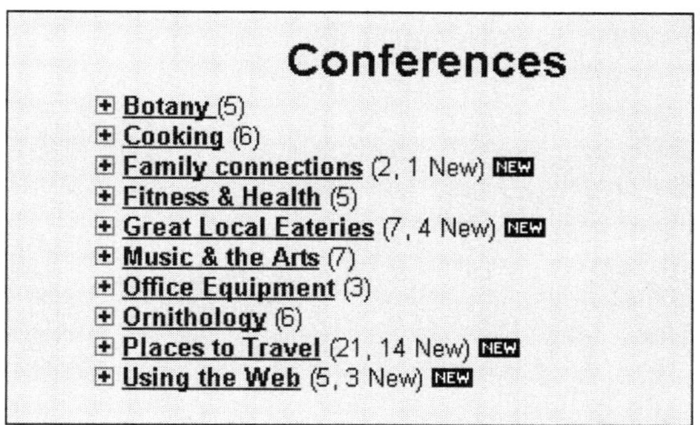

You can expand one conference list to view the topics in a conference. When you expand another conference, the previous topic display in the conference menu collapses. Or, you can close the conference list by clicking the expansion box again.

Viewing the Conference Profiles

If this is a very active WebBoard with many topics and messages, you may find it useful to first check the conference profile before you expand any conferences in the Conferences list, to see what the conference is about (see Figure 9-8). To see a conference profile, select Profiles from the WebBoard menubar and click the conference name.

The conference profile contains a short description of the conference's content, the date it was created, its creator's name, the number of messages, the number of new messages, and whether it is private, read-only, or moderated. From its title and description, you should be able to determine whether or not to explore a conference further. You can also post a message to a conference from its conference profile (also see "Posting a Topic or Message" in the next chapter).

Browsing Topics and Messages

Topics and messages provide the information to your conferences. A conference begins when someone posts a topic to it. Other users can reply to the topic by posting reply messages at any time. All messages in a topic may have the same name as the original topic or a different name; however, reply messages are indented under the topic message. For instance, the conference Places to Travel has African Adventures as the first topic. Several people reply to that topic about their travels in Africa. Someone else adds the topic Frolicking in Liechtenstein, to

Figure 9-8 Conference profile

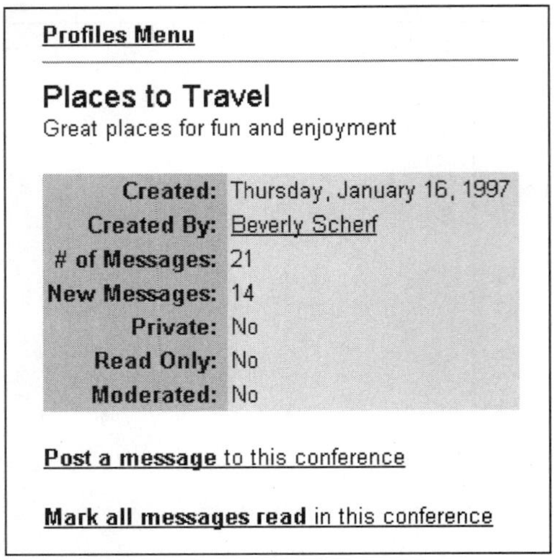

Profiles Menu

Places to Travel
Great places for fun and enjoyment

Created:	Thursday, January 16, 1997
Created By:	Beverly Scherf
# of Messages:	21
New Messages:	14
Private:	No
Read Only:	No
Moderated:	No

Post a message to this conference

Mark all messages read in this conference

which others reply, and so forth. In essence, a topic message starts a discussion, and any replies continue it. WebBoard's ability to let you browse by message or by topic from the Conferences list means you can either follow a subject exhaustively or pick and choose just the messages you want.

When you locate the conference you want to look over, you can read its contents by clicking its name or the expansion box (+ icon) to the left of the conference name in the Conferences list. The list of topics opens, as shown in Figure 9-9. Topics and messages both have hyperlinks that you can click to open them in the right frame.

An expansion box to the left of the topic name indicates that this topic contains more than one message. To the right of each topic and message is the poster's name and date. The poster's name is also a hyperlink to that person's profile.

Notice that Figure 9-10 also shows handy arrows and hyperlinks to quickly navigate through large conferences with many topics. A down arrow appears to the left of the conference name so you can click it to see groups of topics incrementally. At the end of the group of topics, you can click Next and Bottom hyperlinks to bring you to the next level or to the end of the topics. Previous and Top hyperlinks appear at the end of the topics so that you can return up through the topics or back to the top of the conference.

Reading Messages

WebBoard's messages are arranged logically with the earliest (original) message at the top of each topic list. You can follow a thread from its beginning if you desire, or jump in at a later point. When you click a message on the Conferences

Figure 9-9 Topics list with navigational arrows and links

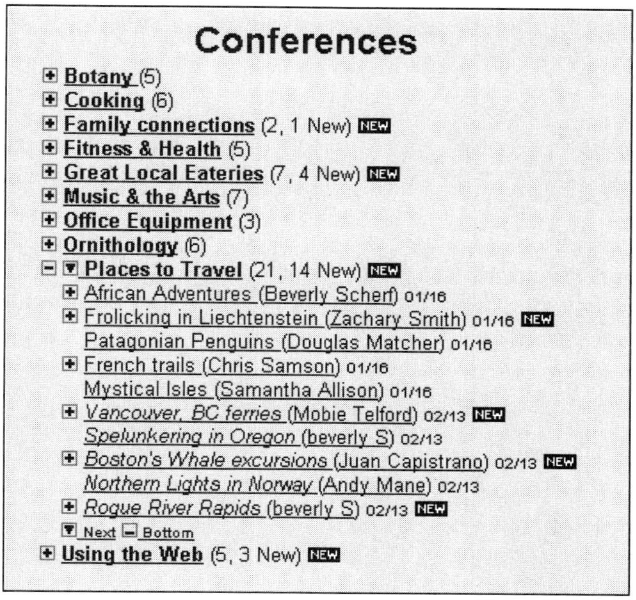

Conferences

- **Botany** (5)
- **Cooking** (6)
- **Family connections** (2, 1 New) NEW
- **Fitness & Health** (5)
- **Great Local Eateries** (7, 4 New) NEW
- **Music & the Arts** (7)
- **Office Equipment** (3)
- **Ornithology** (6)
- **Places to Travel** (21, 14 New) NEW
  - African Adventures (Beverly Scherf) 01/16
  - Frolicking in Liechtenstein (Zachary Smith) 01/16 NEW
  - Patagonian Penguins (Douglas Matcher) 01/16
  - French trails (Chris Samson) 01/16
  - Mystical Isles (Samantha Allison) 01/16
  - *Vancouver, BC ferries* (Mobie Telford) 02/13 NEW
  - *Spelunkering in Oregon* (beverly S) 02/13
  - *Boston's Whale excursions* (Juan Capistrano) 02/13 NEW
  - *Northern Lights in Norway* (Andy Mane) 02/13
  - *Rogue River Rapids* (beverly S) 02/13 NEW
  - Next Bottom
- **Using the Web** (5, 3 New) NEW

list, the message appears in the right frame (unless you are using non-frames mode). If you are using the Full topic view mode, the next messages in the topic are also displayed, as shown in Figure 9-10. Note that you cannot see messages earlier in the list; however, you can click the Previous hyperlink in the Message menu.

Follow these steps to read specific messages:

1. From the Conferences list, select the conference you want to view and click its name or the expansion box (+ icon).
2. Locate the topic you want to read and click its name or the topic expansion box. If you click the topic expansion box, the subsequent messages are displayed.
3. Locate the message you want to read and click its name. The message displays in the Message window. You may need to scroll to read the entire message(s).
4. When you have finished reading the message, you can select another message to read or you can post a message. Posting messages is described in Chapter 10.

Identifying New Messages

If you like to read every message in a conference or only those on specific topics or from specific users, WebBoard's new message notification feature makes it easier for you to quickly see new messages of interest to you. This section shows

Figure 9-10 Reading messages in full topic view

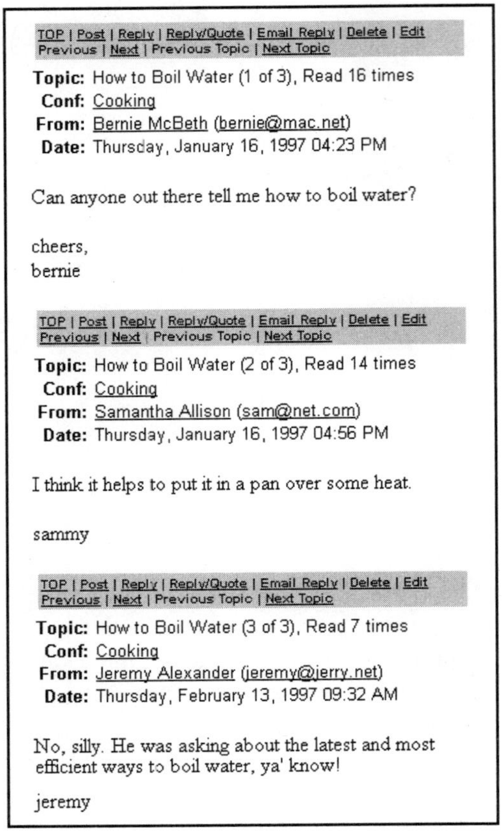

TOP | Post | Reply | Reply/Quote | Email Reply | Delete | Edit
Previous | Next | Previous Topic | Next Topic

Topic: How to Boil Water (1 of 3), Read 16 times
Conf: Cooking
From: Bernie McBeth (bernie@mac.net)
Date: Thursday, January 16, 1997 04:23 PM

Can anyone out there tell me how to boil water?

cheers,
bernie

TOP | Post | Reply | Reply/Quote | Email Reply | Delete | Edit
Previous | Next | Previous Topic | Next Topic

Topic: How to Boil Water (2 of 3), Read 14 times
Conf: Cooking
From: Samantha Allison (sam@net.com)
Date: Thursday, January 16, 1997 04:56 PM

I think it helps to put it in a pan over some heat.

sammy

TOP | Post | Reply | Reply/Quote | Email Reply | Delete | Edit
Previous | Next | Previous Topic | Next Topic

Topic: How to Boil Water (3 of 3), Read 7 times
Conf: Cooking
From: Jeremy Alexander (jeremy@jerry.net)
Date: Thursday, February 13, 1997 09:32 AM

No, silly. He was asking about the latest and most efficient ways to boil water, ya' know!

jeremy

you several ways to identify new messages in WebBoard: the new message hyperlink, NEW icon, Today's Messages, New Messages, and Email Notify. Chapter 11, *What's Happening on Your WebBoard?* goes into further detail for some of these features. Each time you enter WebBoard, the Welcome message has a hyperlink that tells you how many new messages you have (see Figure 9-1 earlier in this chapter). In addition, the Conferences list includes icons next to conferences and topics with new messages. You can also get a list of messages that were posted that day.

As you browse the Conferences list, WebBoard lists the number of messages in a conference and indicates how many of them are new for you. WebBoard also displays the NEW icon (a black box with white text) next to conferences that have new messages. Be sure to use Refresh from your WebBoard menubar to update the Conferences list when you use WebBoard, so that you are aware of current messages being posted.

Tip

You can go directly to the list of your unread messages by clicking the new message hyperlink in the Welcome message (shown in Figure 9-1). Or, you can see what new messages you have daily and also directly link to them from Today's Messages under More Options (discussed in Chapter 11, *What's Happening on Your WebBoard?*)

WebBoard also tracks messages that were in conferences before you first logged in. These are also considered unread or new messages, but to distinguish them from messages that are unread since your last login, WebBoard displays them in the color your browser uses for hyperlinks, and in italic type. When you finish reading new messages, you can select Mark All Read and Refresh from WebBoard's menubar—the italics are removed.

Searching Messages

You can do a simple search for specific text in messages as well as in message and topic names in WebBoard. Your search for a topic needs only a word or part of a word from the title. So, if you search for a topic such as How to Boil Water from the Cooking conference, you enter the word *boil*, and WebBoard returns the match. To do a message search, you enter one or two of the words. For example, if you read some messages about flowers in the Botany conference, you can search to find not just the word, but the context as well. You can search for "spring flowers" and find matches with detailed results showing message matches such as "lovely pink spring flowers," "buying small spring flowers," "daffodils are spring flowers," and so forth.

In a search, you enter the word or words you want to find, tell WebBoard the maximum number of messages to return, and specify whether you want WebBoard to return just the message title or the line of text that contains your search string as well. When WebBoard finds messages that match your search criteria, it lists them by date order, grouped by conference. Each entry in the list is a hyperlink, so you can click on any message and view it.

To search for words within topics and/or message bodies, follow these steps:

1. From the WebBoard menubar, select Search. The Message Search form opens, as shown in Figure 9-11.
2. Enter the word(s) you want to search for in the textbox field, for example, coffee.
3. Select how many matches should be displayed (Display Count). The display count shows matches for you search word in the number you specify. For example, if you want to find the word "coffee" and know that recently you have seen it used frequently in the conferences, specify 120.

Figure 9-11 Message Search form

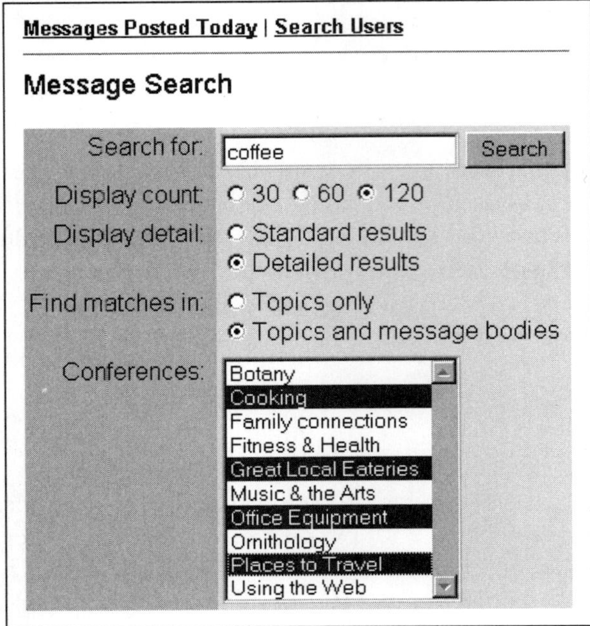

4. Select how the matches should be displayed (Display detail). Standard results shows the match in the topic name only. Detailed results shows the matched word in partial-sentence context of the match. If the word you want to find is frequently used, specify Detailed results to see the context. For example, to find "Bring coffee to the meeting," specify Detailed results so that you can see the context of the word coffee.
5. Select whether matches should be found in topics only or in topics and messages.
6. Select the conference(s) containing the search word. To select more than one conference, hold down the Control key as you select additional conference name(s) with the mouse. (The Shift key also works to select sequential conferences.)
7. Click Search. The Message Search Results form appears, as shown in Figure 9-12, displaying the conference name, the subject, and the date. If you have selected Detailed results, the details of each result appears below the conference name. Click Search Messages to return to the Message Search form.

Getting Online Help

You can find out information immediately about WebBoard's commands and features by using online help. Information about WebBoard is available to you

Figure 9-12 Message Search Results form

Messages Posted Today | Search Messages

Message Search Results for "coffee"

Found 4 messages.

Conference	Subject	Date
Great Local Eateries I drink French coffee with my scones there, Bernie!	Breakfast Spots	2/13/97
Great Local Eateries has wonderful food, but lousy coffee. susan	Serendipity Cafe	2/13/97
Great Local Eateries has questionable food, but really great coffee! be sure to bring some coffee to	Tony's Fry Shack	2/13/97
Office Equipment Please bring coffee to the meeting tomorrow. sammy	Company meeting	1/16/97

not only through the WebBoard menubar, but also from the Chat menubars. Online help gives definitions and specific procedures for you to follow. As in online help for any other Windows-based applications, WebBoard help includes hyperlinks to associated topics and topic searching. WebBoard help is also available at WebBoard Central (*http://webboard.ora.com*).

Exercising Online Etiquette

Before becoming a WebBoard user, you may have participated in some kind of online communication such as an online service forum, a bulletin board system, an electronic mailing list, or a Usenet group. If so, you've probably come in contact with the concept of online etiquette, sometimes called "netiquette." You may even have violated it at one point. If you have, you almost certainly knew about it right away from the responses that flooded your email or from the irate, furious, or insulting posts that dogged your article for the next several days. In short, you've been flamed—that is, been the subject of vitriolic online comments made in the relative safety and anonymity of distant electronic communication.

This section offers some pointers to help make sure you don't get flamed, or at least to let you see why you did. Online communication works best when everyone is working to keep things moving in the same direction. Whether you know it or not, you have a personality and a function in the online community in which you participate. You have a say in how you are perceived online, both by what you say and how you choose to say it.

Five Tips for More Effective Online Communication

In general, it's a good idea to ask yourself the following questions before replying to a posting in WebBoard (or any other online forum, for that matter.)

Does everyone in the conference need to see what I am about to send?

Think of the scope of your posting and of its applicability to the conference, the topic, and the conference participants. If only a few people need to see what you're getting ready to write, don't post it as a reply; rather, send email to the individual(s) who you think would benefit from your observations.

Does anyone need to see what I am about to send?

"Me too" messages should get trapped by this question. Many new users of online services see a question that they've asked, and reply to the message with the single line "me too!" This takes up time, communication processing, and disk space, with no real value to the group at large. If someone in a conference asks a question to which you also want to know the answer, be patient—posting a "me too" message won't make the answer come any faster.

Does what I am about to send further the conversation or add clarity to the discussion?

Peter Egan, a motorsports journalist and author whose self-effacing humor is part of the key to his popularity, once commented in an article that he preferred writing to speaking "because it gives me a chance to edit out nearly half of the really dumb things I have to say." Before you click the button to post your message, take a minute and look over what's about to go out under your name. Will it help the group's efforts? Will it add to someone's understanding of the subject? Is it a question for which the answer will prove useful to the group at large? Is it worded clearly?

Am I reacting emotionally to something personal the message reminds me of?

The oddity of online communication, often called "impersonal," is that it is taken so very personally by so many people. If you find yourself reacting with intense emotion to something in an online message, don't click Reply/Quote and dash off an angry retort. Consider whether you are ready to respond constructively now, the next day, or not at all. If you decide to respond, consider whether the best forum is the conference or in personal email.

Do you really need to include all that text?

One of the biggest space-wasters is the temptation to include everything in a quoted reply. Edit the text you include—not to change the initial meaning or to lose something important, but to keep your reply even more focused on the point of the original message. A common practice is to insert [snip] to indicate lines you have removed.

Five Tips for Less Effective Online Communication

Just as the preceding tips are suggestions for ways you can make your online communication more effective, and more powerful, the following tips are things you should try not to do, or at least are characteristics of messages that you can begin to recognize as bad netiquette.

Include critical comments about the author of a message rather than about the content.

Sometimes called ad hominem (a Latin phrase meaning directed at the person), such comments at best distract from the conversation at hand (social online groups excluded, of course). At worst, they can cause the whole group conversation to lapse into insults and name-calling about the people in the conference, not about the issues and subjects for which you are presumably meeting online in the first place.

Criticize the spelling, phrasing, or other noncontent errors in a message.

The Internet is a strange place, with people from many countries who possess an almost unimaginable range of skills in language, typing, and technology. English may not be the native language of the person at the other end of the line. And many people using slow modems or are under other technological constraints often make odd choices in what they say or how they say it. Pointing these errors out, particularly if you do so in a reply to the whole conference, slows down communication and makes the conference much less effective.

Defend spelling, phrasing, or other noncontent errors in your own messages.

Now, after having apologized for people who can't spell, type, or phrase cogent prose, you're going to be asked to hold yourself to a higher standard. Exactly so; remember the online community will know you by what and how you post. You may sneer at spelling as unnecessary, you may not care about syntax or grammar, you may believe that the technical content of your postings is vastly more important than the way you present them. You can go on believing that, but people will never take you as seriously as they take someone whose postings are well-phrased, spelled correctly, and clearly organized. It's your choice; how do you want people to see you?

Include a large signature file.

WebBoard accepts 2,000 characters in a signature, and those characters can include HTML tags. Thus, you may be tempted to include large or multiple graphics. Be careful. Every time someone loads a message from you, their browser will load that graphics file. If it's a 32K full-page image, you're going to become unpopular in short order and people will learn to skip over your postings because they take too long. Use graphics if they pass the tests included in the previous section (does anyone need to see them, and so forth), but try to keep them small so they load quickly. If WebBoard is on an intranet, graphics are probably less of an issue.

Post messages that are clearly unconnected with the conference or topic.

While the five tips for more effective online communication cover this, it's worth mentioning again here. WebBoard isn't a good place to go fishing. Focus your postings, questions and answers alike, to the groups or conferences where they are pertinent. Occasionally, someone will get the idea that if they send the same message to everyone in the world who has an Internet connection, they'll either get rich, meet the man/woman/space alien of their dreams, or have some other wonderful result. What invariably happens is that less than 1 percent of the Internet actually cares about what they have to say, and chances are these are people they already know; the other 99 percent of the Internet is now annoyed that their online time (and any associated connect charges) has been wasted.

10

Participating in Conferences

Once you are familiar with conferences, you will want to participate in them by posting messages. The heart of WebBoard is its messages. In the previous chapter we likened conferences to book titles, topics to chapter titles, and messages to the content of a book. To develop conferences, you can reply to messages in existing topics or create entirely new topics, like new chapters. You can conveniently participate in WebBoard's conferences in a number of different ways. This chapter describes options that are available to you so that you can become more familiar with navigation on WebBoard. You will see the various methods you can choose to post and reply to topics.

WebBoard users form a community of people who share information and ideas electronically. You can browse through conferences, select topics of interest, look for new messages, post messages for all other users, reply to messages directly through email, and engage in real-time chat sessions. Also, you can learn about the other members of the WebBoard community and give them information about yourself.

Most conferences you participate in will be public—open to anyone who cares to join. Public conferences let you freely read and post messages. Other conferences may be moderated with one or more users exercising editorial control over what messages are posted. Moderated conferences are used to keep discussions focused, such as a conference about a specific event.

Some conferences you participate in may be private. They are limited to specific users who are authorized to read and post messages. Private conferences allow you to discuss confidential or nondisclosure topics, such as new products being developed. The fourth kind of conference you may encounter is a read-only conference. These conferences are used to distribute official information to WebBoard users, such as company policies or product announcements and updates. You can read, but not post messages to a read-only conference.

Whatever types of conferences you participate in, you'll find WebBoard an easy, intuitive way to share information and collaborate with others. The next section will familiarize you with WebBoard's Message menu.

Note

Many of the features presented in this chapter require Netscape Navigator 3.0 or higher or Microsoft Internet Explorer 3.0 or higher, as discussed in Chapter 9, *WebBoard Basics*.

A Quick Look at the Message Menu

After you have read the messages in a conference, you may want to post a new topic or reply to certain messages. To do so, you can select Post from the WebBoard menubar or one of several commands from the menu above messages in the Message window (see Figure 10-1). Notice also that the upper portion of each Message window contains summary information indicating the topic and conference name, number of replies, name and email hyperlinks to the sender, and date.

Before posting messages, take a few minutes to become familiar with the commands on the Message menu. Basic and advanced options are available to make your time on WebBoard more effective. The rest of this section describes these commands. Note that they are also discussed more fully in the remaining sections of this chapter.

Top

appears only if you are in Full topic view and it brings you back to the first message. This option is not available as a hyperlink if you are already at the top. You can change the topic view in your personal profile.

Post

opens the form for posting a new topic to the current conference. A new topic creates a thread, like a chapter in a book, for others to follow by adding more messages to it. The procedure for posting a message is covered in the next section. From this form, you have the following options:

Figure 10-1 Message window with message displayed

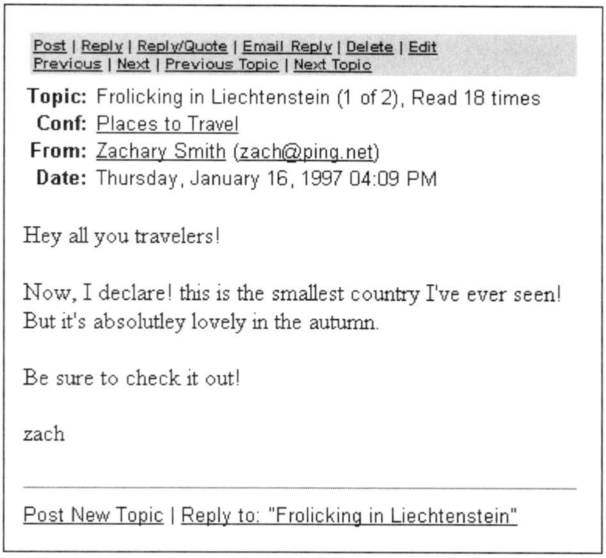

Post | Reply | Reply/Quote | Email Reply | Delete | Edit
Previous | Next | Previous Topic | Next Topic

Topic: Frolicking in Liechtenstein (1 of 2), Read 18 times
Conf: Places to Travel
From: Zachary Smith (zach@ping.net)
Date: Thursday, January 16, 1997 04:09 PM

Hey all you travelers!

Now, I declare! this is the smallest country I've ever seen! But it's absolutley lovely in the autumn.

Be sure to check it out!

zach

Post New Topic | Reply to: "Frolicking in Liechtenstein"

Convert line breaks to HTML breaks
: to use the HTML capabilities of WebBoard. This is a default option. When you use this option, your message will have the capability for you to add more HTML formatting.

Preformatted text (No HTML)
: to insert, or paste in, original material from another source, such as an email message.

Anonymous
: to exclude your name from the post. When you use this option, your message is signed "Anonymous."

Preview message
: to review your message before posting it. When you choose this option, you can edit it again before posting.

Preview/Spell-check
: to use WebBoard's dictionary to check for any misspelled words. This is a default option. When you choose this option, you can edit your message to correct spelling errors before posting.

Attach file
: to attach a file to your message. You can attach the following file types: Unknown, Document, Image, Audio, Multimedia, or Application. WebBoard's file attachment option allows document sharing in workgroups.

Reply

opens a form for replying to the same topic as the current message. Replying to a message lets you add your own opinion, information, or question to an existing topic. The topic of the message remains the same, although you can edit it if you choose, at which time it becomes a new topic thread in the conference.

Reply/Quote

opens the Reply form and includes the text of the current message. The Reply/Quote feature allows you to address specific points in the previous message or answer questions, without retyping its content.

Note

Be selective about the portions of the quote you include. To cut down on long, unnecessary text, make sure they are relevant to your reply.

Email Reply

lets you reply by email to the person who posted the current message. If you have a private response to someone, send email, rather than reply to the entire conference. Since this feature uses your web browser's email capability, your browser must be set up to send email. WebBoard itself does not provide email capability.

Delete

deletes a message you have posted. You cannot delete a message posted by others. While it's useful to have this option, the better choice is to carefully review any message before you post it, so that you don't have to go back later to delete it. For tips on effective online communication, see "Online Etiquette" in Chapter 9.

Edit

opens the Message window and displays a message you have posted, so that you can edit or modify it. Note that edited messages are not marked as new messages when they are reposted.

Previous

displays the previous message from the Conferences list. If there are no previous messages in this conference, this command does not appear as a hyperlink.

Next

displays the next message from the Conferences list. If this is the last message in this conference, this command does not appear as a hyperlink.

Previous Topic

displays the first message of the topic that precedes the current one in this conference, skipping over any intermediate messages in the current topic. If this is the first topic in the conference, this command does not appear as a hyperlink.

Next Topic

displays the first message of the next topic, skipping over any intermediate messages in the current topic. If this is the last topic in the conference, this command does not appear as a link.

Posting a Topic or Message

When you post to a conference, you are either adding to a current topic or starting a new topic. If you want to contribute to a discussion that is underway (say, to add your favorite morning café), then post a message in an existing topic. If you have something to contribute to the general theme of a conference (say, to ask others for good afternoon tea spots), but it doesn't relate to the existing topic, then you can start a new topic. If you are the first visitor to a conference, you will also need to post a new topic message.

Note

It's best to keep your topic and message titles brief and to the point.

You must be in a conference or in the conference profile to post a topic or message. You can select from many options when you post a message, such as spell-checking, converting line breaks to HTML breaks, attaching files, and so forth.

A message must begin with a topic. If a topic doesn't already exist, start a new topic. Figure 10-2 shows the Post a New Topic form. This section shows you how to post a new topic and message.

To post a new topic, follow these steps:

1. Choose from one of these three ways to display the Post form (Figure 10-2):
   - From the Message menu, select Post.
   - From the WebBoard menubar select Post. You must have expanded the conference to which you want to add a new topic.
   - From the WebBoard menubar, select Profiles. From the Conference Profiles list, locate the conference to which you want to add a new topic. From that conference profile, click Post a New Topic to this conference.
2. Enter the new topic name in the Topic field; then enter your message in the textbox.

Figure 10-2 Post a New Topic form

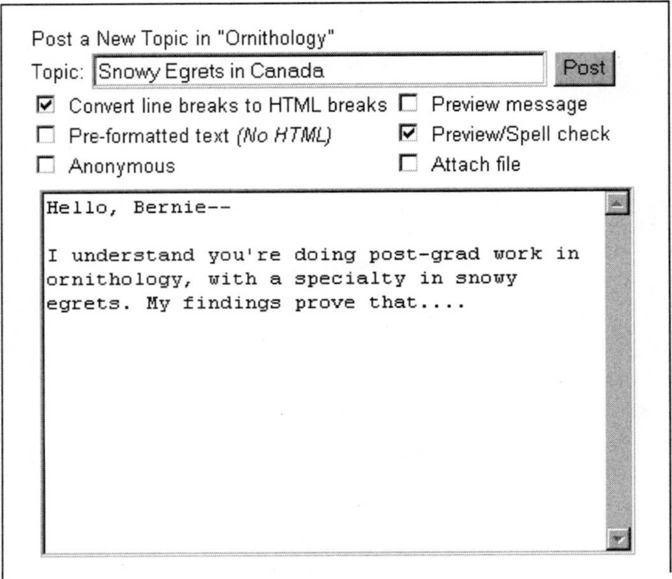

3. Choose any of the following options:
   - *Convert line breaks to HTML breaks* to use HTML features—this is a default setting.
   - *Preformatted text (No HTML)* to turn off HTML features.
   - *Anonymous* to post anonymously.
   - *Preview message* to review your message before you post it.
   - *Preview/Spell-check* to review and spell-check your message—this is a default setting.
   - *Attach File* to attach a file to your message.
4. Type in your message. Scroll the edit box as necessary.
5. When you complete your message, click Post. Depending on which options you have selected, WebBoard will initiate posting your message. If you accepted the default options, WebBoard shows you a preview of your message. If not, the message is posted and WebBoard displays it in your Message window.

   If have Preview selected and are dissatisfied with your message and want to change it, click Back on your browser.

You can refresh your Conferences frame to see your new topic in the conferences list by clicking the Refresh on the WebBoard menubar. The next time you visit this conference, you will see your new topic posted—and perhaps some replies.

Previewing your Message

You can preview any new topic or message before you post it. You may want to preview your messages if they contain HTML or if you are uncertain how your message will appear to other WebBoard users. If you don't preview your message, it will be sent immediately to the conference when you click Post. Choose Preview if you just want to preview your message without spell-checking it.

To preview your message, follow these steps:

1. From the Message menu, select Post. The Post form opens (for example, see Figure 10-2).
2. Check the Preview checkbox on the New Topic/Message form.
3. Enter the topic name, your message, and click Post. WebBoard displays your message as it will appear to other users on WebBoard, as shown in Figure 10-3.

Figure 10-3 Message Preview window

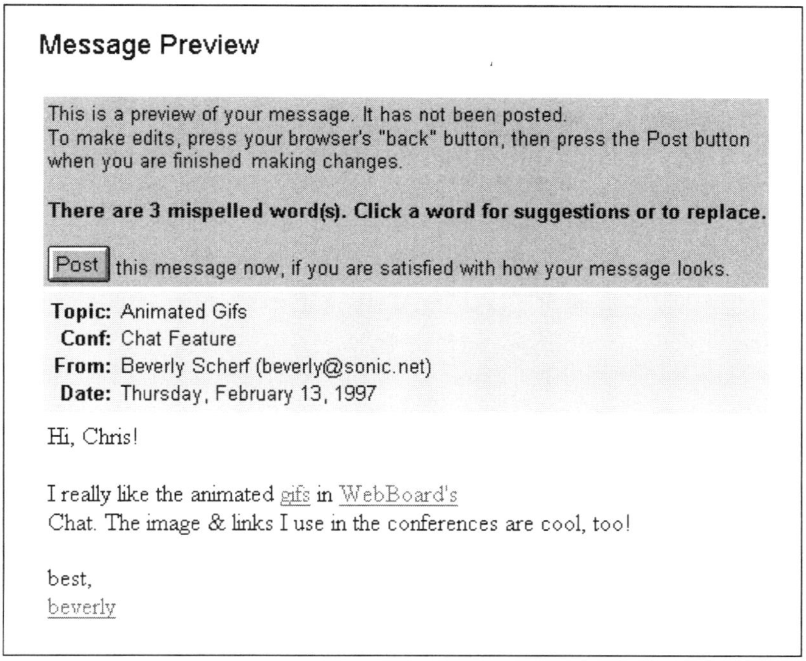

Message Preview

This is a preview of your message. It has not been posted.
To make edits, press your browser's "back" button, then press the Post button when you are finished making changes.

There are 3 mispelled word(s). Click a word for suggestions or to replace.

Post this message now, if you are satisfied with how your message looks.

Topic: Animated Gifs
Conf: Chat Feature
From: Beverly Scherf (beverly@sonic.net)
Date: Thursday, February 13, 1997

Hi, Chris!

I really like the animated gifs in WebBoard's
Chat. The image & links I use in the conferences are cool, too!

best,
beverly

4. If you are dissatisfied with your message and want to change it, click Back on your browser. If you are using a Netscape browser, you can also right-click your mouse, and click Back to get to the previous frame.

5. Once you are satisfied with the appearance of your message, click Post. Your message is immediately posted to the conference and WebBoard displays it in the Message window.

Note

Some versions of Microsoft Internet Explorer may not work correctly with Preview. If the Back button does not display the original message form, we recommend you post the message and then immediately edit or delete it. This problem is caused by a bug in Internet Explorer and may be fixed by Microsoft; it is not a WebBoard problem.

Spell-Checking Your Message

You can spell-check any message you post on WebBoard by using WebBoard's built-in dictionary. Your message will be spell-checked, with each instance of a misspelled word being flagged as a link. When you complete your corrections, you will see a preview of your message.

To spell-check your message, follow these steps:

1. From the Message menu, select Post. The Post form opens (for example, see Figure 10-2).

2. The Preview/Spell-check checkbox is already checked, since this is a default setting.

   If you do not want to spell-check your message, disable spell-checking by clicking the Preview/Spell-check checkbox (removing the check).

3. Enter your message, and click Post. The Message Preview window opens. Your message is spell-checked, with each occurrence of misspelled words being flagged as a hyperlink.

4. Click on each misspelled word to see WebBoard's suggestions for corrections. You can either select a word from the list or enter a new one in the textbox, as shown in Figure 10-4.

5. Click Done to return to the message preview. The corrected word is shown in the message. Repeat Steps 4 and 5 if necessary.

Figure 10-4 Spelling Correction form

Spelling Suggestions for "gifs"

Select a suggested word to replace the misspelled word, or enter another word.
To leave the word as "gifs", hit the back arrow on your browser, or hit the Done button to return.

Done

Change to: Gifs *or use:*

gifts
gigs
gift
gins
ifs

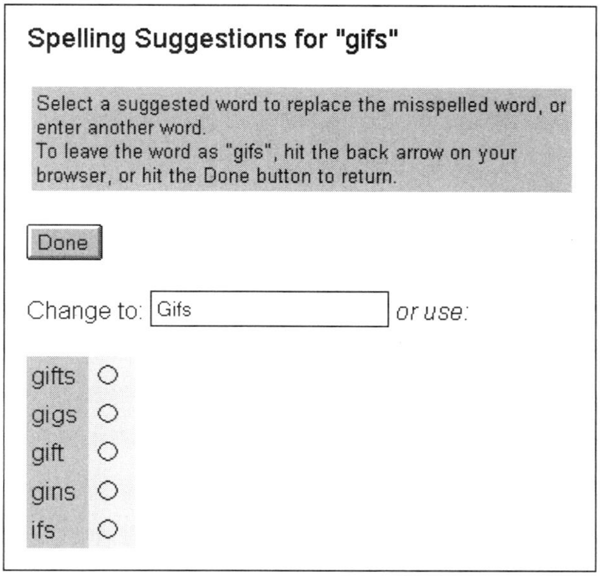

Note

If you are a WebBoard system administrator, manager, or moderator, the spelling correction form also includes a button allowing you to add the misspelled word to the dictionary. This feature is handy for adding words such as proper names or abbreviations.

6. If you are dissatisfied with your message after correcting the spelling errors and want to change it, click Back on your browser to redisplay the original Message form (see notes on previewing in the previous section).
7. Once you are satisfied with your message, click Post. Your message is immediately posted to the conference.

Attaching Files to Your Message

Attaching files to your WebBoard messages is a handy way to give users ready access to your information. For example, you may be doing an annual report and want several people to review it.

Note

File Attachments are available only if WebBoard is using its internal web server or one of the O'Reilly WebSite servers. If you have questions, ask your WebBoard system administrator.

Your browser must support file attachment capability (Netscape Navigator 2.0 or higher) for uploading files. Almost any browser can download file attachments. Additionally, those who want to open the files must have the same or similar applications to open them.

To attach a file to your message, follow these steps:

1. From the Message menu, select Post. A Post form opens (see Figure 10-2).
2. Click the Attach file checkbox, enter your message, and click Post.

   If you have selected Preview/Spell check or Preview, complete the preview and click Post. The Attach a file form opens (see Figure 10-5).

Figure 10-5 Attach a File form

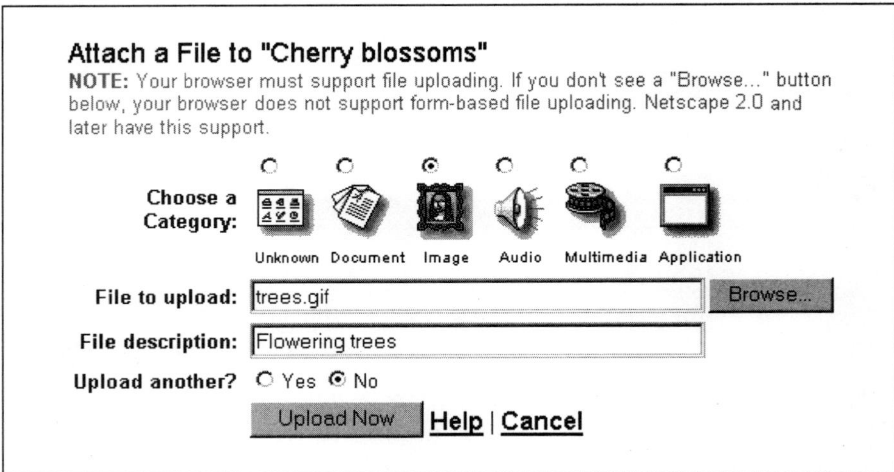

   Click the appropriate Category radio button for your selection(s):

   – *Unknown* if you do not know what type of file this is.
   – *Document* if this is a text file.
   – *Image* if this is a graphics file.
   – *Audio* if this is a sound file.
   – *Multimedia* if this is a multimedia file.
   – *Application* if this is an application.

3. Click Browse to select the attachment you want to upload from your directories. A File Upload dialog opens. Navigate through your directories to select the attachment.

4. Click Open to continue, or click Cancel to cancel the upload (which has the effect of immediately posting your message).
5. Enter the description of the file attachment in the File description field. If you want to attach more files, click the Upload another radio button.
6. For each file attachment you want to upload, repeat this process.
7. When you finish entering your attachments, click Upload Now. Your message is immediately posted to the conference. The attachments appear as hyperlinks at the end of the message. An icon indicates the file type.

Sharing Documents

You can use WebBoard's document-sharing capabilities to collaborate with others when you attach files to messages in conferences (see the previous section). Users can easily track documents and be notified of changes by WebBoard's email notification.

The documents are actually hyperlinks to the attached files. For example, an author posts a message with a rough draft of a chapter as an attached file. Users in the group can download the file to their system and review it. Then they can comment on it, or even make changes directly to it, and attach the modified document in a reply message. This is a convenient way for many users to work on a document in progress. In fact, while writing this book the authors used document sharing to collaborate with WebBoard's development team.

Adding Images and Links

WebBoard's images and links feature can really enhance the messages you post. For example, if you want to customize your message, you can have an image, such as your company logo, appear in your message. This way, your readers can immediately associate your company or product with your posts.

Links are particularly useful, since you can have active links open separate web pages. To add an image to a message, type in its file name location. For example, when you are posting a message, you can type in a URL to an image:

```
http://web.server.name/wsdocs/images/mypicture.jpg
```

Note that *web.server.name* is the fully qualified domain name of the web server where the image resides. Your image will appear in the message.

Similarly, to add a hyperlink, type in the URL to the desired location. For example, typing

```
http://myserver.com/
```

will take WebBoard readers who click on the link to your homepage. WebBoard automatically converts the URL information to an active link.

Posting a Reply

Posting a reply requires the same basic steps as Posting a New Topic. You can post a reply to any message within a topic. For example, if a topic has 10 messages, you can reply to the first message. Replies are displayed chronologically within each topic.

To post a reply, you can choose from the following options:

- Select the Post Reply command from the Message menu to create a reply.
- Select the Reply/Quote command from the Message menu to include text from the original message.
- When you reply to an existing message, WebBoard uses the same topic title. You can, however, edit the topic title, or replace it altogether.

To post a Reply or Reply/Quote, follow the same procedure previously discussed in "Posting a Topic or Message."

Sending a Private Reply

Rather than post a reply to the whole conference, you may prefer to send a reply only to the individual who posted the message. Some replies need to be shared with all the participants of a conference, while others apply only to the individual who posted that message. WebBoard lets you reply privately to the message author by email.

To reply to the author privately, choose Email Reply from the Message menu. Since this function uses your web browser's email capability, your browser must be set up to send email. WebBoard itself does not provide email capability.

Editing Your Messages

You can only edit messages that you have posted. For example, if you want to add or remove information from a message, you can edit it. Or, if you want to change the topic for a message, editing it is the way to do it.

To edit your message, follow these steps:

1. From the Conferences list, locate the message you want to edit and click its name to display it in the Message menu.
2. From the Message menu, click Edit. An Edit Message form opens, as shown in Figure 10-6.

Figure 10-6 Edit Message form

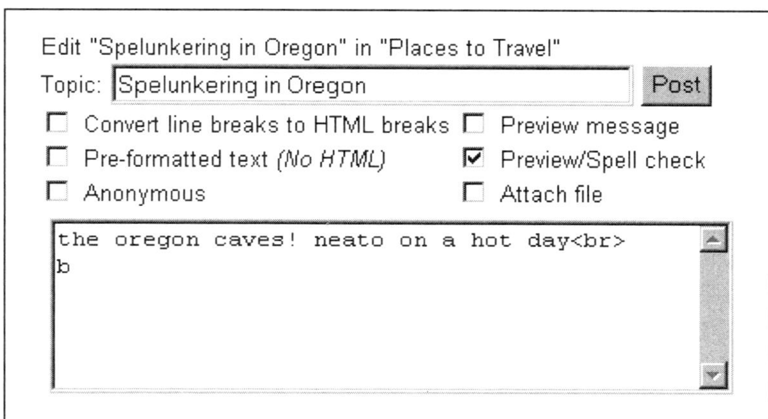

3. Make the desired changes. When you are satisfied with the appearance of your message, click Post. Your message is immediately reposted to the conference.

Deleting Your Messages

Once you have posted a message, you can delete it from the conference. You can only delete your own messages. For example, you posted a message to a conference that you decided would be better sent as a private email reply. You can delete the message.

To delete a message, follow these steps:

1. From the Conferences list, locate the message you want to delete and click its name.
2. From the Message menu, select Delete. WebBoard displays a message asking if you are sure you want to delete the message.
3. Click Yes if you want to delete this message. Your message is immediately deleted from the conference.
4. Click No if you want to keep this message in the conference.

Note

If you accidentally delete a message, the WebBoard system administrator, manager, or the conference moderator can retrieve it from the WebBoard archive. Please contact one of these persons for assistance. Usually there is a limit on how long archived messages are kept, so don't delay if you need the message back.

11

What's Happening on Your WebBoard?

You can keep up with the latest on WebBoard by using commands available from the More Options menu. Whether you want generals or specifics, WebBoard makes it simple and convenient for you to have timely and useful information at your fingertips, whether you want to see new messages or find out more about an interesting WebBoard user. From More Options you can speed up your navigation and see up-to-date statistics about WebBoard and its users.

The following commands and features are available from the More Options menu:

Email Notify
lets you receive email notification of new messages in the conference(s) you specify.

Current Users
lists the users logged in to WebBoard right now, with the login time, users' location, and a hyperlink to their personal profile.

Today's Users
lists the users who have logged in to WebBoard today, with the time, users' location, and a hyperlink to their personal profile.

Search Users
opens a search form to locate users by their first or last name.

Top 10 Users
lists the top 10 WebBoard users with a link to their name and the total number of times they've logged in.

Top 10 Posters
lists the top 10 WebBoard posters with a hyperlink to their name and the total number of their postings.

Today's Messages
lists the messages posted today, with the conference, subject, time, and a hyperlink to each message.

New Messages
lists all your unread messages, with the conference, subject, date, time, and a hyperlink to each message.

Login as a Different User
lets you log in as a different user.

This chapter shows you how to use WebBoard's More Options menu to find out what's happening on WebBoard.

Opening the More Options Menu

The More Options menu is available from the More button on the WebBoard menubar. Simply select More from the WebBoard menubar to display the More Options menu, as shown in Figure 11-1.

Figure 11-1 More Options menu

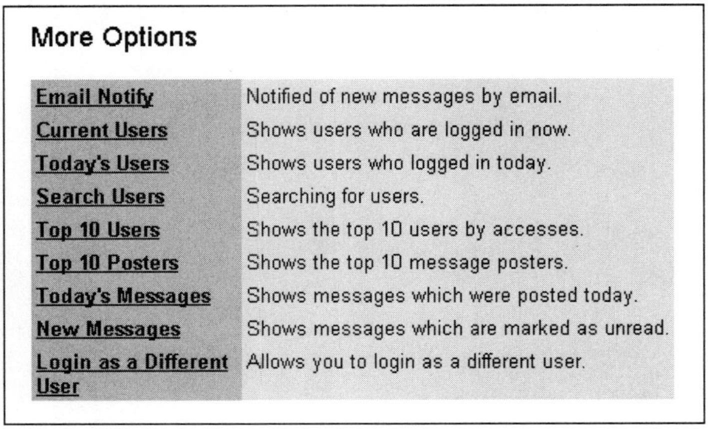

More Options

Email Notify	Notified of new messages by email.
Current Users	Shows users who are logged in now.
Today's Users	Shows users who logged in today.
Search Users	Searching for users.
Top 10 Users	Shows the top 10 users by accesses.
Top 10 Posters	Shows the top 10 message posters.
Today's Messages	Shows messages which were posted today.
New Messages	Shows messages which are marked as unread.
Login as a Different User	Allows you to login as a different user.

Note

Moderators and managers have additional items in the More Options menu and can contact the WebBoard system administrator for more information.

Using Email Notification

If you like, WebBoard will notify you of new messages in conferences. WebBoard sends you an email indicating you have a new message (or messages) in a specific conference. Email notification is sent out daily at a time set by WebBoard's system administrator.

You set email notification on a per conference basis (by default it is off). For example, let's say you're writing your master's thesis on snowy egrets and need up-to-date information on the latest discoveries. Well, you can choose to receive email notification for the Ornithology conference your university has set up. When someone posts a new message or topic to that conference, you receive an email notification so that you can check it out right away.

To receive email notification, follow these steps:

1. From the WebBoard menubar, select More. The More Options menu opens.
2. Click Email Notify. The Email Notification Status form opens, as shown in Figure 11-2. A list displays all the conferences on your WebBoard.

Figure 11-2 Email Notification Status form

More Options

Email Notification Status

Below is a list of the conferences on this board. To receive email notification when new messages are posted to one of these conferences, check the box next to that conference.

Conference	
Botany	☐
Cooking	☑
Family connections	☐
Fitness & Health	☐
Great Local Eateries	☑
Music & the Arts	☑
Office Equipment	☐
Ornithology	☑
Places to Travel	☑
Using the Web	☑

Save

3. To receive email notification when new messages are posted to one of these conferences, check the box next to the name of that conference.

4. Click Save when you complete your selection(s).
5. To return to the More Options menu, click the More Options hyperlink.

Finding Current Users

The Current Users window lists who is using WebBoard right now. You may have some pressing need, or want to participate in real-time chat, so you need to know who is currently logged in. For example, Greg is having a family chat session and wants to see if his brother-in-law in Japan is also currently logged in. So he checks out the Current Users list, which is updated every 60 seconds.

Users who have logged in today for the first time are marked with a NEW icon. You can also find out more about today's users by clicking on their name. A link to their personal profile will open.

To find out who current users are, follow these steps:

1. From the WebBoard menubar, select More. The More Options menu opens.
2. Click Current Users. A list displays all the current users, indicating their location and the time of their last connect, as shown in Figure 11-3.

Figure 11-3 Current Users list

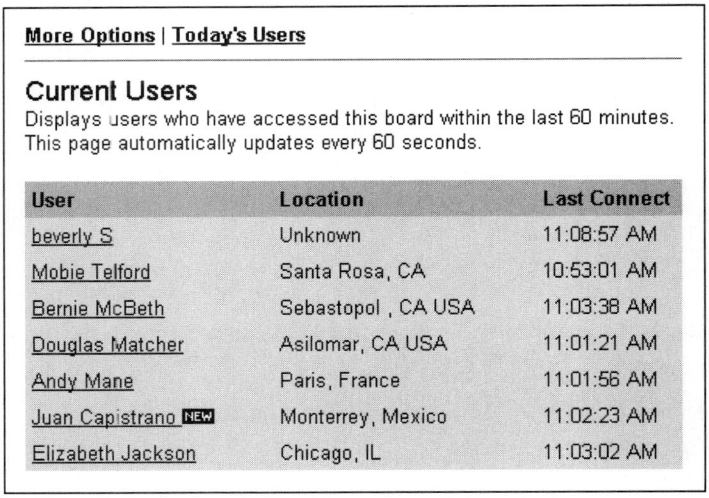

More Options | Today's Users

Current Users

Displays users who have accessed this board within the last 60 minutes. This page automatically updates every 60 seconds.

User	Location	Last Connect
beverly S	Unknown	11:08:57 AM
Mobie Telford	Santa Rosa, CA	10:53:01 AM
Bernie McBeth	Sebastopol , CA USA	11:03:38 AM
Douglas Matcher	Asilomar, CA USA	11:01:21 AM
Andy Mane	Paris, France	11:01:56 AM
Juan Capistrano NEW	Monterrey, Mexico	11:02:23 AM
Elizabeth Jackson	Chicago, IL	11:03:02 AM

3. To return to the More Options menu, click the More Options hyperlink.

Finding Today's Users

WebBoard's Today's Users feature lets you see who has been on WebBoard today. Perhaps you want to see if a particular individual has logged in, in case you are looking for a specific response to one of the conferences.

On this list, users who have logged in today for the first time are marked with a NEW icon. You can also find out more about today's users by clicking on their name. A link to their personal profile will open.

To find out who today's users are, follow these steps:

1. From the WebBoard menubar, select More. The More Options menu opens.
2. Click Today's Users. A list displays all today's users, indicating their location and the time of their last connection, as shown in Figure 11-4.
3. To return to the More Options menu, click the More Options hyperlink.

Figure 11-4 Today's Users list

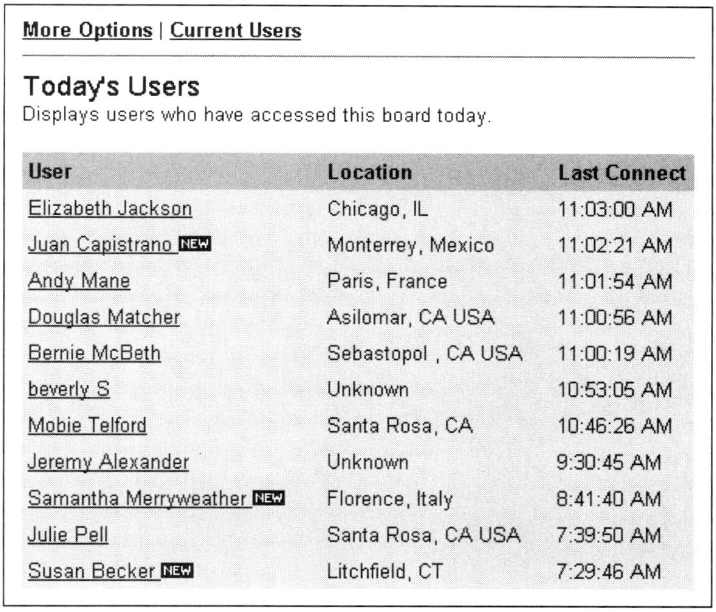

More Options | Current Users

Today's Users

Displays users who have accessed this board today.

User	Location	Last Connect
Elizabeth Jackson	Chicago, IL	11:03:00 AM
Juan Capistrano NEW	Monterrey, Mexico	11:02:21 AM
Andy Mane	Paris, France	11:01:54 AM
Douglas Matcher	Asilomar, CA USA	11:00:56 AM
Bernie McBeth	Sebastopol , CA USA	11:00:19 AM
beverly S	Unknown	10:53:05 AM
Mobie Telford	Santa Rosa, CA	10:46:26 AM
Jeremy Alexander	Unknown	9:30:45 AM
Samantha Merryweather NEW	Florence, Italy	8:41:40 AM
Julie Pell	Santa Rosa, CA USA	7:39:50 AM
Susan Becker NEW	Litchfield, CT	7:29:46 AM

Searching for WebBoard Users

Sometimes you will want to find out more about certain WebBoard users. You have a variety of options to search for a user. You can search by selecting one of the following:

- the first letter of the user's first name
- all users by first or last name
- any letter(s) contained in the user's first or last name

Figure 11-5 shows WebBoard's Search Users form. Each name you see listed in the search results is a hyperlink, which takes you to the personal profile for that user. Users who have logged in today for the first time are marked with a NEW icon.

Figure 11-5 Search Users form

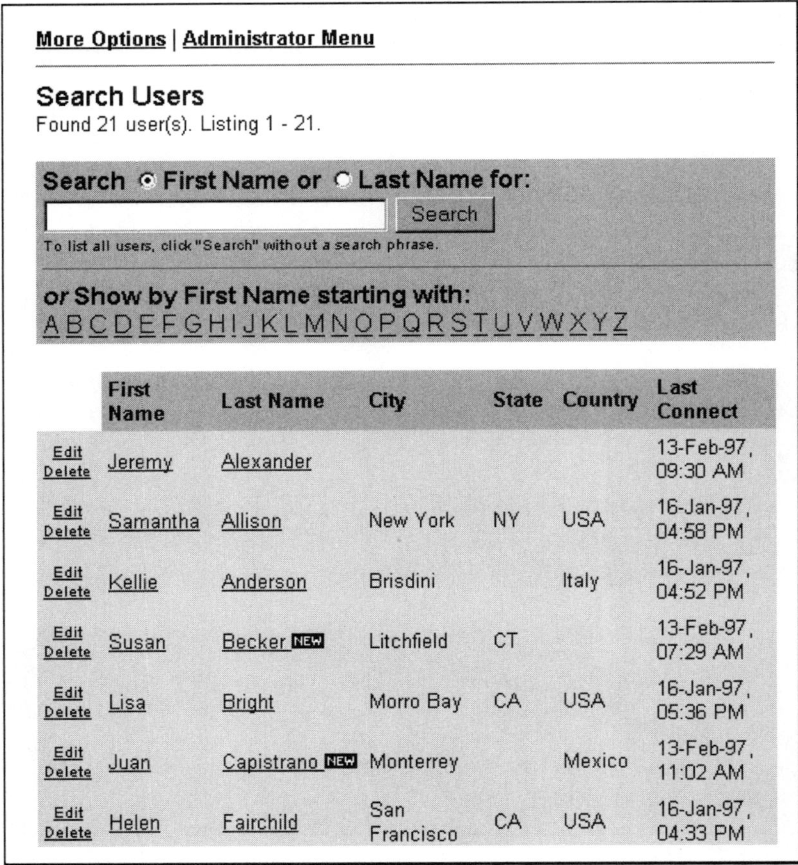

More Options | Administrator Menu

Search Users

Found 21 user(s). Listing 1 - 21.

Search First Name or Last Name for:

Search

To list all users, click "Search" without a search phrase.

or Show by First Name starting with:

A B C D E F G H I J K L M N O P Q R S T U V W X Y Z

	First Name	Last Name	City	State	Country	Last Connect
Edit Delete	Jeremy	Alexander				13-Feb-97, 09:30 AM
Edit Delete	Samantha	Allison	New York	NY	USA	16-Jan-97, 04:58 PM
Edit Delete	Kellie	Anderson	Brisdini		Italy	16-Jan-97, 04:52 PM
Edit Delete	Susan	Becker NEW	Litchfield	CT		13-Feb-97, 07:29 AM
Edit Delete	Lisa	Bright	Morro Bay	CA	USA	16-Jan-97, 05:36 PM
Edit Delete	Juan	Capistrano NEW	Monterrey		Mexico	13-Feb-97, 11:02 AM
Edit Delete	Helen	Fairchild	San Francisco	CA	USA	16-Jan-97, 04:33 PM

To search for a WebBoard user by *first name,* follow these steps:

1. From the WebBoard menubar, select More. The More Options menu opens.
2. Click Search Users. The Search Users form opens.
   - If you know the spelling of the user's first name, click the hyperlinked letter that corresponds to the first letter of the user's first name. For

example, you remember a new user named Zachary Smith who put a cool link in one of his messages, and you want to see his user's profile. You can find him fastest by choosing the First Name radio button and clicking the hyperlink Z, since you know there are a lot of Smiths on your WebBoard. A list displays all the users whose first names begin with that letter.

- If you do not know the spelling of the user's first name, but know some of the letters in it, enter the letters (a string) in the search textbox and click Search. For example, you haven't noticed any postings recently by Jeremy Smith, but don't know if the correct spelling is Geremy or Jeremy. So, you can enter *eremy* in the Search textbox. A list displays all the users whose first name contains those letters.

To search for a WebBoard user by *last name,* follow these steps:

1. From the WebBoard menubar, select More. The More Options menu opens.
2. Click Search Users. The Search Users form opens.
   - If you know the spelling of the user's last name, click the Last Name radio button. Enter the letter(s) in the search textbox and click Search. A list displays all the users whose last names contain those letters.
   - If you do not know the spelling of the user's last name, but know some of the letters in it, click the Last Name radio button. Enter the letters (a string) in the search textbox and click Search. For example, you want to find the user whose name is Monte Smythe, but you can't remember how to spell it. After you click the Last Name radio button, you can enter *Sm* in the search textbox. A list displays all the users whose last names contain those letters.

To search for *all users:*

1. From the WebBoard menubar, select More. The More Options menu opens.
2. Click Search Users. The Search Users form opens.
   - To list all users by *first* name, click the First Name radio button. Do not put any letters in the Search textbox. Click Search. A list displays all the users' first names.
   - To list all users by *last* name, click the Last Name radio button. Do not put any letters in the Search textbox. Click Search. A list displays all the users' last names.

Finding the Top 10 Users

WebBoard keeps track of its users and can tell you who the 10 most active users are. These users are selected by the number of times they log in to WebBoard.

Figure 11-6 shows the Top 10 Users list. You can also find out more about any of the top 10 users by clicking on his or her name. A link to his or her personal profile opens.

Figure 11-6 Top 10 Users list

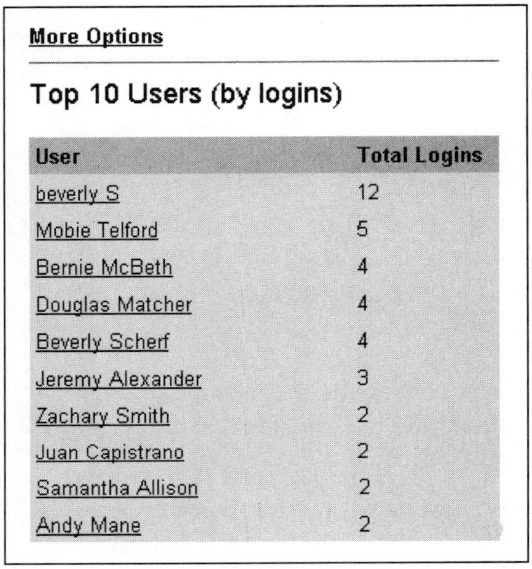

More Options

Top 10 Users (by logins)

User	Total Logins
beverly S	12
Mobie Telford	5
Bernie McBeth	4
Douglas Matcher	4
Beverly Scherf	4
Jeremy Alexander	3
Zachary Smith	2
Juan Capistrano	2
Samantha Allison	2
Andy Mane	2

To find out who the top ten users are, follow these steps:

1. From the WebBoard menubar, select More. The More Options menu opens.
2. Click Top 10 Users. A list displays the top ten users and number of their total log ins.
3. To return to the More Options menu, click the More Options hyperlink.

Finding the Top 10 Posters

You can easily determine who the top 10 posters on your WebBoard are. These users are selected by the number of messages they've posted.

Figure 11-7 shows the Top 10 Posters list. You can also find out more about any of the top 10 posters by clicking on his or her name. A link to his or her personal profile will open.

To find out who the top 10 posters are, follow these steps:

1. From the WebBoard menubar, select More. The More Options menu opens.
2. Click Top 10 Posters. A list displays the ten most frequent posters and number of their total posts.
3. To return to the More Options menu, click the More Options hyperlink.

Figure 11-7 Top 10 Posters list

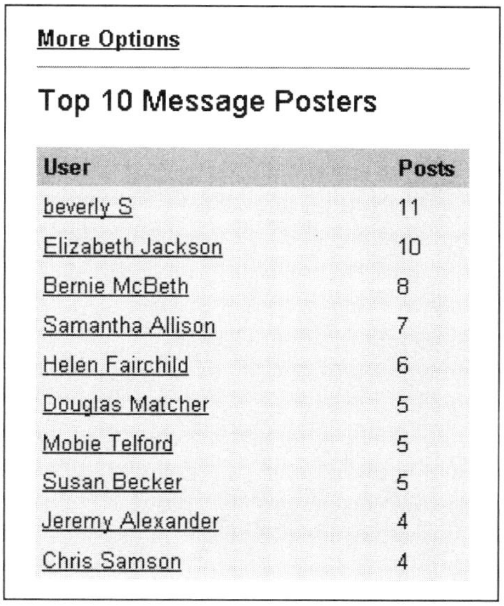

More Options

Top 10 Message Posters

User	Posts
beverly S	11
Elizabeth Jackson	10
Bernie McBeth	8
Samantha Allison	7
Helen Fairchild	6
Douglas Matcher	5
Mobie Telford	5
Susan Becker	5
Jeremy Alexander	4
Chris Samson	4

Finding Today's Messages

Today's Messages lists all messages posted that day, whereas the New Messages feature lets you see all your unread messages, regardless of when they were posted. If you want to see just the most current messages posted, Today's Messages lists them by the conference, subject, and time.

You will most likely want to use this feature every time you use WebBoard, because you can directly link to any messages posted that day from the Today's Messages list (see Figure 11-8). This list is immediately updated, so that you can keep close track of what is going on.

To locate today's messages, follow these steps:

1. From the WebBoard menubar, select More. The More Options menu opens.
2. Click Today's Messages. The Messages Posted Today list displays each message with the conference, the subject, and the time of the post.
3. To open a message, click the linked name under the Subject column. The message opens.
4. To return to Today's Messages, click the Back browser button.

Figure 11-8 Today's Messages list

More Options | Search Messages

Messages Posted Today

Found 41 message(s) that were posted today.

Conference	Subject	Time
Places to Travel	Vancouver, BC ferries	7:09:55 AM
Family connections	Geneology charts	7:19:14 AM
Great Local Eateries	Amelio's Fine Dining	7:19:47 AM
Ornithology	Flight patterns of Whistling Swans	7:20:50 AM
Places to Travel	Spelunkering in Oregon	7:22:15 AM
Using the Web	Chatting in WebBoard	7:22:48 AM
Music & the Arts	Hammered dulcimer duets	7:23:26 AM
Great Local Eateries	Tony's Fry Shack	7:29:15 AM
Great Local Eateries	Serendipity Cafe	7:30:25 AM
Music & the Arts	Celtic harp/Piano duets	7:31:21 AM
Botany	Flowers	7:32:23 AM
Fitness & Health	Jogging in the pines	7:33:43 AM
Places to Travel	Vancouver, BC ferries	7:35:07 AM
Places to Travel	Yukon trails	7:46:56 AM
Fitness & Health	Jogging in the pines	7:47:35 AM
Music & the Arts	Hammered ducilmer duets	7:48:44 AM
Music & the Arts	Hammered ducilmer duets	7:50:59 AM

Finding All New Messages

Today's Messages is probably one of the handiest features in WebBoard, offering you speedy navigation to all your unread messages. New Messages lets you see any messages that you haven't read and lists the conference, subject, and time (see Figure 11-9). This list is immediately updated, so that you can keep close track of what is going on. The messages on the list no longer appear when you click the Mark All Conferences Read hyperlink, but you might want to click the browser Reload button to make sure you're not marking any newly posted messages as well.

Tip

You can also link directly to New Messages from the Welcome page when you log in to WebBoard. Just click *You have x new message(s).*

To locate your new messages, follow these steps:

1. From the WebBoard menubar, select More. The More Options menu opens.
2. Click New Messages. The New Messages list displays each message title with the conference, the subject, and the time of the post.

3. To open a message, click the linked name under the Subject column. The message opens.

4. To return to New Messages, click the Back browser button.

Figure 11-9 New Messages list

More Options | Search Messages

New Messages

New messages since the last time you marked messages read.

Found 25 new message(s).

Conference	Subject	Posted
Botany	Cherry blossoms	2/13/97 10:39:19 AM
Cooking	How to Boil Water	2/13/97 9:32:03 AM
Family connections	Geneology charts	2/13/97 7:19:14 AM
Great Local Eateries	Amelio's Fine Dining	2/13/97 7:19:47 AM
Great Local Eateries	Tony's Fry Shack	2/13/97 7:29:15 AM
Great Local Eateries	Serendipity Cafe	2/13/97 7:30:25 AM
Great Local Eateries	Breakfast Spots	2/13/97 7:59:41 AM
Great Local Eateries	Breakfast Spots	2/13/97 9:44:41 AM
Places to Travel	Vancouver, BC ferries	2/13/97 7:09:55 AM
Places to Travel	Spelunkering in Oregon	2/13/97 7:22:15 AM
Places to Travel	Vancouver, BC ferries	2/13/97 7:35:07 AM
Places to Travel	Boston's Whale excursions	2/13/97 7:36:05 AM
Places to Travel	Northern Lights in Norway	2/13/97 7:38:09 AM
Places to Travel	Rogue River Rapids	2/13/97 7:41:46 AM
Places to Travel	Skiiing in Utah	2/13/97 7:45:52 AM
Places to Travel	Yukon trails	2/13/97 7:46:56 AM
Places to Travel	Yukon trails	2/13/97 7:58:01 AM
Places to Travel	Rogue River Rapids	2/13/97 8:00:29 AM
Places to Travel	Boston's Whale excursions	2/13/97 8:00:48 AM
Places to Travel	Frolicking in Liechtenstein	2/13/97 8:01:11 AM
Places to Travel	Skiiing in Utah	2/13/97 8:03:18 AM
Places to Travel	Rain forests in Amazon	2/13/97 8:03:58 AM
Using the Web	Chatting in WebBoard	2/13/97 7:22:48 AM
Using the Web	WB in Action	2/13/97 8:11:08 AM

12

Chatting in WebBoard

WebBoard's Chat is not only simple to use, it's also attractive. You can have real-time virtual communities when you use Chat. You can exchange information, questions, issues, and concerns with fellow users in your conference chat rooms. You can easily customize some of its options to make your chat contributions really unique. And you can also include images and active links in your chat messages. WebBoard lets you carry on real-time interactive discussions with its Chat feature.

In Chat, you can relate more specifically with others in a conference, and be in the loop about any new developments. Chat rooms are available on a per conference basis; the conference manager determines which conferences will have this feature. Some people like to join chat groups simply to carry on more immediate discussions with fellow users rather than waiting to read new postings in the conferences.

You can schedule a convenient time for chat room members to meet for a chat session. This is particularly useful for designating specific topics to cover that extend beyond current conferences. The Chat feature also permits exclusivity, in that you can *whisper* to select individuals in the room—other users won't see your whispered message.

Let's look at some of the ways to use WebBoard Chat:

- Tech support staff can use Chat to more readily respond to customer queries by discussing particular problems over their local network.
- Offsite customers can benefit from the online connectivity and interactivity that Chat provides, creating a greater sense of community.
- Fellow workers can communicate with one another on specific projects.
- Personnel can use Chat for essential interdepartmental communication.
- Civic groups can carry on real-time discussions about current issues.
- Parents can interact with other parents and gain collective insight regarding their children's health and activities.
- Support group members can benefit from the real-time input they get from others in the group.
- Students can talk with one another to learn more about assignments, lectures, or research projects.
- Chat room participants can alert others in the room to get their immediate attention, rather than calling them on the telephone or sending emails.

This chapter explains how to use WebBoard's features in Chat. The following sections show you how to enter a chat room, send messages, customize your messages, join another chat room discussion, alert other chat users, whisper, and more.

Note

To use the Chat feature you must be using a JavaScript-enabled browser such as Netscape Navigator 3.0 (or higher) or Microsoft Internet Explorer 3.0 (or higher).

Entering a Chat Room

WebBoard makes navigation to chat rooms simple. First, select Chat from the WebBoard menubar to display the list of available chat rooms, as shown in Figure 12-1. This list shows the chat room hyperlink and the number of active users in it. The information in this list updates every 60 seconds.

To participate in Chat, you must first enter a chat room. When you enter an active chat room, you will see the text of the ongoing conversation with the name of the chat room in the Chat window titlebar. Your name appears in the window, with the time you entered. To enter a chat room, follow these steps:

Figure 12-1 Available Chat Rooms list

Available Chat Rooms

Displays available chat rooms and how active they are. This page automatically updates every 60 seconds.

To use the chat feature you must be using a JavaScript enabled browser such as Netscape Navigator 3.0 (or higher) or Microsoft Internet Explorer 3.0 (or higher).

Chat Room	Active Users
Botany	90
Cooking	42
Family connections	10
Fitness & Health	0
Great Local Eateries	0
Music & the Arts	14
Office Equipment	0
Ornithology	2
Places to Travel	0
Using the Web	0

1. From the WebBoard menubar, select Chat. The Available Chat Rooms list displays all the available chat rooms and current activity.
2. To go into a specific chat room, click the hyperlinked conference name. The Chat window appears.

The Chat window is where you see all the activity and dialogue in the chat room, as described in the next section.

Tip

If you seem to have lost your Chat window, simply move or minimize your browser window. Sometimes the browser window covers the Chat window.

A Quick Look at the Chat Window

The Chat window displays a running conversation, as shown in Figure 12-2. As new participants enter the room, their presence is announced to the other participants with the time of their arrival. When members send chat messages, the messages appear in chronological order, the most recent at the top. Figure 12-2 also shows examples of Chat's special features such as Whisper, smileys, and paging.

Chat's features are available from the Chat menubar, at the top of the Chat window. These features are described briefly below and then in more detail in the rest of this chapter.

Figure 12-2 Chat window

Compose

opens the Compose Message window in which you type a chat message. Use this to enter a message in the chat room. You can send longer, or customized messages when you use the Compose window rather than using the Chat window textbox. You can also select text specifications from this window.

Refresh

updates the Chat window. The window updates automatically every 5 seconds. You can change the settings on this by entering a command.

Rooms

displays a list of available chat rooms and their current activity (within 15 minutes). You can enter another chat room by selecting a room in this window. The Rooms window has its own menubar, with Refresh and Close.

Users

displays a list of who is in a current chat room so you know who will be talking (or listening) to you. You can also Whisper, or have a private conversation, with other users in a chat room from the Users window. The Users window has its own menubar, with Refresh and Close.

Close

exits Chat. An alert asks you if you are sure you want to exit.

Help

displays WebBoard's Help menu.

Now that you are familiar with Chat's features, you are probably eager to join a chat session. The next sections describe how you can interact in real-time chat.

Sending Messages

For each chat message you want to send, you can choose one of two methods:

- from the chat room window, use the textbox field
- from the Chat menubar, use the Compose Message window textbox

You can choose from a variety of options, including text colors, and various text specifications when you use the Compose Message window. Using the Chat window textbox allows you to send shorter messages. This section explains how to send messages in Chat using both methods.

> **Tip**
>
> It's good to keep messages brief in chat, since the nature of chat is ongoing conversations and longer messages can slow down the flow.

To Send a Message from a Chat Room

The upper portion of the chat room window contains a textbox to use for sending a message. To send a message from your chat room window, follow these steps:

1. Type your message (up to 500 characters) in the textbox.
2. Click Send to send your message. Your message appears in the chat room at the top of the window, with the time you sent it and your name above it.

To Send a Message from the Compose Message Window

The Compose Message window lets you create customized chat messages. You can choose text options for various sizes, 16 colors, bold, italic, centered, or plain. To send a message from the Compose Message window, follow these steps:

1. From the Chat menubar, select Compose. The Compose Message window opens, as shown in Figure 12-3.
2. Type your message in the textbox. To clear the contents of your textbox, click Clear.

Figure 12-3 Compose Message window

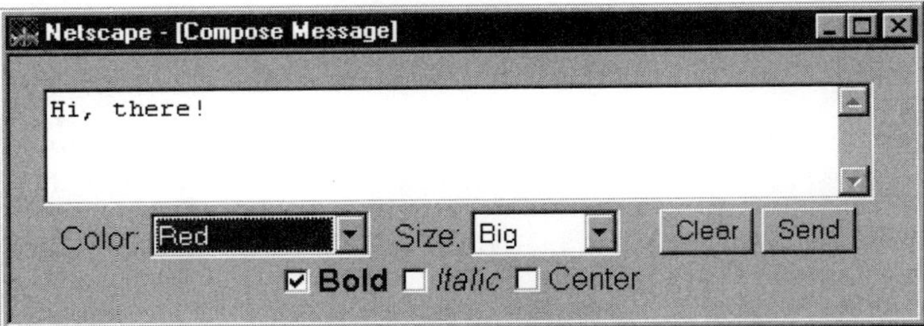

3. Customize your text, if desired (described in the next section).
4. Click Send to send your message. Your message appears in the chat room at the top of the window, with the time you sent it and your name above it.
5. Click the closebox in the window titlebar to close the Compose Message window.

The next sections explain how you can add text enhancement, images, or links to your chat messages.

Customizing Your Chat Message

WebBoard makes it a snap for you to customize the text of each of your chat messages. Sometimes you may want to change the way chat message entries look. For example, if many users are engaged in chat room discussions, you may each want to select a different formatting option, such as text color or size. Thus, it is easy to know who is saying what during a fast interaction, without having to look at all the names.

The customization options you choose affect your entire message entry, not just individual words in the message. Note that your customization of a message affects only your current chat entry.

Note

Note that HTML formatting is not supported in Chat.

Varying Text

You may decide that your messages could be more interesting by using the options available to you in the Compose Message window. You can choose one or any combination of the following options: color, size, bold, italics, and centered.

Get the Word Out in Chat

When you are in a chat session, from time to time you may see a logo, advertisement, or bulletin appear in the Chat window. If so, that means the WebBoard administrator has set up Chat Spots. A Chat Spot is an HTML file that displays in the Chat window at a regular interval. WebBoard supports up to 255 Chat Spot files so you may see a variety of ads or announcements during a chat session. The administrator can also vary how often a Chat Spot is displayed from once every message to every 255 messages.

Chat Spots are a great way for businesses and organizations to promote their products or post announcements to the WebBoard community. If you have a product or service you'd like to advertise or an informational piece you'd like to display during WebBoard chat, contact the WebBoard administrator to set up your Chat Spot file. Then the next time a chat session is active, everyone participating will get the word from your Chat Spot.

To customize your text in Chat, follow these steps:

1. From the Chat menubar, select Compose. The Compose Message window opens, as shown earlier in Figure 12-3.
2. Type your message.
3. From the Compose Message window options, select one of the following, or any combination if you want more than one feature in your text entry:
   - To select a text color (16 are available), click the Color drop-down box.
   - To select Tiny, Normal, Big, Bigger, or Huge for your font size, click the Size drop-down box.
   - To specify bold text, click the Bold checkbox.
   - To specify italic text, click the Italic checkbox.
   - To specify centered text (rather than the default left-justified), click the Center checkbox.
4. Click Send to send your message. Your customized message will appear in the chat room at the top of the window, with the time you sent it and your name above it.
5. Click the closebox in the titlebar to close the Compose Message window.

Adding Smileys

One of the easiest ways to customize your chat messages is to use smileys. Chat messages from both the Chat window textbox and the Compose Message window can contain smileys. To include smileys in chat messages, type the characters as shown in Table 12-1.

Table 12-1 WebBoard smileys

Type these characters	*For this smiley*
:)	
:(	
:o	

Adding Images or Links

Another way to customize your chat messages is to include images and links. For example, Sally wants her friend Lisa to see her new horse. So she includes a small photo of her horse's head (the image link) in her chat message. Lisa sees the photo in the Chat window. Sally also includes a link to her web page so that Lisa can see more pictures. Lisa clicks on the link in the Chat window to go to the web page.

To add an image or link, type in its file name location in your chat message. For example,

```
http://web.server.name/wsdocs/images/mypicture.gif
```

where *web.server.name* is the fully qualified domain name of the web server hosting your WebBoard. Your image or active link will appear in the chat room window.

Clearing the Textbox

If before you send a message you change your mind, you can either edit or cancel it by clearing the textbox. To clear the textbox in the Compose Message window, follow these steps:

1. From the Compose Message window, click Clear. All the text in the textbox is cleared.
2. Type in another message, if desired.
3. Click the closebox in the titlebar to close the Compose Message window.

Finding Active Users in a Chat Room

Before you participate in a chat session, you may want to see who's in the room. You can see this information from the Users window from the Chat menubar, as shown in Figure 12-4. Also from this window, you can whisper private messages to one or more users, as described later in this chapter.

Figure 12-4 Chat Room Users window

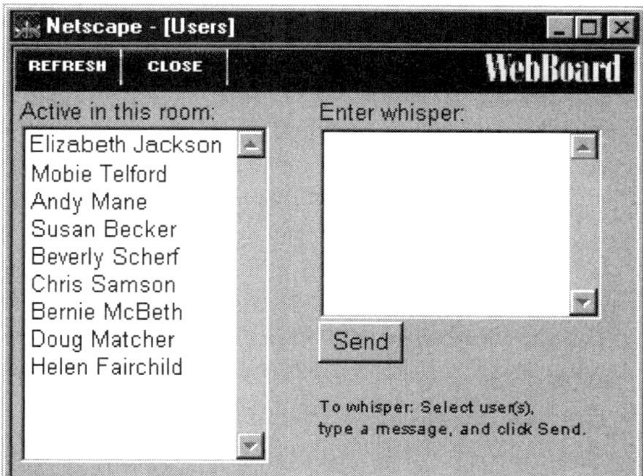

To find out who is active in a chat room, follow these steps:

1. From the Chat menubar, select Users. The Users window opens and displays the currently active users. (Users remain active for 15 minutes after the time of their last message.)

   —OR—

   From the chat room Users window, select Refresh to update any user activity.

2. Select Close from the Users menubar to close the Users window.

Tip

The fastest way to see how many people are active in any chat room is to select Chat from the WebBoard menubar, and then link directly to a room. But the Users window from Chat's menubar lists the names of those in the chat room.

Paging Another Chat User

From time to time, you may need to immediately contact another chat room user without sending a message to the whole chat room. The Page feature lets you do so. Notice the bell by each active user in a chat room. The Page (bell) icon enables you to signal anyone in the room by sending an alert message to the user's screen. Note that this is a written alert, not a sound.

To page another chat room user, follow these steps:

1. From the Chat window, locate the user you want to page.
2. To page that user, click the Page (bell) icon next to the user's name. A Page Alert displays on that user's screen, as shown in Figure 12-5.

Figure 12-5 Page Alert

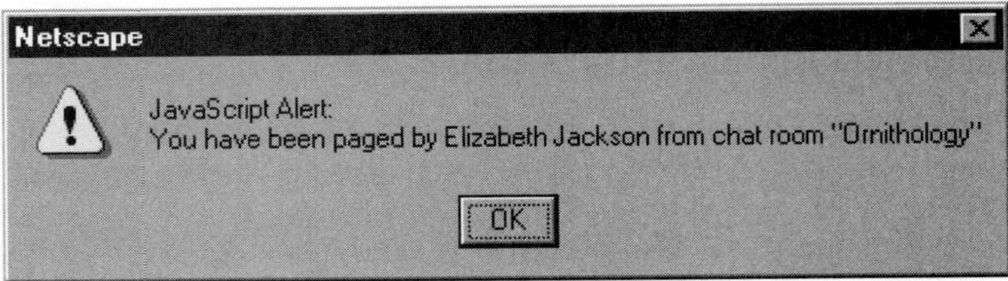

Going to Another Chat Room

You can see a list of available, active chat rooms with ongoing chat discussions from the Chat Rooms list, as shown in Figure 12-6. You can also change to another chat room by selecting a name from the list.

Figure 12-6 Chat Rooms window

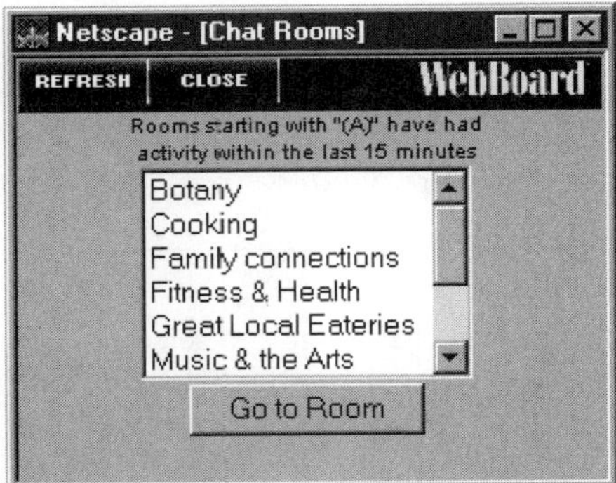

Chat rooms that are currently active have an A (for active) next to the room name in the Chat Rooms window. While in a chat room, you may want to keep the Chat Rooms window open to watch for any activity.

To go to another chat room, follow these steps:

1. From the Chat menubar, select Rooms. The Chat Rooms window opens and displays all the chat rooms. Rooms that have recent activity (within the last 15 minutes) are preceded by an *(A)*.
2. Highlight the room you wish to enter. You may need to scroll to see all the room names.

3. Click Go to Room to enter the room. Note that from the Chat Rooms window, you can select Refresh to update activity information.

4. To close the Chat Rooms window, either select Close from the Chat Rooms menubar, or click the closebox in the titlebar.

Tip

You can also view the activity level of all the chat rooms from selecting Chat from the WebBoard menubar.

Refreshing the Chat Window

If you like to keep your favorite chat room open, you can use Refresh from the Chat menubar to update its contents at certain time intervals that you can specify by typing in a command in the Chat window textbox.

You can refresh your chat room window at intervals by setting the Refresh option from 3 to 120 seconds, or just leave it off (zero). Choose the higher number if you aren't concerned about immediate activity.

To change the refresh settings for your chat room, do one of the following:

- From the Chat window, type in the following command: *r=#* where # is a number of seconds ranging from 3 to 120. The *r* can be upper- or lowercase.
- To turn off automatic refresh, type *r=0* (zero). To manually refresh the chat window, select Refresh from the Chat menubar.

Using Whisper to Send Private Messages

Chat's Whisper feature lets you send private messages to other active chat room participants. Chat rooms are open to all users of a given conference, but you can tailor your chat session to include only those users you specify. From the Chat window, you can whisper to one user at a time. From the Chat Users' window, you can whisper to more than one user at a time. The following sections describe how you can use Whisper.

Note

Chat sessions can be stored to a log file by the conference manager. Although whisper messages may not be seen by anyone besides the chosen recipient, they can be saved to the log file and reviewed by the manager.

Whispering to Another User

You can send a private message to anyone in a chat room. When you want to send long messages to specific user(s), you can use Whisper for private chats, so as not to disrupt the flow in the chat room. To send a message to a particular person in a chat room, you can whisper from the Chat window, as described here, or from the Chat Users room window, as described in the next section.

To whisper to another user from the Chat window, follow these steps:

1. From the Chat window, locate the user's name, and click that user's Whisper (cloud) icon. The Whisper icon prompts you to enter your message, as shown in Figure 12-7.

Figure 12-7 Whisper Message Prompt

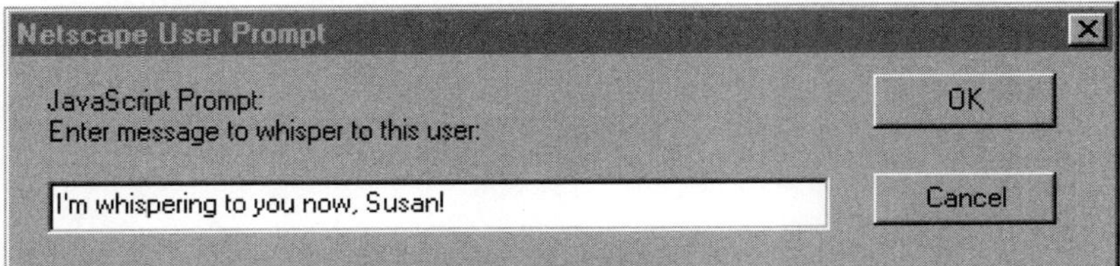

2. Type in your private text.
3. Click Send to send your private message to the chat room. Your message appears only to that user, with the Whisper graphic next to it, and the time and your name preceding it. The Chat window also indicates that you whispered to that individual, with the time you sent the message.

Whispering to Create a Private Chat

To send a message to a group of users in a chat room, you select users to whisper to from the Chat Users window (see Figure 12-4 earlier). To have a private chat with one or more users, follow these steps:

1. From the Chat menubar, select Users. The Users window opens.
2. From the Users list, select one or more users that you want to whisper to by clicking each user's name. To select more than one user, press the Control key while making your selections.
3. Type your message in the Enter message to whisper textbox field.
4. Click Send to send your private message to the chat room. Your message appears only to the users you select, with a Whisper graphic next to it and the time and your name preceding it. Your chat room window indicates the users you whispered to, with the time you sent it.

5. To close the Users window, select Close from the Users menubar.

Ending Your Chat Session

When you are finished chatting, you should close the Chat window.

To exit Chat, follow these steps:

1. From the Chat menubar, select Close. A Confirm Exit prompts you whether you want to exit, as shown in Figure 12-8.

Figure 12-8 Confirm Exit prompt

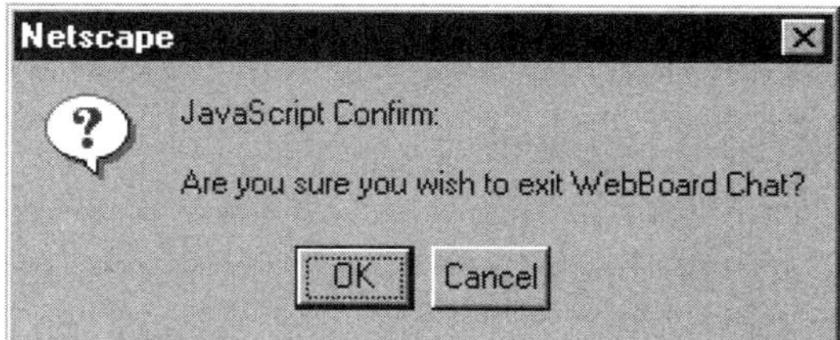

2. Click Yes to exit. This ends your chat session.

Note

You may want to keep the Chat window open in the background or minimized on your desktop so that you are always available to others entering chat rooms.

V

Appendixes

The two appendixes included in this book provide more detailed information about WebBoard. Appendix A covers WebBoard 2.0 XL, the extended license version of WebBoard that supports up to 255 virtual boards and unlimited conferences in addition to all the standard WebBoard features. Appendix B is a collection of Troubleshooting Tips with contributions from O'Reilly Software's technical staff.

Upgrading to WebBoard 2.0 XL

Throughout this book, we have mentioned the extended license version of WebBoard 2.0. This appendix tells you more about this version and how to go about upgrading to it.

The WebBoard software on the CD-ROM in this book supports all WebBoard's features, including message posting, chat, file attachments, spell-checking, and so on. You can also use this version of WebBoard to create a virtual board, so that your WebBoard has two separate boards—the original, "real" board and one virtual board. Virtual boards are discussed in detail in Section 2 of this book. Each board can have up to 10 conferences.

For many WebBoard administrators, two virtual boards and 10 conferences per board may be sufficient. However, if you want to offer more virtual boards or more than 10 conferences per board, you can do so by upgrading to the extended license version of WebBoard 2.0. WebBoard 2.0 XL supports up to 255 virtual boards and unlimited conferences per board. You may upgrade to XL from any previous version of WebBoard.

WebBoard 2.0 XL is available only direct from O'Reilly & Associates. You may order online or by phone, as follows:

- Order online at WebBoard Central, *http://webboard.ora.com*. Follow the links for upgrading to WebBoard 2.0 XL.

- Order by phone from O'Reilly Customer Service, 707-829-0515 or 800-998-9938. Ask for the WebBoard 2.0 XL upgrade.

You will receive instructions by mail for installing WebBoard 2.0 XL. As soon as you implement the upgrade, you can create up to 255 virtual boards and an unlimited number of conferences per board, as described in Section 2 of this book.

Note

If you are upgrading from a previous version of WebBoard 1.0 and have more than two virtual boards or 10 conferences per board, the boards and conferences that exceed the basic license limitation will not be visible until you upgrade to WebBoard 2.0 XL. However, these boards and conferences are converted to the new 2.0 format, as described in Chapter 3.

B

Troubleshooting Tips

This WebBoard troubleshooting appendix is divided into two main sections: a section of specific problems and solutions, and a section of guidelines for diagnosing and solving problems on your own. The problems and solutions have been collected from O'Reilly Technical Support and reflect questions users have had of WebBoard. The guidelines section describes the troubleshooting tools that come with WebBoard, and suggests typical places to look for the causes of problems.

This appendix ends with information regarding other resources that you can use to get help with WebBoard, including O'Reilly Technical Support. We highly recommend that you read this appendix and check the online resources before calling Technical Support.

Problems and Solutions

The following specific problems have been encountered by WebBoard users in earlier versions and during beta tests. The answers are from O'Reilly's Technical Support staff.

Problem

When installing under Windows NT 3.51, a "~Gtmp" error message appears at the end of setup and the installation aborts.

Solution

You must have at least Service Pack 3 installed on your NT 3.51 system. You can obtain service packs from Microsoft at *http://www.microsoft.com*.

Problem

When running WebBoard under NT and using an external web server, the error message "500 Server Error" appears in the browser when the WebBoard URL is requested.

Solution

Both WebBoard and the web server must be running either as a desktop application or as a system service. If one is running as a service and the other as an application, WebBoard will return this error message. See Chapter 3 for instructions on changing WebBoard's run mode.

Problem

When running WebBoard as a service under NT 4.0 and using an external web server, the error message "Document contains no data" or "Server returned an invalid or unrecognized response" appears in the browser when the WebBoard URL is requested.

Solution

Both WebBoard and the web server services must be running to *not* interact with the desktop. If one is set to interact with the desktop and the other is set not to, WebBoard will return these error messages. By default, WebBoard is configured to *not* interact with the desktop; maintain this default and change this option for your web server. The interact with desktop option is available from the Startup button on the Control Panel Services dialog box.

Problem

When running WebBoard with WebSite or WebSite Professional, the error message "404 Not Found. The requested URL was not found on this server: /webboard/$webb.exe (C:/WebSite/htdocs/webboard/$webb.exe)" appears in the browser when the WebBoard URL is requested.

Solution

You probably installed WebBoard while WebSite was running. Stop and restart WebSite to update the CGI and document mappings added to WebSite's configuration during WebBoard installation.

Problem

Since I upgraded from WebBoard 1.0 to WebBoard 2.0, some of my virtual boards and conferences are no longer available.

Solution

WebBoard 2.0 supports two virtual boards and up to 10 conferences per board. During installation, WebBoard upgrades all your existing boards and conferences to the new format. However, you will be able to see only the first two boards and 10 conferences on each board. To have access to the remainder of your virtual boards and conferences, you must purchase the WebBoard 2.0 XL version. This extended license version of the software supports up to 255 virtual boards and unlimited conferences.

Problem

Message preview does not work for some users of Microsoft Internet Explorer. They can preview the message but not back up to edit it again.

Solution

This is a bug in certain Internet Explorer 3.0 browsers for NT. We suggest the following workaround: have the user post the message and then edit it or delete it using the WebBoard message menu.

Problem

The Refresh button on the WebBoard menubar does not always update the Conferences list for some users of Microsoft Internet Explorer.

Solution

This is a bug in certain Internet Explorer 3.0 browsers for NT. We suggest the following workaround: right-click in the Conferences list frame and select Refresh from the menu.

Troubleshooting Guidelines

The following guidelines will help you diagnose and solve problems you may encounter while using WebBoard. Please work through these before calling technical support.

- Restart your computer to ensure that the effects of any unstable or faulty software are removed from memory.
- Make sure you have read and met the WebBoard installation requirements, described in Chapter 2.
- Make sure you have tested WebBoard according to the procedures outlined in Chapter 3.
- Verify the web server mappings for the external web server you are using with WebBoard. See Chapter 3 for this information.
- Browse WebBoard from the local computer and from a different computer. If browsing locally works, but remotely doesn't, you have a network problem. Contact your network administrator.
- Test your network connection with another tool or application, such as *ping* or *telnet*. For example, if you *ping localhost,* the true name it resolves to

should be the same name used in Server Admin (Identity page) and in your TCP/IP configuration (computer name and host/domain name).

- Stop WebBoard and check the error log.
- Stop WebBoard and check the activity log.
- Stop WebBoard and check the mail log if you suspect email problems.
- Check the Application Event Log (from the Windows NT Event Viewer) for information and warnings about problems with the application.
- Look closely at the error messages sent from WebBoard to the browser. For example, in the "Not Found" return, WebBoard or the web server reports both the URL and the physical file pathname for the URL target—information invaluable in diagnosing mapping problems. Not all browsers save error messages. If yours doesn't, we recommend that you try another browser.
- If you have edited WebBoard's HTML files, verify that no tags are missing, improperly entered, or unclosed. We recommend you use an HTML editor's diagnostic capability or a special diagnostic tool.

Other Resources

WebBoard has several online resources for more information. WebBoard Central, the web site maintained for WebBoard users by the technical support staff at O'Reilly & Associates, provides product information, troubleshooting help, advice for particular implementations of WebBoard, ideas for new uses of WebBoard, sample HTML files, helpful utility programs, and opportunities to interact with other WebBoard users in WebBoard conferences.

You can tap the resources at WebBoard Central with your browser, and find out how others have dealt with similar problems. In addition, the Knowledge Base published on WebBoard Central, may provide just the answer you need. You will also find pointers to other resources on the Web, such as specifications and helpful application tools.

Contacting Technical Support

If you've thoroughly tried all the other resources to solve your problem and you still need assistance, O'Reilly & Associates provides technical support for WebBoard as listed below:

- On a per-incident basis. For per-incident tech support, call O'Reilly Technical Support at 707-829-0515. Have your credit card ready.

- On an annual basis with a technical support contract. Contracts are available for a variety of needs and software package combinations. To learn more about annual support contracts, contact O'Reilly & Associates Customer Service at 800-998-9938 or send email to *webboard@ora.com*.

Details of available WebBoard technical support options are posted at WebBoard Central.

Index

More Titles from O'Reilly

Software

WebSite Professional ™

By O'Reilly & Associates, Inc.
Documentation by Susan Peck
1st Edition June 1996
Includes 3 books, ISBN 1-56592-174-7

Designed for the sophisticated user, *WebSite Professional*™ is a complete Web server solution. *WebSite Professional* contains all of *WebSite*'s award-winning features, including remote administration, virtual servers for creating multiple home pages, wizards to automate common tasks, a search tool for Web indexing, and a graphical outline fo Web documents and links for managing your site. New with *WebSite Professional:* support for SSL and S-HTTP, the premier Web encryption security protocols; the WebSite Application Programming Interface (WSAPI); Cold Fusion Standard, a powerful development tool for dynamic linking of database information into your Web documents; and support for client and server-side Java programming.

PolyForm™

By O'Reilly & Associates, Inc.
Documentation by John Robert Boynton
1st Edition May 1996
Two diskettes & 146-pg book
ISBN 1-56592-182-8

PolyForm™ is a powerful 32-bit Web forms tool that helps you easily build and manage interactive Web pages. *PolyForm*'s interactive forms make it easy and fun for users to respond to the contents of your Web with their own feedback, ideas, or requests for more information. *PolyForm*™ lets you collect, process, and respond to each user's specific input. Best of all, forms that once required hours of complicated programming can be created in minutes because *PolyForm*™ automatically handles all of the CGI programming for processing form contents.

Statisphere™

By O'Reilly & Associates, Inc.
Documentation by Jay York
1st Edition May 1997 (est.)
2 diskettes & a 135-page book,
ISBN 1-56592-233-6

Statisphere™ is a Web traffic analyzer that provides precise, graphical reporting on your Web server's usage. Easy-to-read, browser-based reports deliver real-time profiles and long-term trend analysis on who's visiting your site and what they're reading. Whether you're tracking traffic rates for advertising, or steering Web development efforts to where they'll have the most impact, Statisphere gives you the answers you need to make the right decisions about your Web site.

Building Your Own WebSite™

By Susan B. Peck & Stephen Arrants
1st Edition July 1996, 514 pages, 1-56592-232-8

Building Your Own WebSite™ is a hands-on reference for Windows® 95 and Windows NT™ users who want to host a site on the Web or on a corporate intranet. This step-by-step guide will have you creating live web pages in minutes. You'll also learn how to connect your web to information in other Windows applications. *Building Your Own WebSite* is packed with examples and tutorials on every aspect of web management. You also get the highly acclaimed WebSite 1.1 on CD-ROM.

Building Your Own Web Conferences™

By Susan B. Peck & Beverly Murray Scherf
1st Edition March 1997
270 pages, Includes CD-ROM, 1-56592-279-4

Web-based conferencing is rapidly gaining converts from the ranks of computer bulletin board subscribers and members of online service discussion forums. Why? Because web conferences offer any user with a web browser a richer, more accessible set of discussion tools without the hassle of newsreader programs or the cost of proprietary online service memberships. Web conference administrators can easily create an unlimited number of free Internet- or intranet-accessible discussions, allowing anyone on the Web — or just a select few — to participate. *Building Your Own Web Conferences* is a complete guide for Windows 95 and Windows NT webmasters on how to set up and manage dynamic web discussion groups that will keep users coming back to your site.

Building Your Own Win-CGI Programs

By Robert Denny, Andrew Schulman &
Ron Petrusha
1st Edition April 1997 (est.) 350 pages (est.),
Includes CD-ROM, 1-56592-215-8

CGI (Common Gateway Interface) is the "glue" between web servers and custom web-server applications. This book takes an in-depth look at the Windows CGI, or Win-CGI. Win-CGI lets you create a web interface between Windows-based applications, such as relational databases or spreadsheets, and Windows web servers like WebSite Professional and Microsoft IIS. Win-CGI programs can be written in a variety of languages, including Visual Basic, C++, and C. Co-written by Bob Denny, the inventor of Win-CGI, this book provides numerous examples and sample code for these languages.

How to stay in touch with O'Reilly

1. Visit Our Award-Winning Web Site

http://www.ora.com/

★"Top 100 Sites on the Web" —*PC Magazine*
★"Top 5% Web sites" —*Point Communications*
★"3-Star site" —*The McKinley Group*

Our web site contains a library of comprehensiveproduct information (including book excerpts and tables of contents), downloadable software, background articles, interviews with technology leaders, links to relevant sites, book cover art, and more. File us in your Bookmarks or Hotlist!

2. Join Our Email Mailing Lists

New Product Releases

To receive automatic email with brief descriptions of all new O'Reilly products as they are released, send email to:
listproc@online.ora.com
Put the following information in the first line of your message (*not* in the Subject field):
subscribe ora-news "Your Name"of "Your Organization" (for example: subscribe ora-news Kris Webber of Fine Enterprises)

O'Reilly Events

If you'd also like us to send information about trade show events, special promotions, and other O'Reilly events, send email to: **listproc@online.ora.com**
Put the following information in the first line of your message (*not* in the Subject field):
subscribe ora-events "Your Name" of "Your Organization"

3. Get Examples from Our Books via FTP

There are two ways to access an archive of example files from our books:

Regular FTP

- ftp to:
  ftp.ora.com
  (login: anonymous
  password: your email address)
- Point your web browser to:
  ftp://ftp.ora.com/

FTPMAIL

- Send an email message to:
  ftpmail@online.ora.com
  (Write "help" in the message body)

4. Visit Our Gopher Site

- Connect your gopher to:
  gopher.ora.com
- Point your web browser to:
  gopher://gopher.ora.com/
- Telnet to:
  gopher.ora.com
  login: gopher

5. Contact Us via Email

order@ora.com
To place a book or software order online. Good for North American and international customers.

subscriptions@ora.com
To place an order for any of our newsletters or periodicals.

books@ora.com
General questions about any of our books.

software@ora.com
For general questions and product information about our software. Check out O'Reilly Software Online at **http://software.ora.com/** for software and technical support information. Registered O'Reilly software users send your questions to: **website-support@ora.com**

cs@ora.com
For answers to problems regarding your order or our products.

booktech@ora.com
For book content technical questions or corrections.

proposals@ora.com
To submit new book or software proposals to our editors and product managers.

international@ora.com
For information about our international distributors or translation queries. For a list of our distributors outside of North America check out:
http://www.ora.com/www/order/country.html

O'Reilly & Associates, Inc.
101 Morris Street, Sebastopol, CA 95472 USA
TEL 707-829-0515 or 800-998-9938
(6am to 5pm PST)
FAX 707-829-0104

Titles from O'Reilly

Please note that upcoming titles are displayed in italic.

WebProgramming
Apache: The Definitive Guide
Building Your Own Web Conferences
Building Your Own Website
Building Your Own Win-CGI Programs
CGI Programming for the World Wide Web
Designing for the Web
HTML: The Definitive Guide
JavaScript: The Definitive Guide, 2nd Ed.
Learning Perl
Programming Perl, 2nd Ed.
Mastering Regular Expressions
WebMaster in a Nutshell
Web Security & Commerce
Web Client Programming with Perl
World Wide Web Journal

Using the Internet
Smileys
The Future Does Not Compute
The Whole Internet User's Guide & Catalog
The Whole Internet for Win 95
Using Email Effectively
Bandits on the Information Superhighway

Java Series
Exploring Java
Java AWT Reference
Java Fundamental Classes Reference
Java in a Nutshell
Java Language Reference
Java Network Programming
Java Threads
Java Virtual Machine

Software
WebSite™ 1.1
WebSite Professional™
Building Your Own Web Conferences
WebBoard™
PolyForm™
Statisphere™

Songline Guides
NetActivism
NetResearch
Net Law
NetSuccess
NetLearning
NetTravel
Net Lessons

System Administration
Building Internet Firewalls
Computer Crime: A Crimefighter's Handbook
Computer Security Basics
DNS and BIND, 2nd Ed.
Essential System Administration, 2nd Ed.
Getting Connected: The Internet at 56K and Up
Internet Server Administration with Windows NT
Linux Network Administrator's Guide
Managing Internet Information Services
Managing NFS and NIS
Networking Personal Computers with TCP/IP
Practical UNIX & Internet Security. 2nd Ed.
PGP: Pretty Good Privacy
sendmail, 2nd Ed.
sendmail Desktop Reference
System Performance Tuning
TCP/IP Network Administration
termcap & terminfo
Using & Managing UUCP
Volume 8: X Window System Administrator's Guide
Web Security & Commerce

Unix
Exploring Expect
Learning VBScript
Learning GNU Emacs, 2nd Ed.
Learning the bash Shell
Learning the Korn Shell
Learning the UNIX Operating System
Learning the vi Editor
Linux in a Nutshell
Making TeX Work
Linux Multimedia Guide
Running Linux, 2nd Ed.
SCO UNIX in a Nutshell
sed & awk, 2nd Edition
Tcl/Tk Tools
UNIX in a Nutshell: System V Edition
UNIX Power Tools
Using csh & tsch
When You Can't Find Your UNIX System Administrator
Writing GNU Emacs Extensions

Web Review Studio Series
Gif Animation Studio
Shockwave Studio

Windows
Dictionary of PC Hardware and Data Communications Terms
Inside the Windows 95 Registry
Inside the Windows 95 File System
Win95 & WinNT Annoyances
Windows NT File System Internals
Windows NT in a Nutshell

Programming
Advanced Oracle PL/SQL Programming
Applying RCS and SCCS
C++: The Core Language
Checking C Programs with lint
DCE Security Programming
Distributing Applications Across DCE & Windows NT
Encyclopedia of Graphics File Formats, 2nd Ed.
Guide to Writing DCE Applications
lex & yacc
Managing Projects with make
Mastering Oracle Power Objects
Oracle Design: The Definitive Guide
Oracle Performance Tuning, 2nd Ed.
Oracle PL/SQL Programming
Porting UNIX Software
POSIX Programmer's Guide
POSIX.4: Programming for the Real World
Power Programming with RPC
Practical C Programming
Practical C++ Programming
Programming Python
Programming with curses
Programming with GNU Software
Pthreads Programming
Software Portability with imake, 2nd Ed.
Understanding DCE
Understanding Japanese Information Processing
UNIX Systems Programming for SVR4

Berkeley 4.4 Software Distribution
4.4BSD System Manager's Manual
4.4BSD User's Reference Manual
4.4BSD User's Supplementary Documents
4.4BSD Programmer's Reference Manual
4.4BSD Programmer's Supplementary Documents
X Programming
Vol. 0: X Protocol Reference Manual
Vol. 1: Xlib Programming Manual
Vol. 2: Xlib Reference Manual
Vol. 3M: X Window System User's Guide, Motif Edition
Vol. 4M: X Toolkit Intrinsics Programming Manual, Motif Edition
Vol. 5: X Toolkit Intrinsics Reference Manual
Vol. 6A: Motif Programming Manual
Vol. 6B: Motif Reference Manual
Vol. 6C: Motif Tools
Vol. 8 : X Window System Administrator's Guide
Programmer's Supplement for Release 6
X User Tools
The X Window System in a Nutshell

Career & Business
Building a Successful Software Business
The Computer User's Survival Guide
Love Your Job!
Electronic Publishing on CD-ROM

Travel
Travelers' Tales: Brazil
Travelers' Tales: Food
Travelers' Tales: France
Travelers' Tales: Gutsy Women
Travelers' Tales: India
Travelers' Tales: Mexico
Travelers' Tales: Paris
Travelers' Tales: San Francisco
Travelers' Tales: Spain
Travelers' Tales: Thailand
Travelers' Tales: A Woman's World

International Distributors

UK, Europe, Middle East and Northern Africa *(except France, Germany, Switzerland, & Austria)*

INQUIRIES
International Thomson Publishing Europe
Berkshire House
168-173 High Holborn
London WC1V 7AA, United Kingdom
Telephone: 44-171-497-1422
Fax: 44-171-497-1426
Email: itpint@itps.co.uk

ORDERS
International Thomson Publishing Services, Ltd.
Cheriton House, North Way
Andover, Hampshire SP10 5BE, United Kingdom
Telephone: 44-264-342-832 (UK orders)
Telephone: 44-264-342-806 (outside UK)
Fax: 44-264-364418 (UK orders)
Fax: 44-264-342761 (outside UK)
UK & Eire orders: itpuk@itps.co.uk
International orders: itpint@itps.co.uk

France

Editions Eyrolles
61 bd Saint-Germain
75240 Paris Cedex 05
France
Fax: 33-01-44-41-11-44

FRENCH LANGUAGE BOOKS
All countries except Canada
Phone: 33-01-44-41-46-16
Email: geodif@eyrolles.com

ENGLISH LANGUAGE BOOKS
Phone: 33-01-44-41-11-87
Email: distribution@eyrolles.com

Australia

WoodsLane Pty. Ltd.
7/5 Vuko Place, Warriewood NSW 2102
P.O. Box 935, Mona Vale NSW 2103
Australia
Telephone: 61-2-9970-5111
Fax: 61-2-9970-5002
Email: info@woodslane.com.au

Germany, Switzerland, and Austria

INQUIRIES
O'Reilly Verlag
Balthasarstr. 81
D-50670 Köln
Germany
Telephone: 49-221-97-31-60-0
Fax: 49-221-97-31-60-8
Email: anfragen@oreilly.de

ORDERS
International Thomson Publishing
Königswinterer Straße 418
53227 Bonn, Germany
Telephone: 49-228-97024 0
Fax: 49-228-441342
Email: order@oreilly.de

Asia *(except Japan & India)*

INQUIRIES
International Thomson Publishing Asia
60 Albert Street #15-01
Albert Complex
Singapore 189969
Telephone: 65-336-6411
Fax: 65-336-7411

ORDERS
Telephone: 65-336-6411
Fax: 65-334-1617
thomson@signet.com.sg

New Zealand

WoodsLane New Zealand Ltd.
21 Cooks Street (P.O. Box 575)
Wanganui, New Zealand
Telephone: 64-6-347-6543
Fax: 64-6-345-4840
Email: info@woodslane.com.au

Japan

O'Reilly Japan, Inc.
Kiyoshige Building 2F
12-Banchi, Sanei-cho
Shinjuku-ku
Tokyo 160 Japan
Telephone: 81-3-3356-5227
Fax: 81-3-3356-5261
Email: kenji@ora.com

India

Computer Bookshop (India) PVT. LTD.
190 Dr. D.N. Road, Fort
Bombay 400 001
India
Telephone: 91-22-207-0989
Fax: 91-22-262-3551
Email: cbsbom@giasbm01.vsnl.net.in

The Americas

O'Reilly & Associates, Inc.
101 Morris Street
Sebastopol, CA 95472 U.S.A.
Telephone: 707-829-0515
Telephone: 800-998-9938 (U.S. & Canada)
Fax: 707-829-0104
Email: order@ora.com

Southern Africa

International Thomson Publishing Southern Africa
Building 18, Constantia Park
240 Old Pretoria Road
P.O. Box 2459
Halfway House, 1685 South Africa
Telephone: 27-11-805-4819
Fax: 27-11-805-3648

O'REILLY & ASSOCIATES, INC. SOFTWARE LICENSE AGREEMENT

THIS IS A LEGAL AGREEMENT BETWEEN YOU AND O'REILLY & ASSOCIATES ("O'REILLY"). CAREFULLY READ ALL THE TERMS AND CONDITIONS OF THIS AGREEMENT PRIOR TO OPENING THE CD CONTAINER. OPENING THE CD CONTAINER INDICATES YOUR ACCEPTANCE OF THESE TERMS AND CONDITIONS. IF YOU DO NOT AGREE TO THESE TERMS AND CONDITIONS, RETURN THE PACKAGE AND ALL COMPONENTS OF THIS PRODUCT TO THE POINT OF PURCHASE FOR A REFUND. IF PURCHASED FROM O'REILLY, UPON RETURN OF THE PRODUCT WITHIN 30 DAYS OF PURCHASE, A REFUND WILL BE GIVEN. IF PURCHASED FROM ANOTHER SOURCE, FOLLOW THEIR RETURN POLICY.

1. License: This License Agreement ("Agreement") permits you to use one copy of the specified version of the O'Reilly product you have purchased ("Software") on any single computer, provided the Software is in use on only one computer at any time. If you have multiple licenses for the Software, then at any time you may have as many copies of the Software in use as you have licenses. The Software is "in use" on a computer when it is loaded in temporary memory (i.e., RAM) or installed into the permanent memory (e.g. hard disk, CD-ROM, or other storage device) of that computer. If the anticipated number of users of the Software will exceed the number of applicable licenses, then you must have a reasonable mechanism or process in place to assure that the number of persons using the Software concurrently does not exceed the number of licenses. If the Software is permanently installed on the hard disk or other storage device of a computer and one person uses that computer more than 80% of the time it is in use, then that person may also use the Software on a portable or home computer.

2. Backup and Transfer: You may make one copy of the Software solely for backup purposes. You may transfer and license the Software to another party if the other party agrees to the terms and conditions of this Agreement and completes an O'Reilly Enrollment Form available online at O'Reilly Software's web site. If you transfer the Software, you must also transfer or destroy the Documentation and backup copy and you may not retain or use any copy of the Software thereafter.

3. Copyright: The Software and the Building Your Own Web Conferences book are owned by O'Reilly. Components are owned by third parties and licensed to O'Reilly. The Software and Documentation are protected by United States and international copyright and other laws. You may not remove, obscure, or alter any notice of patent, copyright, trademark, trade secret, or other proprietary rights. You may not copy the written materials accompanying the Software, except by prior written permission from the owner of such material, as described above. You may not reverse engineer, disassemble or de-compile the Software nor may you permit anyone else to do so.

This license and your right to use the product terminate automatically if you violate any part of this agreement. In the event of termination, you must immediately destroy all copies of the product or return them to O'Reilly.

4. Term: This license is effective until terminated. You may terminate the Agreement by returning or destroying the Software and Documentation and all copies. You agree upon termination to return or destroy within five days all copies of the Software and Documentation and within two (2) weeks after any such termination you must specify in writing to O'Reilly that you have done so.

5. Limited Warranty (Disclaimer and Limitation of Liability): O'Reilly warrants the media on which the Software is provided to be free from defects in materials and workmanship for 90 days after delivery. Defective media may be returned for replacement without charge during the 90-day warranty period unless the media has been damaged by acts or actions of the Licensee or while under its control.

O'REILLY MAKES NO OTHER WARRANTIES EXPRESSED OR IMPLIED WITH RESPECT TO THE SOFTWARE (INCLUDING ASSOCIATED WRITTEN MATERIALS), ITS MERCHANTABILITY, OR FITNESS FOR ANY PARTICULAR PURPOSE. IN NO EVENT WILL O'REILLY BE LIABLE FOR INDIRECT OR CONSEQUENTIAL DAMAGES, INCLUDING, WITHOUT LIMITATIONS, LOSS OF INCOME, USE, OR INFORMATION, NOR SHALL THE LIABILITY OF O'REILLY EXCEED THE AMOUNT PAID FOR THE SOFTWARE. THIS LIMITED WARRANTY GIVES YOU SPECIFIC LEGAL RIGHTS. YOU MAY HAVE OTHERS, WHICH VARY FROM STATE TO STATE.

Without limitation, O'Reilly does not warrant that the Software is completely error free, will operate without interruption, or is compatible with any equipment or software configurations. The Licensee expressly assumes all risk for use of the Software. Repair, replacement, or refund (at the option of O'Reilly) is the exclusive remedy, if there is a defect.

6. General: You may not sublicense, assign, or transfer the license, Software, or Documentation except as expressly provided in this Agreement. This Agreement constitutes the entire agreement between you and O'Reilly and supersedes any prior written or oral agreement concerning the contents of this package. It shall not be modified except by written agreement dated subsequent to the date of this Agreement and signed by an authorized O'Reilly representative. O'Reilly is not bound by any provision of any purchase order, receipt, acceptance, confirmation, correspondence, or otherwise, unless O'Reilly specifically agrees to the provision in writing. This Agreement is governed by the laws of the State of California as if the parties hereto were both California residents; and you consent to exclusive jurisdiction in the state and federal courts in San Francisco in the event of any dispute.

7. U.S. Government Restricted Rights: The Software and Documentation are provided with RESTRICTED RIGHTS. Use, duplication, or disclosure by the Government is subject to restrictions as set forth in subparagraph ©(1)(ii) of the Rights in Technical Data and Computer Software clause at DFARS 252.227-7013 or subparagraphs ©(1) and (2) of the Commercial Computer Software Restricted Rights at 48 CFR 52.227-19, as applicable. Contractor/manufacturer is O'Reilly & Associates, Inc., 101 Morris Street, Sebastopol, CA 95472.